MACGILLIVRAY ON LAW

CW00402363

RELATING TO ALL RISKS OTHER THAN MARINE

SECOND SUPPLEMENT TO THE FOURTEENTH EDITION

Up to date to August 2020

JOHN BIRDS, LLM

Emeritus Professor of Law, University of Manchester; Honorary Professor of Law, University of Sheffield and Honorary Professor of Law, University of Exeter

BEN LYNCH QC, BA (Oxon), LLM (Columbia)

Of Middle Temple, Barrister

SIMON PAUL, BSc (Hons.), MPhil (Cantab), LLM (Harvard)

Of Gray's Inn, Barrister

SWEET & MAXWELL

THOMSON REUTERS

Fourteenth Edition 2018 by John Birds, Ben Lynch and Simon Paul
First Supplement to the Fourteenth Edition 2019 by John Birds, Ben Lynch
and Simon Paul
Second Supplement to the Fourteenth Edition 2020 by John Birds, Ben
Lynch QC and Simon Paul

Published in 2020 by Thomson Reuters, trading as Sweet & Maxwell.
Thomson Reuters is registered in England & Wales, Company No.1679046.
Registered Office and address for service: 5 Canada Square, Canary Wharf,
London, E14 5AQ.

For further information on our products and services, visit *http://
www.sweetandmaxwell.co.uk*.

Computerset by Sweet & Maxwell.
Printed and bound by CPI Group (UK) Ltd, Croydon, CR0 4YY.
A CIP catalogue record for this book is available from the British Library.

ISBN (print): 978-0-414-08028-7

ISBN (e-book): 978-0-414-08031-7

ISBN (print and e-book): 978-0-414-08029-4

FSC
www.fsc.org
MIX
Paper from
responsible sources
FSC® C013604

HOW TO USE THIS SUPPLEMENT

This is the Second Supplement to the Fourteenth Edition of *MacGillivray on Insurance Law* and has been compiled according to the structure of the main volume.

At the beginning of each chapter of this Supplement, a mini table of contents of the sections in the main volume has been included. Where a heading in this table of contents has been marked with a square pointer, this indicates that there is relevant information in this Supplement to which the reader should refer. Material that is new to the Cumulative Supplement is indicated by the symbol ■. Material that has been included from the previous supplement is indicated by the symbol □.

Within each chapter, updating information is referenced to the relevant paragraph in the main volume.

TABLE OF CONTENTS

CHAPTER 1

NATURE OF INSURANCE AND INSURABLE INTEREST

CHAPTER 2

FORMATION OF THE CONTRACT

CHAPTER 4

THE PERIOD PRIOR TO ISSUE OF THE POLICY

CHAPTER 6

COMMENCEMENT AND TERMINATION OF RISK

CHAPTER 10

WARRANTIES AND OTHER POLICY TERMS

CHAPTER 11

CONSTRUCTION OF POLICIES

CHAPTER 13

CONFLICT OF LAWS

CHAPTER 14

ILLEGALITY

CHAPTER 15

MISTAKE

CHAPTER 16

MISREPRESENTATION

CHAPTER 17

GOOD FAITH AND THE DUTY OF DISCLOSURE

CHAPTER 18

FRAUD, MISREPRESENTATION AND NON-DISCLOSURE BY THIRD PARTIES

CHAPTER 19

CONSUMER INSURANCE (DISCLOSURE AND REPRESENTATIONS) ACT 2012

CHAPTER 20

THE INSURANCE ACT 2015

CHAPTER 21

The Loss

CHAPTER 22

The Claimant

CHAPTER 23

Reinstatement

CHAPTER 24

Subrogation

CHAPTER 25

Rights of Two or More Insurers

CHAPTER 26

Life Insurance

CHAPTER 36

INSURANCE COMPANIES

CHAPTER 38

THE ROLE OF AGENTS IN INSURANCE BUSINESS

TABLE OF CASES

TABLE OF STATUTES

FOREIGN LEGISLATION

TABLE OF STATUTORY INSTRUMENTS

TABLE OF EUROPEAN LEGISLATION

DIRECTIVES

TABLE OF NON-STATUTORY RULES AND REGULATIONS

CHAPTER 1

NATURE OF INSURANCE AND INSURABLE INTEREST

6. INSURABLE INTEREST IN LIVES

(a) Principles of the 1774 Act

Presumption of non-pecuniary interest.

Replace paragraph with:

In the following categories of life assurance, an insurable interest is presumed **1-067** and need not be proved. These are: (i) an insurance by a person on his own life[216]; (ii) insurance by a spouse on the life of his or her spouse; and (iii) insurance by a civil partner on the life of his or her civil partner.[217] In these instances, the law takes the view that the interest of the insured is of higher account than a purely pecuniary interest and is incapable of pecuniary valuation, and accordingly there is no limit

[1]

upon the amount which may be insured upon such lives or upon the number of policies which may be effected.[218]

[216] *Wainwright v Bland* (1835) 1 Moo. & R. 481; (1836) 1 M. & W. 32.

[217] Not surprisingly the authorities (*Reed v Royal Exchange* (1795) Peake Add. Cas. 70; *Griffiths v Fleming* [1909] 1 K.B. 805; *Wight v Brown* (1849) 11 D. 459; *Murphy v Murphy* [2004] Lloyd's Rep. I.R. 744 at 751) concerned only insurances by a married man on the life of his wife or vice versa. The presumption that one spouse has an unlimited interest in the life of the other was extended to registered civil partners of the same sex by s.253 of the Civil Partnership Act 2004. The text reflects the position that now both marriages and civil partnerships can be entered into by members of the opposite or same sexes (see the Marriage (Same Sex Couples) Act 2013; and the Civil Partnership (Opposite-sex Couples) Regulations 2019 (SI 2019/1458)).

[218] *M'Farlane v The Royal London F.S.* (1886) 2 T.L.R. 755; *Shilling v Accidental Death* (1857) 2 H. & N. 42.

(c) Family Relationships

Not per se a ground of interest.

After "Relationship other than", replace "that of husband and wife" with:

1-092   those of spouses and civil partners

(e) Necessity for the Act Today

Replace second paragraph with:

1-117   The English and Scottish Law Commissions produced a Consultation Paper proposing reforms to the law, although this contained nothing so radical as the Australian statute.[364] However, those proposals failed to command sufficient consensus to be included in their Report of July 2014 and hence did not appear in the Bill that became the Insurance Act 2015. In March 2015 they produced a further Issues Paper[365] with revised proposals that they hoped would command such support as to form the basis of an uncontroversial draft Bill to be included in a further Report later in 2015. These later proposals are that insurable interest should exist: (i) where there is a reasonable prospect that the insured will retain an economic benefit on the preservation of the life insured or incur an economic loss on the death of the life insured, with no limit on the amount of cover; (ii) that co-habitants should have an insurable interest in each other's lives, irrespective of showing economic loss when they live together as spouses at the time of effecting the insurance; and (iii) that parents should be entitled to insure the lives of their children of any age without evidence of economic loss. They also consider that trustees of pension schemes and employers effecting group insurance for their members should have an unlimited interest. They propose repealing the requirement in s.2 of the Life Assurance Act and providing that a contract taken out without interests should be void, but not illegal. They have not as yet produced a final Report, but have issued two draft Bills, the latest of which, issued in June 2018, may lead to their final recommendations.[366] However, the delay in this appearing is now so long that it has to be wondered whether there will indeed be such a Report.

[364] LCCP 201/ SLCDP 152.

[365] Available at *https://www.lawcom.gov.uk/project/insurance-contract-law-insurable-interest/* [Accessed 29 June 2020].

[366] See *https://www.lawcom.gov.uk/project/insurance-contract-law-insurable-interest/* [Accessed 29 June 2020].

7. INSURABLE INTEREST IN PROPERTY

(a) Generally

General definition.

Replace first paragraph with:

English law lays down two criteria for the possession of a valid insurable inter- **1-118** est in property. First, the insured must be so situated to the insured property that he will suffer pecuniary loss as the proximate result of its damage or destruction. In his classic description of an insurable interest in the leading case of *Lucena v Craufurd* Lawrence J said[367]:

> "A man is interested in a thing to whom advantage may arise or prejudice happen from the circumstances which may attend it ... and where a man is so circumstanced with respect to matters exposed to certain risks or dangers, as to have a moral certainty of advantage or benefit, but for those risks or dangers, he may be said to be interested in the safety of the thing. To be interested in the preservation of a thing, is to be so circumstanced with respect to it as to have benefit from its existence, prejudice from its destruction."

This passage from his judgment is often interpreted as recognising an insurable interest to exist in any case where the insured has a "moral certainty" of advantage or benefit from the continued preservation of the insured property, regardless of whether he possesses any legal right in it or pertaining to it,[368] so that Lawrence J recognised a well-founded factual expectation of benefit from the continuing existence of property as a sufficient ground of insurable interest.[369] When, however, the passage cited above is placed in the overall context of his entire judgment, it appears more probable that he did not intend it to be a complete definition in itself.[370] It lacked a criterion of "moral certainty", something supplied by the remainder of his judgment. From this it seems that the criterion of "moral certainty" in his view was the insured's possession of a legal right to, or legal responsibility for, the insured property, and there is authority for this interpretation also.[371] At all events there is no doubt that the House of Lords did not regard factual expectation, or moral certainty, of benefit from the preservation of property as a sufficient basis of insurable interest in it, and added the second requirement of a legal relationship between the insured and the subject-matter of the insurance.[372] Giving the leading speech Lord Eldon said[373]:

> "In order to distinguish that intermediate thing between a strict right, or a right derived under a contract, and a mere expectation or hope, which has been termed an insurable interest, it has been said in many cases to be that which amounts to a moral certainty. I have in vain endeavoured, however, to find a fit definition of that which is between a certainty and an expectation; nor am I able to point out what is an interest unless it be a right in the property or a right derivable out of some contract about the property, which in either case may be lost upon some contingency affecting the possession or enjoyment of the party."

In *Routh v Thompson*[374] Lord Ellenborough CJ, who had delivered a short speech in *Lucena v Craufurd* concurring with that of Lord Eldon, described the requirement as possession of a legal or equitable right in property, and Lord Eldon's test was subsequently summarised as requiring a legal or equitable interest in the insured property.[375] If we add the additional ground of insurable interest created by the existence of a legal obligation to bear any loss arising from destruction of, or damage to, the insured property, then we have a substantially accurate definition of insurable interest in property.[376]

[367] *Lucena v Craufurd* (1806) 2 Bos. & P. N.R. 269 at 302.

[368] *Mark Rowlands v Berni Inns* [1986] 1 Q.B. 211 at 228; *The Moonacre* [1992] 2 Lloyd's Rep. 503 at 511; *Glengate-KG Properties v Norwich Union Fire Insurance Society* [1996] 1 Lloyd's Rep. 614 at 621 and 626; *Constitution Insurance Company of Canada v Kosmopoulos* (1987) 34 D.L.R. (4th) 208 at 216; *Cowan v Jeffrey Associates*, 1999 S.L.T. 757; R. Merkin, *Colinvaux & Merkin's Insurance Contract Law* (London: Sweet & Maxwell, 2002), Vol.1, para.A.4.1-19; H. Bennett, *Law of Marine Insurance* (Oxford, Clarendon, 1996), p.17; Hartnett and Thornton, "Insurable Interest in Property" (1948) 48 Col. L. Rev. 1162. This view was followed in earlier editions of this work (see 9th edn, para.1-116).

[369] *Macaura v Northern Assurance* [1925] N.I. 141 at 157–158 per Andrews LJ, approved by Lord Buckmaster on appeal [1925] A.C. 619 at 627. It is unclear precisely what degree of probability is meant by a "moral certainty", which appears to signify something greater than the mere balance of probability and less than complete certainty.

[370] See Legh-Jones in *The Modern Law of Marine Insurance*, edited by D. Rhidian Thomas (2002), Vol.2, at Ch.4.

[371] *Ebsworth v Alliance Marine Insurance Co* (1873) L.R. 9 C.P. 596 at 617 and 621 per Bovill CJ; *Moran, Galloway & Co v Uzielli* [1905] 2 K.B. 555 at 561–562 per Walton J; Mance et al., *Insurance Disputes*, 2nd edn (2003), para.1.12. In *Wilson v Jones* (1867) L.R. 2 Ex. 139 at 150, Blackburn J said he knew no better definition of an interest in an event than that given by Lawrence J, namely that if the event happens the party will gain an advantage, if it is frustrated he will suffer a loss. Citing him in *Griffiths v Fleming* [1909] 1 K.B. 805 at 820, Farwell LJ added: "And the interest must be a legal interest, not a mere chance or expectation".

[372] This last sentence and the previous two sentences were cited with approval in *Comlex Ltd (in Liquidation) v Allianz Insurance Plc* [2016] CSOH 87 at [33].

[373] *Lucena v Craufurd* (1806) 2 Bos. & P. N.R. 269 at 321.

[374] *Routh v Thompson* (1809) 11 East 428 at 433.

[375] Marine Insurance Act 1906 s.5(2); *Moran, Galloway & Co v Uzielli* [1905] 2 K.B. 555 at 562; *Macaura v Northern Assurance* [1925] A.C. 619 at 630. The words "a right derivable out of some contract about the property" are apt to cover such cases as the insurable interest possessed by licensees and others with a legal right to occupy and enjoy property—see para.1-127 below.

[376] *Stock v Inglis* (1884) 12 Q.B.D. 564 at 578 per Lindley LJ; *Glengate-KG Properties Ltd v Norwich Union Fire Insurance Society* [1996] 1 Lloyd's Rep. 614 at 623 per Auld LJ. This case concerned the interpretation of the word "interest" in a consequential loss policy, but the judgments contain obiter observations on the nature of insurable interest required by law in property insurance.

Replace first paragraph with:

1-120   Other common law jurisdictions have dispensed with the requirement of a legal or equitable interest. In *Constitution Insurance Company of Canada v Kosmopoulos*[383] the Supreme Court of Canada decided not to follow its earlier decision in *Guarantee Co of North America v Aqua-Land Exploration Ltd*[384] and held that a moral certainty of economic advantage from property was a sufficient ground of insurable interest therein. The courts in a number of American jurisdictions have adopted a test based upon a factual expectation of benefit from the continuing existence of property, regardless of the existence of a legal or equitable relationship to it.[385] In Australia the legislature has intervened, and s.17 of the Insurance Contracts Act 1984 provides that, when the insured suffers pecuniary or economic loss because insured property has been damaged or destroyed, the absence of an interest at law or in equity in the property at the time of loss does not relieve the insurer from liability. These developments notwithstanding, it is submitted that the English law requirement of a legal interest or obligation regarding the property cannot be dispensed with except by a reforming statute or by restatement of the law by the Supreme Court.[386] Although the Law Commissions were at one time minded to recommend reform of the law along the lines that other common law jurisdictions have taken, they have most recently taken the view that reform of insurable interest so far as property insurance is concerned is unnecessary.[387] This will leave any development or change in the law subject to litigation, which, on the evidence of recent years, is likely to raise the point very infrequently. It may be thought that the view of the Law Commissions represents a missed opportunity to restate the law in a clearer manner.

[383] *Constitution Insurance of Canada v Kosmopoulos* (1987) 34 D.L.R. (4th) 208. See also, for example, *Broadgrain Commodities Inc v Continental Casualty Co* [2017] ONSC 4721, which is discussed in R. Merkin, "Marine insurance: insurable interest" (February 2019) 31(2) *Insurance Law Monthly* 6. Although it is argued there that this marine insurance case construed the Canadian provisions equivalent to those in the Marine Insurance Act 1906 in a broad way, this is hardly surprising given the decision of the Canadian Supreme Court in the *Kosmopoulos* case. In any event, the insured in that case, the seller under a CIF contract from whom title to and risk in the goods in question had passed, still had an interest by virtue of a term providing for the seller to retain a security interest "until all buyers' accounts are settled".

[384] *Guarantee Co of North America v Aqua-Land Exploration Ltd* (1965) 54 D.L.R. (2d) 299. The Supreme Court had approved and followed the statement of the English law at para.445 of the 5th edition of this work.

[385] See, for instance, cases in which a creditor has been held to have an insurable interest in the property of his debtor after a judgment has been obtained for an unsecured debt, such as *American Equitable Assurance Co v Powderly Coal & Lumber Co* 128 So. 225 (1930); *Spare v Home Mutual Insurance Co* 15 Fed.Rep. 707 (1883); *Rohrbach v Germania Fire Insurance Co*, 62 N.Y. 47 (1875). See para.1-149, below. So also a person named in the will of a living person as a devisee of property has an insurable interest in the property left to him—*Home Insurance Co v Mendenhall* 45 N.E. 1078 (1897)—cf. Lord Eldon's example of the heir at law in *Lucena v Craufurd* (1806) 2 Bos. & P. N.R. 269 at 324–325. Further illustrations are *Liverpool & London Globe Insurance Co v Bolling* 10 S.E. 2d 578 (Va., 1940); *Womble v Dubuque Fire & Marine Insurance Co* 37 N.E. 2d 263 (Mass. 1941); *N. British & Mercantile Insurance Co v Sciandia* 54 So. 2d 764 (Ala. 1951); *Putnam v Mercantile Marine Insurance Co* 46 Mass. (5 Met.) 386 (1843). For further detail see Hartnett and Thornton (1948) 48 Co.L.Rev. 1162–1188 and Note on *Castle Cars Inc v United States Fire Insurance Co* 221 Va., 773 (1981) in (1982) 68 Va., L. Rev. 651. Other authorities are cited in *Constitution Insurance of Canada v Kosmopoulos* (1987) 34 D.L.R. (4th) 208.

[386] The suggestion made in *Sharp v Sphere Drake Insurance* [1992] 2 Lloyd's Rep. 503 at 511–512 and in *National Oilwell (UK) Ltd v Davy Offshore Ltd* [1993] 2 Lloyd's Rep. 582 at 611 that it is unnecessary to establish a proprietary legal or equitable interest in the insured property, is unexceptionable so long as it is recognised that the insured without a proprietary title in it must possess a legal right or liability relating to the insured property—see paras 1-116 to 1-117, above. This sentence was cited in *Comlex Ltd (in Liquidation) v Allianz Insurance Plc* [2016] CSOH 87 at [37].

[387] See their latest paper produced in June 2018 and available at *https://www.lawcom.gov.uk/project/insurance-contract-law-insurable-interest/* [Accessed 29 June 2020]. For their earlier views see the Joint Consultation Paper of the English and Scottish Law Commissions, LCCP 201/SLCDP 152, December 2011, Pt 12 and the Issues Paper issued in March 2015 and the draft Bill produced in April 2016, available at *http://www.lawcom.gov.uk/wp-content/uploads/2016/04/draft_Insurable_Interest_Bill_April_2016.pdf* [Accessed 29 June 2020].

(c) Insurances Effected by the Insured on Behalf of Others

Real property.

Replace paragraph with:

Doubts about this construction of the Act were, however, expressed in Com- **1-166**
monwealth cases[573] and by commentators.[574] In *Davjoyda Estates Ltd v National Insurance Co of New Zealand*[575] an alternative construction was suggested whereby s.2 applied generally only where the named insured himself had no interest in the property and contracted solely for the benefit of another. If he had an interest, so that s.1 and the aim of the Act to strike down gambling policies were satisfied, there was no need to name the other parties interested in the property. In other cases the possibility of the Act applying to realty was discreetly circumvented[576] or simply ignored.[577] More recently in *Siu Yin Kwan v Eastern Insurance Co Ltd*[578] the Privy

Council held, approving dicta of Kerr LJ in *Mark Rowlands Ltd v Berni Inns Ltd*,[579] that the 1774 Act was not intended to apply, and does not apply, to indemnity insurance of any kind, but only to insurances which provide for the payment of a specified sum upon the happening of an insured event. The earlier dicta of Lord Denning MR to the contrary were disapproved.[580] While technically it is still open to an English court to take a different view, especially as the decision in *Siu Yin Kwan* was concerned with a liability insurance policy, it seems realistic to conclude that all insurances on buildings and realty generally will be regarded as outside the scope of the Act so long as they have the character of indemnity insurance.[581]

[573] e.g. *British Traders' Insurance Co v Monson* (1964) 111 C.L.R. 86 at 103 per Menzies J. The question in that case whether the tenant had insured on behalf of the lessor as undisclosed principal was resolved against the lessor on the ground of the absence of intention on the part of the tenant to cover the lessor's interest, and not by reference to the 1774 Act.

[574] J.N. Quarterly 1971 S.L.T. (News) 141; *Halsbury's Laws*, 4th edn (1978), Vol. 25, p.328. E.R. Ivamy, *Fire and Motor Insurance*, 4th edn (Lexis Law Publisher, 1984), p.184.

[575] *Davjoyda Estates Pty Ltd v National Insurance Co of New Zealand* (1967) 65 S.R. (N.S.W.) 381 at 428 per Manning J.

[576] *Petrofina (UK) Ltd v Magnaload Ltd* [1984] Q.B. 127 at 136.

[577] *Mumford Hotels Ltd v Wheler* [1964] Ch. 117; *Lonsdale & Thompson Ltd v Black Arrow Group Plc* [1993] Ch. 361; *National Oilwell (UK) Ltd v Davy Offshore Ltd* [1993] 2 Lloyd's Rep. 582. The Canadian courts ignored the possibility of the Act's application to policies on buildings in *Keefer v Phoenix Insurance Co* (1898) 29 Ont. R. 394 and *Caldwell v Stadacona Fire & Life Insurance Co* (1883) 11 S.C.R. 212. See also the unreported decision of the High Court of Ireland in *Church General Insurance Co v Connolly*, 7 May 1981, discussed (by Birds) in (1983) 5 Dublin University Law. Jo. at 291.

[578] *Siu Yin Kwan v Eastern Insurance Co Ltd* [1994] 2 A.C. 199.

[579] *Mark Rowlands Ltd v Berni Inns Ltd* [1986] 1 Q.B. 211 at 227.

[580] *Re King* [1963] Ch. 459 at 485.

[581] In particular the judgments in *Hodson v Observer Life Assurance Society* (1857) 8 E. & B. 40 and *Williams v Baltic Insurance Association* [1924] 2 K.B. 282 were not cited to the Privy Council. The arguments to the contrary are rehearsed in J. Birds, *Birds' Modern Insurance Law*, 11th edn (London: Sweet & Maxwell, 2019), para.3.14.

FORMATION OF THE CONTRACT

1. GENERAL PRINCIPLES

(b) Offer and Acceptance

Silence not acceptance.

Replace footnote 48 with:

[48] *Taylor v Allon* [1966] 1 Q.B. 304 at 311. In that case there was no evidence offered to show that the insured sufficiently knew of the insurers' offer to accept it in this way. See also *Danbol Pty Ltd v Swiss Re International Se* [2020] V.S.C. 23.

2-016

THE PERIOD PRIOR TO ISSUE OF THE POLICY

1. TEMPORARY COVER

(a) Grant of Temporary Cover

Nature of interim insurance.

After "... and takes effect subject to its own particular terms.", add new footnote 2a:

4-002   [2a] For a recent example of a situation where there was no acceptance of an offer of a temporary contract, see *Danbol Pty Ltd v Swiss Re International Se* [2020] V.S.C. 23.

COMMENCEMENT AND TERMINATION OF RISK

1. RISK COMMENCING WITH REFERENCE TO DATE OR EVENT

(a) Commencement of Cover

Specified date.

Replace footnote 9 with:

[9] *Cartwright v MacCormack* [1963] 1 W.L.R. 18 at 21; *Dunn and Tarrant v Campbell* (1920) 4 Lloyd's **6-004**
Rep. 36.

Specified hour.

After the first paragraph, add new paragraph:
   In the New Zealand case of *QBE Insurance (International) Ltd v Allianz* **6-006**
Australia Insurance Ltd,[15a] a property insurance contract issued by QBE was
expressed to expire on 4 September 2010 at 16.00. When QBE indicated that it
would not be interested in renewal of that contract, the insured's broker approached Allianz and obtained a policy stating "effective date: 04/09/2010" and
"expiry date: 4 pm on 04/09/2011". As the evidence was quite clear that the broker
and Allianz had agreed that the latter would take over the insurance when QBE's
policy expired, it was held that the Allianz policy did not commence until 16.00 on
4 September 2010 and hence Allianz was not liable for the loss which occurred at
04.35 on that day.

[15a] *QBE Insurance (International) Ltd v Allianz Australia Insurance Ltd* [2018] NZCA 239.

2. RISK COMMENCING UPON PAYMENT OF PREMIUM

(a) Termination of Cover

Statutory rules as to cancellation.

After "The insured", delete "under a long-term insurance contract, that is most **6-022**
forms of life and related insurance,".

Replace paragraph with:

6-023   The Financial Conduct Authority[57a] has promulgated rules[58] dealing with cancellation of, and withdrawal from, various types of contract.[59] The individual customer is given a right to cancel investment-related and non-investment-related insurance contracts.[60] Broadly, where there is a right of cancellation, it is to be exercised, either within 30 days or within 14 days of the conclusion of the contract, depending on the type of contract and the circumstances of sale. There are various exceptions to this right, and detailed provisions as to its exercise. Reference should be made to the rules for the full details of the cancellation regime which they implement.

[57a] Previously the Financial Services Authority.

[58] The rules are published on the FCA website, and are subject to change from time to time. The Conduct of Business Sourcebook (COBS) applies to life insurance, and the separate Insurance Conduct of Business Sourcebook (ICOBS) applies to general insurance. Note that, although statutory cancellation rules for life insurance have existed for many years, they became in effect the implementation of requirements imposed by the EC Directives on life insurance, now contained in arts 185 and 186 of the Solvency II Directive 2009/138/EC [2009] OJ L335/1. As to how they are to be interpreted as a matter of EU law, see *Rust-Hackner v Nürnberger Versicherung Aktiengesellschaft Österreich* (C-355/18) EU:C:2019:1123. Here one key ruling was that, unless and until the insured had been informed of the right to cancel, which had to be by the insurer not a third party, the period allowed for cancellation did not start to run. However, where the insured was informed, albeit with incorrect information as in the case where the insured had been told wrongly that cancellation had to be in writing under the national law, it was for the national court to decide if the mistake operated as an essential limitation on the right to cancel. It was also held that national law restricting the insured's rights, following cancellation, to receipt of the surrender value only was contrary to the Directive.

[59] COBS 15 and ICOBS 7.

[60] COBS 15.2.1 and ICOBS 7.1.

CHAPTER 10

WARRANTIES AND OTHER POLICY TERMS

1. CLASSIFICATION OF TERMS

After "The work of the Law Commissions has", delete "now".   **10-001**

Suspensive condition.

Replace footnote 29 with:

[29] *Roberts v Anglo Saxon Insurance Co* (1926) 26 Ll. L. Rep. 154 at 157 (Div. Ct.) where MacKinnon   **10-007**
J said: "Now, nothing turns upon the use of the word 'warranted' ... always used with the greatest
ambiguity in a policy ...". Cp. however *AC Ward & Sons v Catlin (Five) Ltd* [2008] EWHC 3585
(Comm), upheld on appeal at [2009] EWCA Civ 1098; [2010] Lloyd's Rep. I.R. 301, where the use of
the word warranty, combined with a definitions clause which stated that a warranty was a fundamental
term or condition of the insurance the breach of which voids the contract from the time of the breach,
was held to have the effect of making clear that the term was indeed a true warranty. Compare *Bluebon
Ltd v Ageas (UK) Ltd* [2017] EWHC 3301 (Comm); [2017] 2 C.L.C. 890, where an electrical inspec-
tion warranty in a policy insuring a hotel, which contained a general condition providing that the due
observance and fulfilment of the terms of the policy imposing obligations on the insured "shall be conditions precedent to any liability of the Insurers to make any payment under this Policy", was held to be
suspensive.

Exceptions clauses.

After "... of loss being excluded. Nonetheless it", replace "is" with:
   was traditionally   **10-009**

[11]

2. WARRANTIES—DETAILED SURVEY

(a) Definition and How Created

No technical words necessary.

Replace footnote 129 with:

10-030   [129] *Newcastle Fire v Macmorran* (1815) 3 Dow. 255; *Ellinger v Mutual Life* [1905] 1 K.B. 31 at 38. *Sugar Hut Group Ltd v Great Lakes Reinsurance (UK) Plc* [2011] EWHC 2636 (Comm); [2011] Lloyd's Rep. I.R. 198, where Burton J held that the use of the word warranty, whilst not decisive, was a "good starting point" in favour of construing the clause as a warranty. Cp. too *AC Ward & Sons v Catlin (Five) Ltd* [2008] EWHC 3585 (Comm), upheld on appeal at [2009] EWCA Civ 1098; [2010] Lloyd's Rep. I.R. 301, where the use of the word "warranty", combined with a definitions clause which stated that a warranty was a fundamental term or condition of the insurance the breach of which voids the contract from the time of the breach, was held to have the effect of making clear that the term was indeed a true warranty. Compare *Bluebon Ltd v Ageas (UK) Ltd* [2017] 2 C.L.C. 890 (see final footnote at para.10-007).

3. THE EFFECT OF THE INSURANCE ACT 2015 ON THE LAW OF WARRANTIES AND OTHER TERMS

Terms not relevant to the actual loss.

Replace footnote 425 with:

10-126   [425] See Law Com No.353, Scot Law Com No.238 at 18.24. For an interesting discussion of the meaning of terms defining the risk as a whole, see Ö. Gürses, "Section 11 of the Insurance Act 2015: when does a term define the risk as a whole in an insurance contact?" [2020] J.B.L. 184. The author suggests that risk defining terms, as opposed to what she calls risk mitigating terms, are similar to "core terms" under the Consumer Rights Act 2015 (see para.10-019) and explores the impact of s.54 of the Australian Insurance Contracts Act 1984, to which s.11 was intended to have a similar effect. Ultimately, though, the distinction depends on the proper construction of terms.

CHAPTER 11

CONSTRUCTION OF POLICIES

5. ADMISSIBILITY OF EXTRINSIC EVIDENCE

Replace footnote 169 with:

169 *Wood v Capita Insurance Services Ltd* [2017] UKSC 24; [2017] 2 W.L.R. 1095. The other notable **11-040**
cases are *Rainy Sky SA v Kookmin Bank* [2011] UKSC 50; [2011] 1 W.L.R. 2900 and *Arnold v Britton*
[2015] UKSC 36; [2015] A.C. 1619, both referred to in the extract below. The approach in *Wood v Capita
Insurance Services Ltd* in particular was followed in *Financial Conduct Authority v Arch Insurance (UK)
Ltd* [2020] EWHC 2448 (Comm) at [61]–[79], as to which see para.33-001A, below.

CHAPTER 13

CONFLICT OF LAWS

1. JURISDICTION

Brussels, Lugano and 2007 Lugano Conventions.

Replace paragraph with:

13-002 These Conventions are no longer relevant in cases involving EC Member States, but form an important part of the background to the current jurisdictional regime. The Civil Jurisdiction and Judgments Act 1982[2] gave effect in the law of the UK to the 1968 Convention on Jurisdiction and the Enforcement of Judgments in Civil and Commercial Matters as amended,[3] which contained special provisions dealing with the jurisdiction of courts in insurance cases.[4] Schedule 1 to the 1982 Act contained the text of the 1968 Convention. The 1982 Act also implemented a parallel convention, the Lugano Convention, which extended the scheme of the 1968 Convention to EFTA States and potentially to other states. The Lugano Convention applied to Iceland, Norway and Switzerland. On 30 October 2007 a new convention with (amongst others) those three countries was entered into; the Convention on jurisdiction and the recognition and enforcement of judgments in civil and commercial matters ([2009] OJ L147/5), ratified by the Council of Ministers on 18 May 2009 (the 2007 Lugano Convention).[4a] This replaces the original Lugano Convention. Its provisions are generally parallel to reg.44/2001 and reg.1215/2012. The signatories are the Swiss Confederation,[4b] the European Community, the Kingdom of Denmark, the Kingdom of Norway and the Republic of Iceland.[4c] It entered into force for the EC, Denmark and Norway on 1 January 2010. Switzerland ratified the 2007 Lugano Convention on 20 October 2010, with effect from 1 January 2011. For Iceland it entered into force on 1 May 2011. Consequen-

[14]

tial legislative amendments and amendments to the Civil Procedure Rules in the UK were made by the Civil Jurisdiction and Judgments Regulations 2009 (SI 2009/3131).

[2] Civil Jurisdiction and Judgments Act 1982 c.27.

[3] The Convention, often referred to as the Brussels Convention, was signed in 1968. The original parties were Belgium, France, Germany, Italy, Luxembourg, and The Netherlands. The Accession Convention of 1978, by which Denmark, Ireland and the UK became parties, led to amendment of the text of the 1968 Convention. The 1982 Act came into force on 1 January 1987. The 1968 Convention was further amended as a result of further accessions. Greece acceded to the Convention by an Accession Convention of 1982. In 1989, Spain and Portugal did likewise by an Accession Convention, often referred to as the San Sebastian Convention, which involved amendment of the original 1968 Convention. The amendments resulting from the San Sebastian Convention came into force in the UK on 1 December 1991, being implemented by SI 1990/2591. By an Accession Convention in 1996 Austria, Finland and Sweden became parties.

[4] Section 3 of the Brussels Convention.

[4a] On 8 April 2020, the UK submitted its application to accede to the 2007 Lugano Convention (in accordance with the UK Government's previous statements of intention) from the end of the Brexit implementation period.

[4b] On 24 January 2019, Switzerland and the UK signed the Agreement between the UK and the Swiss Confederation on direct insurance other than life assurance. See the Joint Statement on Signing the Agreement between the UK and the Swiss Confederation on direct insurance other than life insurance, a Treasury policy paper setting out a bilateral Agreement between the UK and the Swiss Confederation to provide continuity when the UK is no longer subject to the EU-Swiss Direct Insurance Agreement.

[4c] As noted above, on 8 April 2020, the UK submitted its application to accede to the 2007 Lugano Convention (in accordance with the UK Government's previous statements of intention) from the end of the Brexit implementation period.

Regulations 44/2001 and 1215/2012 and the Conventions: general points.

Replace footnote 14 with:

[14] art.1(2)(d) of the Regulations, and recital 12 and art.73(2) of the Recast Regulation; *The Atlantic Emperor* [1989] 1 Lloyd's Rep. 548; [1992] 1 Lloyd's Rep. 342 (English court proceedings relating to appointment of arbitrator fell within Convention exclusion); *The Atlantic Emperor (No.2)* [1992] 1 Lloyd's Rep. 624 (submission to jurisdiction); *Partenreederei M/S Heidberg v Grosvenor Grain & Feed Co Ltd* [1994] 2 Lloyd's Rep. 287; *Toepfer International GmbH v Molino Boschi SRL* [1996] 1 Lloyd's Rep. 510; *Toepfer International GmbH v Societe Cargill France* [1997] 2 Lloyd's Rep. 98; *Vale do Rio Doce Navegacao SA v Shanghai Bao Steel Ocean Shipping Co Ltd* [2000] CLC 1200; *Through Transport Mutual Insurance Association (Eurasia) Ltd v New India Assurance Co Ltd (The Hari Bhum) (No.1)* [2005] 1 Lloyd's Rep. 67 (declaratory relief and anti-suit injunctions). This last case is now in part no longer good law as a result of the decision of the ECJ in *Allianz SpA (formerly Riunione Adriatica di Sicurta SpA) v West Tankers Inc* (C-185/07) [2009] 1 A.C. 1138 (incompatible with reg.44/2001 to grant anti-suit injunction to restrain proceedings in another Member State on the ground that such proceedings were in breach of an arbitration agreement), and note the effect of recital 12 and art.73(2) of the Recast Regulation: see further discussion below. See also *CMA CGM SA v Hyundai MIPO Dockyard Co Ltd* [2009] 1 Lloyd's Rep. 213 at [41]–[46] (arbitral tribunal applying English law not obliged to recognise judgment given in a Member State); *Youell v La Reunion Aerienne* [2009] 1 Lloyd's Rep. 586 (negative declaratory relief); *National Navigation Co v Endesa Generacion SA (The Wadi Sudr)* [2010] 1 Lloyd's Rep. 193 (incorporation of London arbitration clause, declaratory relief and anti-suit injunction). For a recent insurance case considering anti-suit injunctions, see *Enka Insaat ve Sanayi AS v OOO Insurance Co Chubb* [2020] EWCA Civ 574; [2020] 3 All E.R. 577.

13-004

A primary aim of reg.44/2001 and reg.1215/2012 and the discretion to stay.

Replace third paragraph with:

However, it appears that *Owusu* has significantly restricted the ability of a third state domiciled defendant to seek a stay of proceedings where jurisdiction under the Regulation has been established against one or more co-defendants. In *Lungowe v Vedanta Resources Plc*,[50] the Court of Appeal confirmed that position since *Owusu*

13-007

is clear "and the debate has moved on"; the effect of the ECJ decision in *Owusu* is that art.4 of the Recast Regulation precludes the English court from declining what is a mandatory jurisdiction where the defendant is a company domiciled in England and Wales. The court also refused to grant a stay against a Zambian domiciled defendant on forum non conveniens grounds, concurring with the editors of *Dicey, Morris & Collins on the Conflict of Laws* that the indirect effect of *Owusu* is that the ability of those co-defendants to obtain a stay (or to resist service out of the jurisdiction) by pointing to the courts of a non-Member State which would otherwise represent the forum conveniens, will be reduced, for to grant jurisdictional relief to some but not to others will fragment what ought to be conducted as a single trial.[51]

[50] *Lungowe v Vedanta Resources Plc* [2017] EWCA Civ 1528; [2018] 1 W.L.R. 3575. The Supreme Court dismissed the appeal from the Court of Appeal: [2019] UKSC 20; [2019] 2 W.L.R. 1051. It is, of course, important to have regard to the full judgment of the Supreme Court, which is beyond the scope of this work.

[51] *Lungowe v Vedanta Resources Plc* [2017] EWCA Civ 1528; [2018] 1 W.L.R. 3575 at [113], citing *Dicey, Morris & Collins on the Conflict of Laws*, 15th edn (2015), para.12-033. The Supreme Court dismissed the appeal from the Court of Appeal: [2019] UKSC 20; [2019] 2 W.L.R. 1051. It is, of course, important to have regard to the full judgment of the Supreme Court, which is beyond the scope of this work.

Special jurisdiction.

Replace first paragraph with:

13-009   Alternatives to domicile as a basis of jurisdiction are provided by arts 5–6 of the Regulation (arts 7–8, Recast Regulation). Article 5(1) (art.7(1), Recast Regulation) provides for the defendant to be sued in the courts for the place of performance of the obligation in question, i.e. the obligation which forms the basis of the action.[58] The obligation must be contractual as between the parties to the claim:

> "It is ... not enough for Article 7(1) purposes to show that there is a contract with freely assumed obligations which is somewhere in the background, or even one which is a stepping stone to the ultimate liability of the defendant. It must be the basis for the obligation actually relied upon by the claimant as against the defendant."[59]

The obligation to exercise good faith prior to the conclusion of an insurance contract comes within the scope of art.5(1) (art.7(1), Recast Regulation).[60] The court must be satisfied that there is a good arguable case to establish jurisdiction.[61] In this context, applying the "good arguable case" standard, the party asserting the English court's jurisdiction must show that they have a much[62] better argument on the material available than the party denying jurisdiction, on the material available at the time of the jurisdictional challenge, that the requirements of the Regulations (or Convention, as applicable) are met.[63] In *Brownlie v Four Seasons Holdings Inc*, the Supreme Court confirmed (obiter) that "good arguable case" remained the correct test, but noted that that the reference to "a much better argument on the material available" should not be read as a reversion to the civil burden of proof. What is meant is: (i) that the claimant must supply a plausible evidential basis for the application of a relevant jurisdictional gateway; (ii) that if there is an issue of fact about it, or some other reason for doubting whether it applies, the court must take a view on the material available if it can reliably do so; but (iii) the nature of the issue and the limitations of the material available at the interlocutory stage may be such that no reliable assessment can be made, in which case there is a good arguable case for the application of the gateway if there is a plausible (albeit contested) evidential basis for it.[64]

[58] See, for example, *Union Transport Plc v Continental Lines SA* [1992] 1 W.L.R. 15 (failure to nominate vessel for charter). Note that the Regulation introduced special sub-rules for sales of goods and provision of services; these do not appear to be relevant to a contract of insurance. It is settled law that the relevant obligation in a reinsurance contract is the obligation of the reinsurer to pay, and the normal default rule under English law that this payment obligation is to be performed in the creditor's location applies to reinsurance contracts governed by English law: *Gard Marine & Energy Ltd v Tunnicliffe* [2009] EWHC 2388 (Comm); [2010] Lloyd's Rep. I.R. 62 at [36]–[44] (this issue did not arise on appeal: [2010] EWCA Civ 1052; [2011] I.L.Pr. 10). Cf. *Youell v La Reunion Aerienne* [2009] Lloyd's Rep. I.R. 405 at [17] where the applicable law was French law, under which the payment obligation is to be performed in the debtor's location.

[59] *XL Insurance Co SE (formerly XL Insurance Co Ltd) v AXA Corporate Solutions Assurance* [2015] EWHC 3431 (Comm); [2016] Lloyd's Rep. I.R. 420 at [28]. In that case, Judge Waksman QC held that a claim for contribution in a case of double insurance was not a matter relating to contract within the meaning of art.7(1). For a commentary on the decision in *XL Insurance v AXA Corporate Solutions*, see "Contribution: Jurisdiction over contribution claims" (2016) 28 I.L.M. 4. For an equivalent approach in respect of the Rome I and Rome II Regulations see para.13-094 below.

[60] In *Trade Indemnity Plc v Forsakrings A.B. Njord* [1995] 1 All E.R. 796 (a reinsurance case where it was accepted that the special rules as to insurance in s.3 of the Convention did not apply) it was held by Rix J that the obligation did not come within art.5(1). However, the opposite conclusion was reached by Mance J in *Agnew v Lansforsakringsbolagens A.B.* [1996] L.R.L.R. 392. The decision in *Agnew* was affirmed by the Court of Appeal, [1997] L.R.L.R. 671, and by the House of Lords: [2001] 1 A.C. 223. By contrast, a claim to recover moneys pursuant to a contract subsequently admitted to be void is not a matter relating to a contract within art.5(1), *Kleinwort Benson Ltd v Glasgow City Council* [1999] 1 A.C. 153 HL. Presumably, a claim by the insurer to avoid a contract, coupled with a claim for repayment of moneys previously paid to the insured, would fall within art.5(1), although the point is not free from difficulty. In *Fisher v Unione Italiana de Riassicurazione SpA* [1999] Lloyd's Rep. I.R. 215, a claim for rescission based on an alleged breach of the duty of disclosure was held to be within art.5(1). Where a reinsurer principally claimed a declaration of non-liability to its Greek reinsured based upon a failure to comply with an obligation to notify loss under a claims co-operation clause, it was held that art.5(1) applied to give the English Court jurisdiction, notwithstanding an alternative claim for damages: *AIG Europe (UK) Ltd v The Ethniki* [2000] Lloyd's Rep. I.R. 343.

[61] *Canada Trust Co v Stolzenberg* [1998] 1 W.L.R. 547 at 553–559 CA; [2000] 4 All E.R. 481 HL; *Deutsche Ruckversicherung A.G. v La Fondiara* [2001] 2 Lloyd's Rep. 621.

[62] The word "much" has been regarded as adding little of substance to the test, but emphasises the fact that if, in the rare case, there were a dead-heat between the parties' rival cases, the claimant's assertion of jurisdiction would fail: *Joint Stock Co Aeroflot Russian Airlines v Berezovsky* [2013] EWCA Civ 784; [2013] 2 Lloyd's Rep. 575 at [50]; *Kaefer Aislamientos SA de CV v AMS Drilling Mexico SA de CV* [2017] EWHC 2598 (Comm); [2017] 2 Lloyd's Rep. 575 at [57]—decision affirmed on appeal: [2019] EWCA Civ 10; [2019] 1 W.L.R. 3514, and see the Court of Appeal's helpful analysis and guidance at [57]–[80]. It should not be taken as suggesting a superior standard of conviction: *Brownlie v Four Seasons Holdings Inc* [2017] UKSC 80; [2018] 1 W.L.R. 192 at [7]. Now see the decision of the Supreme Court in *Aspen Underwriting Ltd v Credit Europe Bank NV* [2020] UKSC 11; [2020] 2 W.L.R. 919 at [21].

[63] *Bols Distilleries BV (t/a Bols Royal Distilleries) v Superior Yacht Services Ltd* [2006] UKPC 45; [2007] 1 W.L.R. 12 at [28], *Gard Marine & Energy Ltd v Tunnicliffe* [2009] EWHC 2388 (Comm); [2010] Lloyd's Rep. I.R. 62 at [19] (this issue did not arise on appeal: [2010] EWCA Civ 1052; [2011] I.L. Pr. 10) and *Joint Stock Co Aeroflot Russian Airlines v Berezovsky* [2013] EWCA Civ 784 at [47]–[48] (relating to the 2007 Lugano Convention).

[64] *Brownlie v Four Seasons Holdings Inc* [2017] UKSC 80; [2018] 1 W.L.R. 192 at [7] (per Lord Sumption) and [33] (per Baroness Hale). See also the decision of the Court of Appeal in *Aspen Underwriting Ltd v Kairos Shipping Ltd* [2018] EWCA Civ 2590; [2019] 1 Lloyd's Rep. 221 at [34], in relevant part as follows: "... nothing said in *Brownlie* invalidated the approach adopted by the judge to the applicable standard of proof to be satisfied by Underwriters – on whom the burden of proof rested – to come within the relevant Brussels Recast jurisdictional gateways. As is clear from *Brownlie*, the test remains that of 'a good arguable case'. A majority of the Supreme Court deprecated any 'glossing' of that test but said, in terms, that Lord Sumption's 'explication', at para 7, did not constitute any such impermissible gloss. Accordingly, a good arguable case remains something more than a prima facie case and something less than a case satisfying a balance of probabilities test. Where there is a dispute as to the applicability of a gateway, unless prevented by reason of some consideration relating to the interlocutory stage of the proceedings, the court 'must take a view on the material available if it can reliably do so'. With regard to the disputed issues on this appeal, there does not seem to me to be any reason why the court cannot make a reliable assessment. For my part, I think that is what the judge did: on the mate-

rial available, he took a view and made an assessment. I would be content to say that in asking himself who had the better of the argument on the material available, the judge may be seen to give effect to the test as subsequently formulated in *Brownlie*; but it suffices to conclude, as I do, that if any distinction can be drawn between the judge's approach and the *Brownlie* formulation, it is a distinction without any meaningful difference. ..." Now see the decision of the Supreme Court in *Aspen Underwriting Ltd v Credit Europe Bank NV* [2020] UKSC 11; [2020] 2 W.L.R. 919 at [21]. See also *Griffin Underwriting Ltd v Varouxakis* [2019] 1 W.L.R. 2529 at [62] and the Court of Appeal's detailed and careful analysis and guidance in [2019] EWCA Civ 10; [2019] 1 W.L.R. 3514 at [57]–[80].

Jurisdiction in matters relating to insurance.

Replace paragraph with:

13-011   Section 3 of reg.44/2001, comprising arts 8–14 (arts 10–16 in the Recast Regulation), contains special jurisdictional rules[72] for "matters relating to insurance".[73] Unlike the rules relating to consumer and employment contracts, the rules in s.3 have not been altered in the Recast Regulation.[74] The rules in s.3 are not applicable to reinsurance.[75] Nor do the rules in s.3 apply to actions between insurers, whether they are the assignee of the insured or not.[76] They also do not, it is submitted, apply to subrogated claims brought on behalf of insurers against third parties. The rules are not restricted to consumer contracts of insurance, nor to contracts where there is inequality of bargaining power.[77] They apply without prejudice to arts 4 and 5(5) of reg.44/2001 (arts 6 and 7(5), Recast Regulation).[78] They do not apply to the jurisdictional regime for different parts of the UK which is contained in Sch.2 of the Civil and Jurisdiction and Judgments Order 2001.[79] Article 9 of the Regulation (art.11, Recast Regulation) contains a special rule as to domicile under which an insurer who would not otherwise be domiciled in a Member State but has a branch, agency or other establishment in that Member State is, in disputes arising out of the branch, agency or establishment, deemed to be domiciled in that State.[80] If a judgment conflicts with rules in s.3, that will be a ground for the judgment not to be recognised or enforced in other Member States.[81]

[72] The rules have been described as a "self-contained and exclusive code governing insurance": *Baltic Insurance Group v Jordan Grand Prix* [1999] Lloyd's Rep. I.R. 93 at 95.

[73] On this issue, now see the decision of the Supreme Court in *Aspen Underwriting Ltd v Credit Europe Bank NV* [2020] UKSC 11; [2020] 2 W.L.R. 919, summarised in para.13-011A below. The following should be read in light of that decision: in determining whether a matter "relates to insurance" the court will consider whether the subject matter of the dispute relates to insurance "in a broad and common-sense manner". However, the mere fact that an insurance policy features in the history or pathology of the claim may not be enough to cause the subject-matter of the dispute to relate to insurance: *Aspen Underwriting Ltd v Kairos Shipping Ltd* [2017] EWHC 1904 (Comm); [2017] 2 Lloyd's Rep. 295 at [68]–[70]. At [61], Teare J noted that although the meaning of "matters relating to insurance" will no doubt have an autonomous meaning and will not be dependent upon national laws, he considered it helpful to look at three English cases for the guidance they give: *Jordan v Baltic* [1999] 2 A.C. 127; *The Ikarian Reefer (No.2)* [2000] 1 Lloyd's Rep. 129; and *Mapfre v Keefe* [2016] Lloyd's Rep. I.R. 94. The Court of Appeal dismissed the appeal from Teare J's decision: [2018] EWCA Civ 2590; [2019] 1 Lloyd's Rep. 221. The Court of Appeal held that the underwriters' claim was a "matter relating to insurance" within art.10 of the Recast Regulation, but the bank in that case could not take advantage of the principle in art.14 that the underwriters could only bring an action in the Netherlands courts, where the bank was domiciled. The Court of Appeal held (at [77]) that: "However, as a matter of reality and substance, the foundation of Underwriters' claims lies in the Policy. Central to Underwriters' claims, as the Judge explained (at [69] – [70], set out above), was the question of Underwriters' liability or non-liability to indemnify Owners under the Policy. The crucial (if not the only) question is whether the Vessel was lost by reason of a peril insured against under the Policy or whether the loss arose by reason of wilful misconduct on the part of Owners. On this footing, there is the most material nexus between Underwriters' claims and the Policy. Further still, a consideration of the Policy is indispensable to the determination of the claim. As a matter of common sense, having regard to the autonomous meaning to be given to Section 3 and fortified by *Brogsitter* and *Arcadia*, notwithstanding the interposition of the Settlement Agreement, Underwriters' claims come squarely within the heading 'matters relating to insurance'." As set out above, now see the decision of the Supreme Court in *Aspen Underwriting Ltd v Credit Europe Bank NV* [2020] UKSC 11; [2020] 2 W.L.R. 919, summarised at para.13-011A below.The matter is understood now to be proceeding to the Supreme Court. See also the recent decision of Butcher J in

London Steam-ship Owners' Mutual Insurance Association Ltd v Spain (The Prestige) (No.4) [2020] EWHC 1920 (Comm).

[74] Note however the new requirement that under art.26(2) of the Recast Regulation where the policyholder, the insured, a beneficiary of the insurance contract, the injured party, the consumer or the employee is the defendant, the court shall, before assuming jurisdiction under art.26(1), ensure that the defendant is informed of his right to contest the jurisdiction of the court and of the consequences of entering or not entering an appearance.

[75] *Group Josi Reinsurance Co SA v Universal General Insurance Co* (C-412/98) [2001] Lloyd's Rep. I.R. 483, anticipated by the House of Lords in *Agnew v Lansforsakringsbolagens AB* [2001] 1 A.C. 223. See the consideration of the *Group Josi* case by the Supreme Court in *Aspen Underwriting Ltd v Credit Europe Bank NV* [2020] UKSC 11; [2020] 2 W.L.R. 919, summarised at para.13-011A above. For prior consideration of the point, see Schlosser report [1979] OJ C59/1, para.151; *Citadel Insurance Co v Atlantic Union Insurance Co* [1982] 2 Lloyd's Rep. 543; *Arkwright Mutual Insurance Co v Bryanston Insurance Co Ltd* [1990] 2 Q.B. 649; *Overseas Union Insurance Ltd v New Hampshire Insurance Co* (C-351/89) [1992] Q.B. 434; *New Hampshire Insurance Co v Strabag Bau AG* [1992] 1 Lloyd's Rep 361; *Trade Indemnity v Forsakrings A.B. Njord* [1995] 1 All E.R. 796.

[76] *Youell v La Reunion Aerienne* [2009] Lloyd's Rep. I.R. 405 at [19]–[23] (unchallenged on this point on appeal, [2009] 1 Lloyd's Rep. 586).

[77] *New Hampshire Insurance Co v Strabag Bau AG* [1990] 2 Lloyd's Rep. 61; affirmed [1992] 1 Lloyd's Rep. 361.

[78] reg.44/2001 art.8 (reg.1215/2012 art.10).

[79] Civil and Jurisdiction and Judgments Order 2001 (SI 2001/3929).

[80] art.9(2) (reg.1215/2012 art.11(2)), applied in *Berisford v New Hampshire Insurance Co* [1990] 2 Q.B. 631. If the State is the UK, the insurer will be deemed to be domiciled in the part of the UK in which the branch, agency or establishment is situated: s.44 of the 1982 Act and s.11 of Sch.1 of (SI 2001/3929). "Part of the UK" means England and Wales, Scotland or Northern Ireland: s.50 of the 1982 Act.

[81] reg.44/2001 art.35(1) (reg.1215/2012 art.45(1)).

After para.13-011, add new paragraphs:

The recent decision of the Supreme Court in *Aspen Underwriting Ltd v Credit Europe Bank NV*[81a] is important in a number of respects and is addressed here as a whole for convenience.[81b]   **13-011A**

[81a] *Aspen Underwriting Ltd v Credit Europe Bank NV* [2020] UKSC 11; [2020] 2 W.L.R. 919.

[81b] See also the recent decision of Butcher J in *London Steam-ship Owners' Mutual Insurance Association Ltd v Spain (The Prestige) (No.4)* [2020] EWHC 1920 (Comm).

In summary of the factual background, Aspen Underwriting Ltd (the Insurers) insured the Atlantik Confidence (the Vessel) pursuant to an insurance policy which contained a clause giving exclusive jurisdiction to the courts of England and Wales. Credit Europe NV (the Bank), a Dutch bank which held a mortgage over the vessel, was named as loss payee in the insurance policy and took an assignment of it. The Vessel sank and the Insurers entered into a settlement agreement with the owners and managers of the Vessel, to which the Bank was not a party, pursuant to which the Insurers paid a sum to the Bank. Three years later the Admiralty Court held that the owners of the Vessel had deliberately sunk her. The Insurers commenced proceedings in the High Court against the owners, the managers and the Bank seeking damages for misrepresentation and restitution of the money which they had paid out. The Bank challenged the jurisdiction of the English courts, contending that the claim was a "matter relating to insurance", within art.14(1) of the Recast Regulation, with the consequence that the Insurers could bring proceedings only in the courts of the Member State of the Bank's domicile, namely the Netherlands. The Insurers contended that the English courts had jurisdiction pursuant to arts 15 or 25 of the Recast Regulation (on the basis that the exclusive jurisdiction clause in the policy fell within those articles) and/or pursuant to art.7(2) of the

Recast Regulation (on the basis that the claims were "matters relating to tort" and the harmful event had occurred in England).

At first instance, Teare J held that: (i) the bank was not bound by the exclusive jurisdiction clause; (ii) the claim was a "matter relating to insurance", within art.14(1); but (iii) the Bank could not rely on art.14 because the provisions of s.3 of Ch.II of the Recast Regulation, which contained art.14, were available only to protect a weaker party, which the Bank was not; and (iv) the English courts had jurisdiction in respect of the claim for damages, although not the claim for restitution, under art.7(2). The Court of Appeal upheld that decision. Both the Insurers and the Bank appealed. The Supreme Court dismissed the Insurers appeal, allowed the Bank's appeal and declared that the High Court does not have jurisdiction over the Insurers' claims against the Bank.

Lord Hodge gave the judgment of the court. At [3], Lord Hodge noted that the appeals raise four issues which concern the interpretation of the Recast Regulation. The issues are: (i) Does the High Court have jurisdiction pursuant to the exclusive jurisdiction clause contained in the Policy? (ii) Are the Insurers' claims against the Bank "matters relating to insurance" within s.3 of Ch.II of the Recast Regulation? (iii) If the answer to (ii) is yes, is the Bank entitled to rely on s.3 by virtue of it falling within a class of persons who are entitled to the protection afforded by that Section? (iv) Are the Insurers' claims for restitution matters relating to tort, delict or quasi-delict under art.7(2) of the Recast Regulation?

13-011B Before discussing the issues raised in the appeals, Lord Hodge made some general comments about the structure of the Recast Regulation. At [19], Lord Hodge noted that in order to promote the free circulation of judgments within Member States, the Recast Regulation seeks to set out rules which are highly predictable and are founded on the principle that jurisdiction is generally based on the defendant's domicile. At [20], Lord Hodge also noted that it is only in well-defined circumstances that jurisdiction based on domicile is replaced by a different connecting factor based on the subject matter of the dispute or the autonomy of the parties (recital (15)). The CJEU has repeatedly held that articles which provide for the exclusion of jurisdiction based on domicile are to be narrowly interpreted. Subject to certain exclusive grounds of jurisdiction, the Regulation also respects the autonomy of parties to a contract to determine the courts to have jurisdiction but it restricts that autonomy in insurance, consumer and employment contracts (recital (19)). It appears to me that when a court comes to interpret an article in the Regulation it must consider whether on the one hand the rule contained in the article supports the general rule of jurisdiction based on the defendant's domicile, or on the other hand purports to exclude or provide an alternative to that general rule.

Importantly, at [21] Lord Hodge addressed "the relevant test" and stated that although there was a challenge in the Court of Appeal, there was now no disagreement between the parties that in relation to the preliminary question of the jurisdiction of the English courts it is for the Insurers to show that they have a good arguable case in the sense that they have the better of the argument.

Issue 1 ("Does the High Court have jurisdiction pursuant to the exclusive English jurisdiction clause contained in the Policy?") is addressed at [22]–[30]. The Supreme Court found that Teare J and the Court of Appeal did not err on this issue.

At [24], Lord Hodge noted (by reference to various EU law authorities) that under EU law a jurisdiction agreement in a contract will bind a defendant only if there is actual consensus between the parties which is clearly and precisely demonstrated. Thus, a jurisdiction agreement in an insurance contract does not bind a third-party beneficiary of insurance who is domiciled in a different contracting state and who has not expressly subscribed to the clause. Nor does such an agreement bind a victim of insured damage who wishes to bring an action directly against the insurer. However, at [25], Lord Hodge noted that EU law recognises that a person who is not a party to a jurisdiction agreement may be taken to have consented to it if, under the applicable national law, it became "the successor" to the rights and obligations under the contract. Lord Hodge noted that the first paragraph of (old) art.17 (now art.25 of the Recast Regulation) required that an agreement on jurisdiction had to be in writing or evidenced in writing, or in a form which accorded with practices which the parties had established between themselves, or in international trade or commerce in a form which conformed with an established trade usage of which the parties were or ought to have been aware. In the *Aspen* case it was not suggested that there was an agreement in any of those forms. The court therefore had to look to national law to determine whether the Bank can be seen in EU law as "the successor" of the owners and managers who are subject to the jurisdiction clause.

In summary of Lord Hodge's reasoning in [26]–[30], it was held that the Bank's **13-011C** entitlement to receive the proceeds of the Policy in the event that there was an insured casualty rests on its status as an equitable assignee. It is trite law that an assignment transfers rights under a contract but, absent the consent of the party to whom contractual obligations are owed, cannot transfer those obligations. As Sir Robert Megarry V-C stated in *Tito v Waddell (No.2)*,[81c] "you take the right as it stands, and you cannot pick out the good and reject the bad". This concept, which has often been described as "conditional benefit", is to the effect that an assignee cannot assert its claim under a contract in a way which is inconsistent with the terms of the contract. In Lord Hodge's view, the formulation of the principle by Hobhouse LJ in *The Jay Bola*,[81d] which the Court of Appeal approved in *The Yusuf Cepnioglu*, is the best encapsulation. This formulation emphasises the constraint on the assertion of a right as being the requirement to avoid inconsistency and, whether the clause is an arbitration clause, as in *The Jay Bola*, or an exclusive jurisdiction clause, as in *Youell*, it is the assertion of the right through legal proceedings which is in conflict with the contractual provision that gives rise to the inconsistency.

[81c] *Tito v Waddell (No.2)* [1977] Ch. 106 at 290.

[81d] *The Jay Bola* [1997] 2 Lloyd's Rep. 279.

In conclusion on this issue, at [29]–[30], Lord Hodge held that in the present case the Bank did not commence legal proceedings to enforce its claim. The Bank was not a party to the Settlement Agreement and the Bank derived no rights from that agreement. At the time of payment of the proceeds of the Policy there was no dispute as to the Bank's entitlement and no need for legal proceedings. There was therefore no inconsistency between the Bank's actions and the exclusive jurisdiction clause. The Bank therefore was not bound by an agreement as to jurisdiction under art.15 or art.25 of the Recast Regulation.

Turning to issues 2 and 3 ("Are the Insurers' claims against the Bank matters relating to insurance within s.3 of Ch.II of the Recast Regulation and if so, is the Bank entitled to rely on that Section?"), these are addressed at [31]–[61]. The background to these issues is explained atin [31]–[32], including that s.3 of Ch.II of the Recast Regulation is entitled "Jurisdiction in matters relating to insurance". The Section sets out rules which govern jurisdiction in matters relating to insurance. The relevant article in this appeal was art.14(1) which provides (so far as relevant):

[21]

"an insurer may bring proceedings *only* in the courts of the member state in which the defendant is domiciled, irrespective of whether he is the policyholder, the insured or a beneficiary" (emphasis added). It is noteworthy that the article, unlike many articles in the Recast Regulation, is not creating an alternative ground of jurisdiction in addition to domicile of the defendant, nor is it purporting to exclude the domicile of the defendant as an available ground. On the contrary, it makes that ground of jurisdiction, which is the same as the principal ground of jurisdiction under art.4, the exclusive ground in those circumstances in which art.14 applies.

13-011D   Teare J had held that the nature of the Insurers' claim against the Bank was so closely connected with the question of the Insurers' liability to indemnify for the loss of the Vessel under the Policy that the subject matter of the claim can fairly be said to relate to insurance. The Court of Appeal, agreeing with Teare J, stated[81e]:

> "as a matter of reality and substance, the foundation of the underwriters' claims lies in the policy ... The crucial (if not the only) question is whether the vessel was lost by reason of a peril insured against under the policy or whether the loss arose by reason of wilful misconduct on the part of the owners. On this footing, there is the most material nexus between the underwriters' claims and the policy."

However, the Bank did not obtain the protection of art.14 of the Recast Regulation because (although their reasoning diverged) both Teare J and the Court of Appeal held that that protection was available only to the weaker party in circumstances of economic imbalance between the claimant insurer and the defendant.

[81e] *Aspen Underwriting Ltd v Credit Europe Bank NV* [2019] 1 Lloyd's Rep. 221 at [78].

Addressing issue 2 (i.e. are the Insurers' claims against the Bank matters relating to insurance within s.3 of Ch.II of the Recast Regulation) at [33]–[41], the Supreme Court was not persuaded that Teare J or the Court of Appeal had erred in their approach. Lord Hodge set out five reasons for reaching this conclusion, only the first two of which are addressed here: first, the title to s.3 "Jurisdiction in matters relating to insurance" is broader than the words of art.7(1) "matters relating to *a contract*" (emphasis added). Similarly, it is wider than the titles of s.4 "Jurisdiction over consumer contracts" and s.5 "Jurisdiction over individual contracts of employment". The difference in wording is significant as it would require to be glossed if it were to be read as "Matters relating to an insurance contract". Such a gloss would not be consistent with the requirement of a high level of predictability of which recital (15) speaks. Secondly, the scheme of s.3 is concerned with the rights not only of parties to an insurance contract, who are the insurer and the policyholder, but also beneficiaries of insurance and, in the context of liability insurance, the injured party, who will generally not be parties to the insurance contract. The Supreme Court therefore concluded on issue 2 that the Insurers' claims against the Bank were matters relating to insurance within s.3 of Ch.II of the Recast Regulation.

It was on issue 3 where the Supreme Court disagreed with the conclusion of Teare J and the Court of Appeal. Lord Hodge stated, at [43], that there is no "weaker party" exception[81f] which removes a policyholder, an insured or a beneficiary from the protection of art.14. Lord Hodge came to this view for the following six reasons:

1)   First, the reason why art.14 protects the policyholder, the insured and the beneficiary of an insurance policy is because they are generally the weaker

    party in a commercial negotiation with an insurance company and are as a matter of course presented with a standard form contract: see [44].

2)   Secondly, while recital (18) explains the policy behind, among others, s.3 of Ch.II of the Recast Regulation, it is the words of the relevant articles which have legal effect and the recitals are simply an aid to interpretation of those articles: see [45].

3)   Thirdly, derogations from the jurisdictional rules in matters of insurance must be interpreted strictly: see [46].

4)   Fourthly, the CJEU in its jurisprudence has set its face against a case-by-case analysis of the relative strength or weakness of contracting parties as that would militate against legal certainty. Instead, it has treated everyone within the categories of the policyholder, the insured or the beneficiary as protected unless the Recast Regulation explicitly provides otherwise: see [47]–[49] and Lord Hodge's analysis of the cases of *KABEG*[81g] and *Peloux*.[81h]

5)   Fifthly, the CJEU looks to recital (18) not to decide whether a particular policyholder, insured or beneficiary is to be protected by s.3 but in the context of reaching a decision whether by analogy those protections are to be extended to other persons who do not fall within the list of expressly protected persons. As expanded upon from [50] onwards, Lord Hodge held that the case law of the CJEU, to which the Court of Appeal referred for support of the view that the Bank should be excluded from the protection of art.14 of the Recast Regulation because there was not an economic imbalance between it and the Insurers, does not support that conclusion. Lord Hodge then carefully considered and analysed the cases of *Group Josi*[81i]; *Vorarlberger*[81j]; *KABEG*; and *Hofsoe*.[81k] Lord Hodge concluded, at [56], that in none of these cases where the CJEU has relied on the "weaker party" criterion to rule on applications to extend the scope of the s.3 protections beyond those parties who were clearly the policyholder, the insured, the beneficiary or the injured party, did the court call into question the entitlement of those expressly-named persons to that protection by reason of their economic power. On the contrary, the CJEU has treated the exceptions to the entitlement of those persons as confined to the exceptions expressly stated in arts 15(5) and 16 of the Recast Regulation.

6)   Sixthly, the policy which underlies the jurisprudence of the CJEU when it decides whether to extend the protection to persons not expressly mentioned in s.3 is that the court seeks to uphold the general rule in art.4 that defendants should be sued in the courts of the Member State of their domicile and allows extensions to the protection of s.3 only where such an extension is consistent with the policy of protecting the weaker party.

[81f] On this issue see also the recent decision of Butcher J in *London Steam-ship Owners' Mutual Insurance Association Ltd v Spain (The Prestige) (No.4)* [2020] EWHC 1920 (Comm).

[81g] *Landeskrankenanstalten-Betriebsgesellschaft-KABEG v Mutuelles du Mans Assurances IARD SA* (C-340/16) EU:C:2017:576; [2017] I.L.Pr. 31.

[81h] *Peloux* (C-112/03) EU:C:2005:280; [2006] Q.B. 251.

[81i] *Group Josi Reinsurance Co SA v Universal General Insurance Co* (C-412/98) EU:C:2000:399; [2001] Q.B. 68.

[81j] *Vorarlberger Gebietskrankenkasse v WGV-Schwabische Allgemeine Versicherungs AG* (C-347/08) EU:C:2009:561; [2010] Lloyd's Rep. I.R. 77.

[81k] *Hofsoe v LVM Landwirtschaftlicher Versicherungsverein Munster AG* (C-106/17) EU:C:2018:50; [2018] I.L.Pr. 12.

Lord Hodge noted, at [57], that the CJEU has repeatedly stated that derogations from the principle of the jurisdiction of the defendant's domicile must be exceptional in nature and be interpreted strictly: *Group Josi* (at [36] and [49]–[50]); *Vorarlberger* (at [36]–[39]); and *Hofsoe* (at [40]). The jurisdiction of the forum actoris, which arts 11(1)(b) and 13(2) of the Recast Regulation confer, is a derogation from the general principle of the jurisdiction of the defendant's domicile. Article 14, which requires the insurer to bring proceedings only in the courts of the Member State of the domicile of the insured, involves no such derogation but on the contrary supports the general principle. As set out at [59], in Lord Hodge's view, under the test laid down in *CILFIT Srl v Ministero della Sanita*,[811] it is acte clair that a person which is correctly categorised as a policyholder, insured or beneficiary is entitled to the protection of s.3 of Ch.II of the Recast Regulation, whatever its economic power relative to the insurer. It was not necessary to refer a question to the CJEU on this issue. Therefore, the Bank as the named loss payee under the Policy was the "beneficiary" of the Policy. It was entitled to benefit from the protections of s.3, including the requirement under art.14 that it must be sued in the courts of the Member State of its domicile. It followed that the Insurers could not assert jurisdiction under art.7(2) of the Recast Regulation in respect of the claims for misrepresentation. Further, issue 4, the question whether claims in unjust enrichment fall within art.7(2), did not arise. As a result, it was held that the courts of England and Wales had no jurisdiction in respect of the Insurers' claims against the Bank.

[811] *CILFIT Srl v Ministero della Sanita* (C-283/81) EU:C:1982:335; [1982] E.C.R. 3415 at [21].

Actions against insurers.

Replace footnote 92 with:

13-013   [92]   reg.44/2001 art.11/reg.1215/2012 art.13. See *Société financière et Industrielle du Peloux v Axa Belgium* EU:C:2005:280; [2006] Q.B. 251, where the insurer was not permitted to rely on a jurisdiction clause in favour of another state. See the consideration of this decision by the Supreme Court in *Aspen Underwriting Ltd v Credit Europe Bank NV* [2020] UKSC 11; [2020] 2 W.L.R. 919, summarised at para.13-011A above; and by Andrews J in *Hutchinson v Mapfre Espana Compania de Seguros y Reaseguros SA* [2020] EWHC 178 (QB). For a recent case concerning reg.44/2001 art.11, see *Hoteles Pinero Canarias SL v Keefe* [2015] EWCA Civ 598, addressed in more detail at para.13-014 below.

Replace footnote 97 with:

[97]   *Vorarlberger Gebietskrankenkasse v WGV-Schwäbische Allgemeine Versicherungs AG* (C-347/08) [2010] Lloyd's Rep. I.R. 77. The ECJ's decision was based on the view that the special rules in respect of jurisdiction in insurance matters are a departure, designed to protect the economically weaker party, from the primary jurisdictional rules, and since the social security institution was not argued to be the economically weaker party, no special protection was justified and it could not rely on the combined effect of arts 9(1)(b) and 11(2) of the Regulation: [40]–[47]. The ECJ suggested that, by contrast, the executors of an injured party who dies, again statutory assignees, would be able to take advantage of the insurance jurisdiction rules: at [44]. See the consideration of this decision by the Supreme Court in *Aspen Underwriting Ltd v Credit Europe Bank NV* [2020] UKSC 11; [2020] 2 W.L.R. 919, summarised at para.13-011A above; and by Butcher J in *London Steam-ship Owners' Mutual Insurance Association Ltd v Spain (The Prestige) (No.4)* [2020] EWHC 1920 (Comm). In *Landeskrankenanstalten-Betriebsgesellschaft–KABEG v Mutuelles du Mans Assurances IARD SA* (C-340/16) EU:C:2017:576; [2018] C.E.C. 114 the CJEU held that employers who have paid the salary of an employee and have the right to claim for that compensation may rely on the special rules of jurisdiction in arts 8–10. See the consideration of this decision by the Supreme Court in *Aspen Underwriting* [2020] 2 W.L.R. 919, summarised at para.13-011A above; and by Butcher J in *London Steam-ship* [2020] EWHC 1920 (Comm). In *Hofsoe v LVM Landwirtschaftlicher Versicherungsverein Munster AG* (C-106/17) EU:C:2018:50; [2018] I.L.Pr. 12, the CJEU held that the special rules of jurisdiction laid down in art.11(1)(b) and art.13(2) are not to be extended to persons for whom that protection was not justified. Accordingly, no special protection was justified where the assignee was an individual active in the insurance sector whose professional activity consisted in recovering claims for damages from insurers: [41]–[42]. See the consideration of this decision by the Supreme Court in *Aspen Underwriting* [2020] 2

W.L.R. 919, summarised at para.13-011A above. In the context of art.14 of the Recast Regulation, and with reference to Recital 18 (protection of "the weaker party"), and considering the position of the assignee Bank in that case, see the recent decision of the Supreme Court in *Aspen Underwriting* [2020] 2 W.L.R. 919, summarised at para.13-011A above. See also the recent decision of Butcher J in *London Steam-ship* [2020] EWHC 1920 (Comm). See also *Youell v La Reunion Aerienne* [2009] Lloyd's Rep. I.R. 405 at [22]–[23] (unchallenged on this point on appeal, [2009] 1 Lloyd's Rep. 586); and *Assens Havn v Navigators Management (UK) Ltd* (C-368/16) EU:C:2017:546; [2018] Q.B. 463, addressed in more detail at para.13-019 below; and considered briefly by the Supreme Court in *Aspen Underwriting* [2020] 2 W.L.R. 919, summarised at para.13-011A above.

Replace footnote 99 with:

[99] *Hoteles Pinero Canarias SL v Keefe* [2015] EWCA Civ 598; [2016] 1 W.L.R. 905. The decision in **13-014** *Keefe* was recently followed in *Bonnie Lackey v Mallorca Mega Resorts SL, Generali Espana De Seguros Y Reaseçuros SA* [2019] EWHC 1028 (QB); [2019] Lloyd's Rep. I.R. 525 where it was held that the English court had jurisdiction over a personal injury claim brought by a holidaymaker who was injured at a Spanish hotel while on holiday as part of a group. Master Davison held that there was no requirement under the Recast Regulation for the existence of any policy dispute before art.13(3) could operate to join the insured hotel to the claim against the insurer, nor was the term "consumer" in art.17 and art.18 to be interpreted restrictively so as to exclude the claimant on the basis that another member of the group concluded the holiday contract on its behalf. Even more recently, in *Cole v IVI Madrid SL* unreported 21 September 2019 QBD (Birmingham) the Birmingham District Registry considered whether it had jurisdiction to determine claims brought by claimants against a Spanish fertility clinic and its liability insurer. The court considered two exceptions to the general rule that a defendant should be sued in the Member State in which it was domiciled. In relation to the "insurance exception", the court referred to the CJEU the question of whether it was a requirement of art.13(3) that, for an injured person to make a parasitic claim against the insured, the claim against the insured had to involve "a matter relating to insurance". The court considered the *Keefe* case and the *Lackey* case. However, there had been a number of recent developments which cast doubt on the issue, including that the Supreme Court hearing the *Keefe* appeal had referred questions to the CJEU as to whether it was a requirement of art.13(3) that, for an injured person to make a parasitic claim against the insured, the claim against the insured had to involve "a matter relating to insurance". The European Commission supported the contention that the claim had to involve "a matter relating to insurance", and Advocate General Bobek's opinion in *KABEG* (C-340/16) [2018] I.L.Pr. 12 also supported the view that there was at least uncertainty on the issue. Therefore, it could not be said that "the matter was equally obvious to the courts of the other Member States and to the Court of Justice". The question of whether, under art.13(3), the claims must concern "a matter relating to insurance" (or at least questions that enabled that question to be answered) were referred to the CJEU.

Replace footnote 105 with:

[105] On 7 March 2017, the Supreme Court heard the appeal in the *Hoteles* case. It is understood that the matter settled. For a commentary on the *Hoteles Pinero* case (that pre-dates the Supreme Court hearing), see "Conflict of laws: Jurisdiction within the EU" (2015) 27 I.L.M. 11.

Actions by insurers.

Replace second paragraph with:

Jurisdiction in all other actions by an insurer against a policyholder, insured or **13-015** beneficiary domiciled in a Member State[107] is subject to the special rules in s.3 of reg.44/2001 and reg.1215/2012.[108] The primary rule is that an insurer may bring such proceedings in the English courts only if the defendant is domiciled in England.[109] To this there are a number of exceptions. If the dispute arises out of the operations of a branch, agency or other establishment, the action may be brought in England if the branch, agency or other establishment is situated in England, even if the defendant is domiciled in another contracting state.[110] The English courts will also have jurisdiction in the case of a counterclaim if proceedings against the insurer based on the same contract or facts have been commenced in England.[111]

[107] If the defendant is domiciled in a state which is a party to the 2007 Lugano Convention, s.3 of that Convention applies.

[108] See para.13-011 above in relation to the meaning of "matters relating to insurance" and the recent decision of the Supreme Court in *Aspen Underwriting Ltd v Credit Europe Bank NV* [2020] UKSC 11; [2020] 2 W.L.R. 919, summarised at para.13-011A above.

[109] reg.44/2001 art.12(1), Recast Regulation art.14(1). See the decision of the Supreme Court in *Aspen*

Underwriting Ltd v Credit Europe Bank NV [2020] UKSC 11; [2020] 2 W.L.R. 919, summarised at para.13-011A above.

[110] reg.44/2001 art.5(5) as expressly saved by art.8 (arts 7(5) and 10, Recast Regulation).

[111] reg.44/2001arts 6(3), 12(2) (arts 8(3) and 14(2), Recast Regulation).

Jurisdiction clauses.

Replace paragraph with:

13-016   A clause by which the parties agree that disputes are to be resolved in the English courts will generally be effective in conferring jurisdiction upon those courts.[115] The clause must on its true construction oblige the parties to resort to the English jurisdiction.[116] Consent to the clause must be clearly and precisely demonstrated.[117] General words of incorporation will normally not demonstrate that the parties to a reinsurance contract intend to incorporate a jurisdiction clause from the underlying insurance.[118] The agreement must be either in writing or evidenced in writing, or in a form which accords with practices which the parties have established between themselves, or, in international trade or commerce, in a form which accords with a usage of which the parties are or ought to have been aware and which in such trade or commerce is widely known to, and regularly observed by, parties to contracts of the type involved in the particular trade or commerce concerned.[119] The agreement can be concluded through an authorised agent.[120]

[115] See *Dicey, Morris & Collins on the Conflict of Laws*, 15th edn and 4th supplement (London: Sweet & Maxwell, 2017), Vol.1, p.599; CPR r.6.37(1)(a) and PD 6B para.3.1(6)(d); Civil Jurisdiction and Judgments Act 1982 Sch.4, art.12, as enacted by the Civil Jurisdiction and Judgments Order 2001 (SI 2001/3929) Sch.2, Pt II, s.4 (where the defendant is domiciled in Scotland or Northern Ireland). The choice must be express: *New Hampshire Insurance Co Ltd v Strabag Bau AG* [1992] 1 Lloyd's Rep. 361 at 371. For a recent case addressing the position of subrogated insurers, see *Airbus SAS v Generali Italia SpA* [2019] EWCA Civ 805; [2019] Bus. L.R. 2997.

[116] *Berisford v New Hampshire Insurance Co* [1990] 2 Q.B. 631. But it does not have to refer exclusively to the English jurisdiction: *Kurz v Stella Musical Veranstaltungs GmbH* [1992] Ch. 196. See also *Aspen Underwriting Ltd v Kairos Shipping Ltd* [2017] EWHC 1904 (Comm); [2017] 2 Lloyd's Rep. 295, where the exclusive jurisdiction clauses in neither the settlement agreement nor the policy were held to be binding on the bank. The Court of Appeal dismissed the appeal from Teare J's decision: [2018] EWCA Civ 2590; [2019] 1 Lloyd's Rep. 221. Now see the decision of the Supreme Court in *Aspen Underwriting Ltd v Credit Europe Bank NV* [2020] UKSC 11; [2020] 2 W.L.R. 919, summarised at para.13-011A above.

[117] See [2019] EWCA Civ 10; [2019] 1 W.L.R. 3514 at [81]. In the context of consumer contracts and reg.44/2001 art.23(1)(a) (Recast Regulation art.25(1)(a)), see the decision of the Court of Appeal in *Sherdley v Nordea Life and Pensions SA* [2012] EWCA Civ 88; [2012] Lloyd's Rep. I.R. 437 at [47]–[57]. See also the decision of the Supreme Court in *Aspen Underwriting Ltd v Credit Europe Bank NV* [2020] UKSC 11; [2020] 2 W.L.R. 919, summarised at para.13-011A above.

[118] *AIG Europe (UK) Ltd v The Ethniki* [2000] Lloyd's Rep. I.R. 343; *AIG Europe SA v QBE International Ins Ltd* [2001] 2 Lloyd's Rep. 268; *Prifti v Musini S.A. de Seguros y Reaseguros* [2004] Lloyd's Rep. I.R. 528; *Markel Intl Insurance Co Ltd v La Republica Comp. Argentina de Seguros* [2005] Lloyd's Rep. I.R. 90; *Dornoch Ltd v Mauritius Union Assurance Co Ltd* [2006] Lloyd's Rep. I.R. 786.

[119] Regulation 44/2001 art.23(1) (Recast Regulation art.25(1)). In the 2007 Lugano Convention the relevant provision is also art.23(1), which mirrors art.23(1) of reg.44/2001. In the Brussels and Lugano Conventions the relevant provision is art.17(1). The wording in the text reflects changes to art.17 agreed in negotiations concerning the Lugano Convention and the 1989 Accession Convention. Although the relevant article (i.e. art.23(1) in the Regulation and art.25 in the Recast Regulation) is in effect subject to the special insurance rules in arts 13 and 14 (arts 15 and 16 of the Recast Regulation), its formal requirements apply in all cases. Note that the Recast Regulation, unlike the Regulation, does not require either party to be domiciled in a Member State for a jurisdiction clause to be effective under art.25. See *Gerling v Treasury Administration* (C-201/82) [1983] E.C.R. 2503; and *Berisford v New Hampshire Insurance Co* [1990] 2 Q.B. 631 at 643. For the interpretation of those requirements, see *Dicey, Morris & Collins on the Conflict of Laws*, 15th edn (2015), Vol.1, pp.623 and following; *Standard Steamship Owners Protection & Indemnity Association (Bermuda) Ltd v GIE Vision Bail* [2005] Lloyd's Rep. I.R. 407. For decisions in respect of the Brussels Convention art.17, see *Denby v Hellenic Mediterranean Line Co Ltd* [1994] 1 Lloyd's Rep. 320 at [322]; cf. *Lloyd's Syndicate 457 v Shifco (Somali High Seas*

International Fishing Co) [2009] I.L.Pr. 18 at [19]–[31] (a decision of the Italian Court of Cassation), both cases which concerned whether the English jurisdiction clause contained in a MAR standard form policy incorporated by a slip resulted in an agreement to English jurisdiction. For a case concerning art.23 of the 2007 Lugano Convention, see *Joint Stock Co Aeroflot - Russian Airlines v Berezovsky* [2013] EWCA Civ 784; [2013] 2 Lloyd's Rep. 242, which was applied in *R+V Versicherung AG v Robertson & Co SA* [2016] EWHC 1243 (QB); [2016] 4 W.L.R. 106. See also the decision of the Supreme Court in *Aspen Underwriting Ltd v Credit Europe Bank NV* [2020] UKSC 11; [2020] 2 W.L.R. 919, summarised at para.13-011A above.

[120] *Standard Steamship v Gie Vision Bail* [2005] Lloyd's Rep. I.R. 407.

Replace footnote 121 with:

[121] *R+V Versicherung AG v Robertson & Co SA* [2016] EWHC 1243 (QB); [2016] 4 W.L.R. 106. See also the decision of the Supreme Court in *Aspen Underwriting Ltd v Credit Europe Bank NV* [2020] UKSC 11; [2020] 2 W.L.R. 919, summarised at para.13-011A above. **13-017**

Replace first paragraph with:

In insurance cases within s.3 of the Regulation, the agreement must also comply **13-018** with the special rules in arts 13 and 14 of the Regulation (arts 15 and 16 of the Recast Regulation).[123] Under those rules an agreement allowing the policyholder, the insured or a beneficiary to bring proceedings in courts other than those indicated in s.3 of the Regulation will be effective. An agreement allowing an insurer to bring proceedings in such courts will only be effective if:

(a) it is entered into after the dispute has arisen;
(b) it is concluded between a policyholder and an insurer, both of whom are at the time of the conclusion of the contract domiciled or habitually resident in the same Member State and which has the effect of conferring jurisdiction on the courts of that State even if the harmful event were to occur abroad, provided the agreement is not contrary to the law of that State;
(c) it is concluded with a policyholder who is not domiciled in a Member State, except in so far as the insurance is compulsory or relates to immoveable property in a Member State; or
(d) it relates to a contract of insurance in so far as it covers certain risks to ships, aircraft and goods in transit.[124] Those risks are as follows[125]:
   (i) any loss of or damage to sea-going ships, installations situated offshore or on the high seas, or aircraft arising from perils which relate to their use for commercial purposes, or to goods in transit other than passengers' baggage where the transit consists of or includes carriage by such ships or aircraft;
   (ii) any liability, other than for bodily injury to passengers or loss of or damage to their baggage, arising out of the use or operation of such ships,[126] installations or aircraft (in so far as the law of the Member State in which such aircraft are registered does not prohibit agreements on jurisdiction regarding insurance of such risks), or for loss or damage caused by goods in such transit;
   (iii) any financial loss connected with the use or operation of such ships, installations or aircraft, in particular loss of freight or charter-hire;
   (iv) any risk or interest connected with any of those listed above, and
   (v) all "large risks".[127]

[123] In so far as the Lugano or Brussels Convention applies, art.12 is the relevant provision. In so far as the 2007 Lugano Convention applies, the relevant provisions are arts 13 and 14, which mirror arts 13 and 14 of reg.44/2001. For a recent example of a case concerning art.13, see *Sherdley v Nordea Life and Pension SA (Societe Anonyme)* [2012] EWCA Civ 88; [2012] Lloyd's Rep. I.R. 437 at [47]–[57]. For the position of assignees, see the recent decision of the Supreme Court in *Aspen Underwriting Ltd v Credit Europe Bank NV* [2020] UKSC 11; [2020] 2 W.L.R. 919, summarised at para.13-011A above.

[124] reg.44/2001 art.13 (reg.1215/2012 art.15). A jurisdiction clause will bind a beneficiary who has not

expressly subscribed to it, and who is domiciled in a contracting state other than that in which the policyholder and insurer are domiciled: *Societe Financiere et Industrielle du Peloux v Axa Belgium* (C-112/03) EU:C:2005:280; [2006] Q.B. 251. See the consideration of this decision by the Supreme Court in *Aspen Underwriting Ltd v Credit Europe Bank NV* [2020] UKSC 11; [2020] 2 W.L.R. 919, summarised at para.13-011A above; and by Andrews J in *Hutchinson v Mapfre Espana Compania de Seguros y Reaseguros SA* [2020] EWHC 178 (QB). See para.13-019 for the recent CJEU case of *Assens Havn v Navigators Management (UK) Ltd* (C-368/16) EU:C:2017:546.

[125] reg.44/2001 art.14 (reg.1215/2012 art.16).

[126] For the application of this rule, see *Standard Steamship v Gie Vision Bail* [2005] Lloyd's Rep. I.R. 407, where the insured was a concessionaire which did not actually operate ships, and it was held that the liabilities in respect of which it sought cover arose out of the use or operation of ships.

[127] As defined by Council Directive 73/239/EEC, as amended by Directives 88/357/EEC, and 90/618/EEC. "Large risks" are defined to include a wide range of risks where the policyholder satisfies specified tests for minimum balance sheet figures, turnover or numbers of employees. The inclusion of "large risks" in the category of contracts in which the insurer is permitted to rely on a jurisdiction clause was achieved by reg.44/2001. The result is that insurers of substantial commercial risks will be increasingly likely to be able to rely on jurisdiction clauses.

Replace paragraph with:

13-019   In the recent CJEU case of *Assens Havn v Navigators Management (UK) Ltd* (C-368/16),[128a] the essential question for the CJEU was, whether the combined effect of art.13(5) and art.14(2)(a) of the Regulation must be interpreted as meaning that a victim entitled to bring a direct action against the insurer of the party which caused the harm suffered may be bound by an agreement on jurisdiction concluded between the insurer and that party.[129] The CJEU held[130] that an agreement on jurisdiction made between an insurer and an insured party cannot be invoked against a victim of insured damage who wishes to bring an action directly against the insurer before the courts for the place where the harmful event occurred. Otherwise, the extension to victims of the constraints of agreements on jurisdiction based on the combined provisions of arts 13 and 14 of the Regulation could compromise the objective pursued by Ch.II, s.3, thereof, namely to protect the economically and legally weaker party. The CJEU therefore concluded that art.13(5) of the Regulation, considered in conjunction with art.14(2)(a), must be interpreted as meaning that a victim entitled to bring a direct action against the insurer of the party which caused the harm he has suffered is not bound by an agreement on jurisdiction concluded between the insurer and that party.

[128a] See also *Hutchinson v Mapfre Espana Compania de Seguros y Reaseguros SA* [2020] EWHC 178 (QB).

[129] *Assens Havn v Navigators Management (UK) Ltd* (C-368/16) EU:C:2017:546 at [27]. See the brief consideration of this decision by the Supreme Court in *Aspen Underwriting Ltd v Credit Europe Bank NV* [2020] UKSC 11; [2020] 2 W.L.R. 919, summarised at para.13-011A above. See also *Hutchinson v Mapfre Espana Compania de Seguros y Reaseguros SA* [2020] EWHC 178 (QB).

[130] *Assens Havn v Navigators Management (UK) Ltd* (C-368/16) EU:C:2017:546 at [40]–[42].

2. THE PROPER LAW OF THE CONTRACT

Replace footnote 141 with:

13-024   [141] [2008] OJ L177/6. Depending on how Brexit progresses, see the Law Applicable to Contractual Obligations and Non-Contractual Obligations (Amendment etc.) (EU Exit) Regulations 2019 (SI 2019/834) (not yet in force), the purpose of which is to ensure that EU rules that determine the law applicable to contractual and non-contractual obligations continue to operate effectively in domestic law after the UK's exit from the EU. As a result of these Regulations, from exit day, the substantive rules in Rome I, Rome II and the 1980 Rome Convention will continue to apply (as amended) as domestic law in all parts of the UK to determine the law applicable to contractual and non-contractual obligations.

Various complications are envisaged in relation to matters including insurance, however, and the Explanatory Memorandum to these Regulations is helpful in this regard.

(b)   Proper Law: The Statutory Rules

Replace footnote 175 with:

[175] [2008] OJ L177/6. Depending on how Brexit progresses, see the Law Applicable to Contractual Obligations and Non-Contractual Obligations (Amendment etc.) (EU Exit) Regulations 2019 (SI 2019/834) (not yet in force), the purpose of which is to ensure that EU rules that determine the law applicable to contractual and non-contractual obligations continue to operate effectively in domestic law after the UK's exit from the EU. As a result of these Regulations, from exit day, the substantive rules in Rome I, Rome II and the 1980 Rome Convention will continue to apply (as amended) as domestic law in all parts of the UK to determine the law applicable to contractual and non-contractual obligations. Various complications are envisaged in relation to matters including insurance, however, and the Explanatory Memorandum to these Regulations is helpful in this regard.   **13-034**

(d)   Contracts Entered into on or after 17 December 2009

The Rome I Regulation.

After "The Solvency II Directive came into effect on 1 January 2016.", add new footnote 253a:

[253a] This will apparently be subject to change, in terms of domestic application and legislation, in light of "Brexit". See, for example, the Risk Transformation and Solvency 2 (Amendment) (EU Exit) Regulations 2019 (SI 2019/1233), largely not yet in force.   **13-073**

Scope of the Rome I Regulation.

Replace footnote 259 with:

[259] [2007] OJ L199/40. Depending on how Brexit progresses, see the Law Applicable to Contractual Obligations and Non-Contractual Obligations (Amendment etc.) (EU Exit) Regulations 2019 (SI 2019/834) (not yet in force), the purpose of which is to ensure that EU rules that determine the law applicable to contractual and non-contractual obligations continue to operate effectively in domestic law after the UK's exit from the EU. As a result of these Regulations, from exit day, the substantive rules in Rome I, Rome II and the 1980 Rome Convention will continue to apply (as amended) as domestic law in all parts of the UK to determine the law applicable to contractual and non-contractual obligations. Various complications are envisaged in relation to matters including insurance, however, and the Explanatory Memorandum to these Regulations is helpful in this regard.   **13-075**

3.   OTHER RELATED MATTERS

Rights of third parties.

Replace footnote 284 with:

[284] Article 12(2) of the Rome Convention; *Raiffeisen Zentralbank Osterreich AG v Five Star General Trading* [2001] Lloyd's Rep. I.R. 460. For a case concerning assignment, the Rome Convention and the Contracts (Applicable Law) Act 1990, see the decision of the Court of Appeal in *Cox v Ergo Versicherung AG (formerly Victoria)* [2012] EWCA Civ 1001. See now also *Roberts (A Child) v Soldiers, Sailors, Airmen and Families Association-Forces Help* [2019] EWHC 1104 (QB), the trial of a preliminary issue concerning the pure question of law as to whether the Civil Liability (Contribution) Act 1978 (the 1978 Act) has mandatory/ overriding effect and applies automatically to all proceedings for contribution brought in England and Wales, without reference to any choice of law rules. It was held that the 1978 Act has such effect and application. The decision is at the time of writing on appeal to the Court of Appeal.   **13-087**

Proof of foreign law.

Replace footnote 310 with:

[310] To a limited extent the court may take judicial notice of a foreign law: Civil Evidence Act 1972 s.4(2).   **13-092**

On the approach of an appellate court to disputed issues of foreign law, see *Grupo Torras SA v Sheikh Fahad Mohammed Al-Sabah* [1996] 1 Lloyd's Rep. 7 at 18. See also *Mamancochet Mining Ltd v Aegis Managing Agency Ltd* [2018] EWHC 2643 (Comm); [2018] 2 Lloyd's Rep. 441 at [56].

Tort claims.

Replace footnote 326 with:

13-093   326 See art.32 of Regulation 864/2007. Depending on how Brexit progresses, see the Law Applicable to Contractual Obligations and Non-Contractual Obligations (Amendment etc.) (EU Exit) Regulations 2019 (SI 2019/834) (not yet in force), the purpose of which is to ensure that EU rules that determine the law applicable to contractual and non-contractual obligations continue to operate effectively in domestic law after the UK's exit from the EU. As a result of these Regulations, from exit day, the substantive rules in Rome I, Rome II and the 1980 Rome Convention will continue to apply (as amended) as domestic law in all parts of the UK to determine the law applicable to contractual and non-contractual obligations. Various complications are envisaged in relation to matters including insurance, however, and the Explanatory Memorandum to these Regulations is helpful in this regard.

CHAPTER 14

ILLEGALITY

1. CLAIMS TAINTED BY ILLEGALITY

General principles.

Replace first paragraph with:

Previous editions of this work have stated that the courts will not permit a person **14-002** to enforce his rights under a contract of any kind if it is tainted by illegality,[1] but this statement must now be understood in light of the decision of the Supreme Court in *Patel v Mirza*.[2] The principle of public policy is expressed in the familiar Latin maxim ex turpi causa non oritur actio.[3] Although this maxim is lacking in precise legal definition,[4] it is reflected in two rules affecting the enforceability of rights under contracts of insurance. First, a claim is unenforceable when the grant of relief to the claimant would enable him to benefit from his criminal conduct.[5] Secondly, a claim is unenforceable when the claimant either has to found his claim on an illegal contract or to plead its illegality in order to support his claim.[6] The text of the 13th edition of this work stated that once a court has determined that one or other rule applies to the facts of a given case, it has no discretion whether or not to apply the rule depending upon the degree to which the claimant has affronted the public conscience.[7] Again, this statement must now be seen in light of the approach taken in the recent decision of the Supreme Court in *Patel v Mirza*.[8]

[1] Footnote 1 to para.14-002 of the 13th edition of this work referred to *Tinsley v Milligan* [1994] 1 A.C. 340 at 354 and 363 per Lord Goff, citing *Holman v Johnson* (1775) 1 Cowp. 341 at 343. However, the majority in *Patel v Mirza* [2016] UKSC 42; [2017] A.C. 467 has held the rule in *Tinsley v Milligan* is no longer to be followed.

[2] *Patel v Mirza* [2016] UKSC 42; [2017] A.C. 467. For a recent decision of the Grand Court of the Cayman Islands applying *Patel* in a case concerning aviation hull insurance, see *Toby v Allianz Global Risks US Insurance Company* FSD 152 of 2013 (IMJ).

[3] The maxim was considered by the House of Lords in *Stone & Rolls Ltd (In Liquidation) v Moore Stephens (A Firm)* [2009] UKHL 39; [2009] 1 A.C. 1391; and *Gray v Thames Trains Ltd* [2009] UKHL 33; [2009] 1 A.C. 1339; and more recently by the Supreme Court in *Patel v Mirza* [2016] UKSC 42;

[31]

[2017] A.C. 467; *Hounga v Allen* [2014] UKSC 47; [2014] 1 W.L.R. 2889; *Les Laboratoires Servier v Apotex Inc* [2014] UKSC 55; [2015] A.C. 430; and *Bilta (UK) Ltd (in liquidation) v Nazir* [2015] UKSC 23; [2016] A.C. 1. On 17 March 2010, the Law Commission published its report, *The Illegality Defence* (The Stationery Office, 2010), Law Com. No.320, HC Paper No.412, and concluded that in the areas of contract, unjust enrichment and tort, recent case law is already bringing about the improvements that are needed. The Law Commission concluded that the judges in these cases showed a willingness to take into account the policy factors that lie behind the illegality defence, and to explain their reasoning accordingly. In view of these trends within the case law, the Law Commission did not recommend legislative reform in relation to the illegality defence as it applies to claims for breach of contract, tort or unjust enrichment. The Law Commission's report was considered in detail by the Supreme Court in *Patel* (above) and by the Court of Appeal in *ParkingEye Ltd v Somerfield Stores Ltd* [2012] EWCA Civ 1338; [2013] Q.B. 840, and to some extent by the Supreme Court in *Hounga*, *Les Laboratoires* and *Bilta*, above. See now also the decision of the Court of Appeal in *Henderson v Dorset Healthcare University NHS Foundation Trust* [2018] EWCA Civ 1841; [2018] 3 W.L.R. 1651 and para.14-034A below, noting that the Supreme Court gave permission to appeal in the *Henderson* case, the appeal hearing was held in May 2020 and judgment is currently awaited.

4 *Beresford v Royal Insurance Co* [1937] 2 K.B. 197 at 219–220. Prior to the decision of the Supreme Court in *Patel* (above), the position on the potentially conflicting authorities as to the proper approach to the defence of illegality was neatly summarised by Lord Neuberger in *Bilta* (above) at [17]. The position has, however, moved on in light of the decision in *Patel* (above).

5 *Cleaver v Mutual Reserve Fund Life Association* [1892] 1 Q.B. 147; *Beresford v Royal Insurance Co* [1938] A.C. 586; *Hardy v Motor Insurers' Bureau* [1964] 3 W.L.R. 433; [1964] 2 Q.B. 745 at 760, 762 and 769; *Geismar v Sun Alliance & London Insurance Ltd* [1978] 1 Q.B. 383; [1978] 2 W.L.R. 433; *Euro-Diam Ltd v Bathurst* [1988] 2 W.L.R. 517; [1990] 1 Q.B. 1 at 19 per Staughton J, and 35 per Kerr LJ. It is submitted that this established category of ex turpi causa has survived the decision in *Tinsley v Milligan* [1994] 1 A.C. 340, although note that (as set out at para.14-002 above) the majority held in *Patel v Mirza* [2016] UKSC 42; [2017] A.C. 467 that the rule in *Tinsley v Milligan* [1994] 1 A.C. 340 is no longer to be followed. The "public conscience" test, to which Staughton LJ referred in *Group Josi Re v Wallbrook Insurance Co Ltd* [1996] 1 Lloyd's Rep. 345; [1996] 1 W.L.R. 1152 at 1164, related to the court's supposed discretion whether or not to give effect to a defence of illegality depending upon whether the public conscience was affronted. Lord Sumption stated (at [62]) in *Bilta* (above) that "the illegality defence is based on a rule of law on which the court is required to act ... [i]t is not a discretionary power on which the court is entitled to act, nor is it dependent upon a judicial value judgment about the balance of the equities in each case". See also Lord Sumption in *Les Laboratoires* (at [14]–[15]) stating that the "public conscience" test had been "decisively rejected" in *Tinsley v Milligan*. Compare this with the judgment of Lord Wilson in *Hounga* (at [30] and [42]–[43]), although note the views of Lords Toulson and Hodge in *Bilta* (at [173]) and Sales LJ in *R. (on the application of Best) v Chief Land Registrar* [2015] EWCA Civ 17; [2016] Q.B. 23 that the decision in *Les Laboratoires* is not inconsistent with the ratio of *Hounga*. However, see now the approach taken by the Supreme Court in *Patel v Mirza* [2016] UKSC 42; [2017] A.C. 467, summarised at para.14-002 above. The principle may apply even where the criminal conduct in question is yet to take place but it is found as a fact it will do so: *Agheampong v Allied Manufacturing (London) Ltd* [2009] Lloyd's Rep. I.R. 379 at [136]–[137]. It will also apply to deny the recovery of a loss suffered in consequence of a criminal act: *Gray v Thames Trains Ltd* [2009] UKHL 33; [2009] 1 A.C. 1339 at [51]–[55] per Lord Hoffmann, and at [85]–[88] per Lord Rodger of Earlsferry. See now the decision Court of Appeal in *Henderson v Dorset Healthcare University NHS Foundation Trust* [2018] EWCA Civ 1841; [2018] 3 W.L.R. 1651 considering the decision in *Gray* in detail. The decision in *Henderson* is summarised at para.14-034A below, also noting that the Supreme Court gave permission to appeal in the *Henderson* case, the appeal hearing was held in May 2020 and judgment is currently awaited.

6 *Bowmakers Ltd v Barnet Instruments Ltd* [1945] K.B. 65; *Euro-Diam Ltd v Bathurst* [1990] 1 Q.B. 1 at 18 and 35; *Tinsley v Milligan* [1994] 1 A.C. 340 at 366 and 369. See also *Stone & Rolls Ltd (In Liquidation) v Moore Stephens (A Firm)* [2009] 1 A.C. 1391 at [83] per Lord Phillips of Worth Matravers, and at [98]–[103] per Lord Scott of Foscote. See more recently, the decisions of the Supreme Court in *Hounga*, *Les Laboratoires* and *Bilta*, above. Note the extensive criticism of the decision in *Stone & Rolls*: see, for example, the judgment of Lord Neuberger in *Bilta* at [30]. See, now, the analysis of these cases and the approach taken by the Supreme Court in *Patel v Mirza* [2016] UKSC 42; [2017] A.C. 467, summarised at para.14-002 above.

7 See, previously, *Tinsley v Milligan* [1994] 1 A.C. 340 and the judgment of Lord Sumption in *Les Laboratoires Servier v Apotex Inc* [2014] UKSC 55; [2015] A.C. 430 at [14] and [15]. Now see the approach taken by the Supreme Court in *Patel v Mirza* [2016] UKSC 42; [2017] A.C. 467, summarised at para.14-002 above. The majority held in *Patel* that the rule in *Tinsley v Milligan* is no longer to be followed.

8 *Patel v Mirza* [2016] UKSC 42; [2017] A.C. 467.

Replace sixth paragraph with:
    This approach has begun to be applied in a number of decisions.[14]

[32]

[14] For a useful application of the "trio of necessary considerations" (albeit obiter), see *Singularis Holdings Ltd (in liquidation) v Daiwa Capital Markets Europe Ltd* [2017] EWHC 257 (Ch); [2017] 1 Lloyd's Rep. 226 at [216]–[220] per Rose J. The reasoning of Rose J was endorsed by the Court of Appeal (again, obiter)—see [2018] EWCA Civ 84; [2018] 1 Lloyd's Rep. 472 at [61]–[67] per Sir Geoffrey Vos, Chancellor of the High Court. The order of the judge was also upheld by the Supreme Court: [2019] UKSC 50; [2019] 3 W.L.R. 997. In the Court of Appeal in *Singularis*, Sir Geoffrey Vos considered (at [64]–[65]) the approach an appellate court should take to a review of a trial judge's decision on illegality based on the *Patel v Mirza* test, and held that, in common with other evaluative decisions involving a proportionality assessment, an appellate court should only interfere if the trial judge's decision has proceeded on an erroneous legal basis, has taken into account irrelevant considerations, or failed to take into account relevant considerations. This indicated that, given the breadth of considerations relevant to the proportionality assessment (see *Patel* at [107] per Lord Neuberger), it was likely appellate courts would show a high degree of deference to decisions applying the test in *Patel v Mirza*. However, Baroness Hale (giving the judgment of the Supreme Court) in *Singularis* held, at [21], that: "I should, however, record my reservations about the view expressed by the Court of Appeal as to the role of an appellate court in relation to the illegality defence: that 'an appellate court should only interfere if the first instance judge has proceeded on an erroneous legal basis, taken into account matters that were legally irrelevant, or failed to take into account matters that were legally relevant' (para 65). Daiwa point out that applying the defence is 'not akin to the exercise of discretion' (citing Lord Neuberger in *Patel v Mirza*, at para 175) and an appellate court is as well placed to evaluate the arguments as is the trial judge. It is not necessary to resolve this in order to resolve this appeal and there are cases concerning the illegality defence pending in the Supreme Court where it should not be assumed that this court will endorse the approach of the Court of Appeal". The approach of appellate courts to this issue, therefore, remains to be seen. For other cases considering and applying the approach in *Patel*, see also *Harb v Prince Abdul Aziz* [2018] EWHC 508 (Ch) at [226]–[228]; *Gujra v Roath* [2018] EWHC 854 (QB); [2018] 1 W.L.R. 3208; *Geddes (D) (Contractors) Ltd v Neil Johnson Health & Safety Services Ltd* [2017] CSOH 42; [2018] Lloyd's Rep. I.R. 264; *McHugh v Okai-Koi* [2017] EWHC 1346 (QB) at [18]–[22]; and *Stoffel & Co v Grondona* [2018] EWCA Civ 2031; [2018] P.N.L.R. 36. The Supreme Court gave permission to appeal in the *Stoffel* case and the appeal was heard in May 2020. It appears that, so far, first instance judges have continued to regard themselves as bound by illegality cases decided in specific contexts such as joint enterprise notwithstanding the Supreme Court's judgment in *Patel v Mirza*—see *Blake v Croasdale* [2017] EWHC 1336 (QB) at [14]; and *Clark v Farley, MIB, Edmonds* [2018] EWHC 1007 (QB); [2018] Lloyd's Rep. I.R. 645 at [31]–[35]. Both these judgments are considered further at the seventh footnote to para.14-042 below. See also *Wallett v Vickers* [2018] EWHC 3088 (QB); [2019] Lloyd's Rep. I.R. 205 at [56], summarised at para.14-042 below. On the suitability of the *Patel v Mirza* test to summary determination of a claim, see *Ronelp Marine Ltd v STX Offshore and Shipbuilding Co* [2016] EWHC 2228 (Ch); [2017] B.P.I.R. 203 at [36]–[37]; *Gujra v Roath* [2018] 1 W.L.R. 3208 at [35]. On the suitability of *Patel v Mirza* as a universal test for the operation of the illegality defence across all areas of the law, or whether in tortious claims the courts must apply a different approach, see the decision Court of Appeal in *Henderson v Dorset Healthcare University NHS Foundation Trust* [2018] EWCA Civ 1841; [2018] 3 W.L.R. 1651 and para.14-034A below, noting that the Supreme Court gave permission to appeal in the *Henderson* case, the appeal was heard in May 2020 and judgment is currently awaited.

Other statutory provisions.

After the third paragraph, add new paragraph:

14-009   As noted in the Home Office's Counter-Terrorism and Border Security Act 2019 "Extension of Terrorism Reinsurance Fact Sheet", the 2019 Act (which received Royal Assent on 12 February 2019) amends the Reinsurance (Acts of Terrorism) Act 1993 to enable Pool Re, the government-backed terrorism reinsurer, to extend its business interruption cover. The 1993 Act limited the Government's guarantee of Pool Re to covering losses that were caused by damage to commercial property during a terrorist attack. The 2019 Act enables Pool Re to extend its business interruption cover to include losses from terrorist attacks that are not contingent on damage to commercial property by amending s.2 of the 1993 Act.

Property unlawfully employed.

Replace footnote 66 with:

14-016   [66] *Euro-Diam Ltd v Bathurst* [1990] 1 Q.B. 1. For a recent decision of the Grand Court of the Cayman Islands briefly considering *Euro-Diam*, see *Toby v Allianz Global Risks US Insurance Company* FSD

152 of 2013 (IMJ) at [614] and [619]. The court applied the three-stage test in *Patel v Mirza* [2016] UKSC 42; [2017] A.C. 467.

(v) Illegal user of property prior to inception of risk.

Replace footnote 75 with:

14-023   ⁷⁵ *Geismar v Sun Alliance and London Insurance Ltd* [1978] Q.B. 383. For a recent decision of the Grand Court of the Cayman Islands briefly considering Geismar, see *Toby v Allianz Global Risks US Insurance Company* FSD 152 of 2013 (IMJ) at [611], [612], [619] and [626]–[627]. The court applied the three-stage test in *Patel v Mirza* [2016] UKSC 42; [2017] A.C. 467.

Replace footnote 77 with:

14-024   ⁷⁷ *Euro-Diam Ltd v Bathurst* [1990] 1 Q.B. 1, discussed at para.14-016, above. For a recent decision of the Grand Court of the Cayman Islands briefly considering *Euro-Diam*, see *Toby v Allianz Global Risks US Insurance Company* FSD 152 of 2013 (IMJ) at [614] and [619]. The court applied the three-stage test in *Patel v Mirza* [2016] UKSC 42; [2017] A.C. 467.

Performance contrary to foreign law.

Replace footnote 83 with:

14-025   ⁸³ *Rossano v Manufacturers' Life Insurance Co* [1963] 2 Q.B. 352 at 372. *Contrast Euro-Diam Ltd v Bathurst* [1990] 1 Q.B. 1 where the claim under an English policy to be performed in England was enforced, although the insured had participated in actions that contravened German law. For a recent decision of the Grand Court of the Cayman Islands briefly considering *Euro-Diam*, see *Toby v Allianz Global Risks US Insurance Company* FSD 152 of 2013 (IMJ) at [614]. The court applied the three-stage test in *Patel v Mirza* [2016] UKSC 42; [2017] A.C. 467.

Replace footnote 88 with:

14-026   ⁸³ *Brokaw v Seatrain UK Ltd* [1971] 2 Q.B. 476. In *Euro-Diam Ltd v Bathurst* [1990] 1 Q.B. 1 it was not necessary to decide the point, but the Court of Appeal was unimpressed by the distinction between revenue laws and other laws. For a recent decision of the Grand Court of the Cayman Islands briefly considering *Euro-Diam*, see *Toby v Allianz Global Risks US Insurance Company* FSD 152 of 2013 (IMJ) at [614]: "The fact that the illegal conduct in question was a breach of a Brazilian revenue law is irrelevant. As a matter of comity, while the Cayman courts may not enforce a foreign revenue law, they will not assist in the breach of foreign revenue law (see *Euro-Diam v Bathurst* [1990] QB 1 at 40C-F)". The court in *Toby* applied the three-stage test in *Patel v Mirza* [2016] UKSC 42; [2017] A.C. 467.

2.   LOSS CAUSED BY INSURED'S UNLAWFUL ACT

Loss caused by deliberate act.

Replace footnote 98 with:

14-029   ⁹⁸ See, for example, *Gray v Thames Trains Ltd* [2009] UKHL 33; [2009] A.C. 1339; *Laboratoires Servier v Apotex Inc* [2014] UKSC 55; [2015] A.C. 430 at [19]. However, now see the decision of the Supreme Court in *Patel v Mirza* [2016] UKSC 42; [2017] A.C. 467, summarised at para.14-002 above. Both *Gray* and *Laboratoires Servier* were analysed by their Lordships in *Patel* and the approach taken by the majority is summarised above. For a recent case considering *Gray v Thames Trains Ltd* in detail, and also considering *Patel v Mirza*, see *Henderson v Dorset Healthcare University NHS Foundation Trust* [2018] EWCA Civ 1841; [2018] 3 W.L.R. 1651, summarised at para.14-034A below, in which the claimant's negligence claim was held to be barred by illegality as a result of her conviction for manslaughter, notwithstanding that the claimant's personal responsibility for the offence was low. The judgment of Jay J provides a very helpful and detailed analysis of the decision in *Gray v Thames Trains Ltd*. The decision of the Supreme Court in *Henderson* is currently awaited. For a recent Scottish case considering the application of *Gray v Thames Trains Ltd* to a claim to recover as damages a fine imposed for a strict liability offence, see *Geddes (D) (Contractors) Ltd v Neil Johnson Health & Safety Services Ltd* [2017] CSOH 42; [2018] Lloyd's Rep. I.R. 264, in which the Court of Session held (at [18]) that the key concept, in deciding whether the doctrine of illegality precluded recovery in such circumstances, was "responsibility", not whether the wrongdoing was intentional.

Loss caused by criminal or tortious act.

Replace footnote 111 with:

[111] *Beresford v Royal Insurance Co* [1938] A.C. 586; *Hardy v Motor Insurers' Bureau* [1964] 2 Q.B. **14-033**
745 at 760, 762 and 769; *Cleaver v Mutual Reserve Fund Life Association* [1892] 1 Q.B. 147; and *In
the Estate of Crippen* [1911] P. 108. In relation to tortious acts and the maxim ex turpi causa, see paras
14-034A and 14-046 below.

Replace footnote 113 with:

[113] *Gray v Thames Trains Ltd* [2009] 1 A.C. 1339 at [51]–[55] per Lord Hoffmann, at [85]–[88] per Lord
Rodger of Earlsferry; *Laboratoires Servier v Apotex Inc* [2014] UKSC 55; [2015] A.C. 430 at [19] and
[23]–[29] and see further, para.14-046 below. Now see the decision of the Supreme Court in *Patel v
Mirza* [2016] UKSC 42; [2017] A.C. 467, summarised at para.14-002 above. Both *Gray* and
Laboratoires Servier were analysed by their Lordships in *Patel* and the approach taken by the majority
is summarised above. For a recent case considering *Gray v Thames Trains Ltd* in detail, and also
considering *Patel v Mirza*, see *Henderson v Dorset Healthcare University NHS Foundation Trust* [2018]
EWCA Civ 1841; [2018] 3 W.L.R. 1651, summarised at para.14-034A below.

Replace footnote 116 with:

[116] *Chaplin v Royal London Mutual* [1958] I.A.C.Rep. 2. See also *Gray v Thames Trains Ltd* [2009]
UKHL 33; [2009] 1 A.C. 1339 at [8]–[18] per Lord Phillips of Worth Matravers in respect of hospital
orders and restrictions under ss.37, 41 and 45A of the Mental Health Act 1983, and at [83] per Lord
Rodger of Earlsferry. For a recent case considering *Gray v Thames Trains Ltd* in detail, see *Henderson
v Dorset Healthcare University NHS Foundation Trust* [2018] EWCA Civ 1841; [2018] 3 W.L.R. 1651,
summarised at para.14-034A below. Although the claimant in *Henderson* had pleaded guilty to
manslaughter by reason of diminished responsibility, Mr Justice Jay held that the damages claims were
precluded on the ground of the illegality inherent in the claimant's conviction. The Court of Appeal
dismissed the appeal, holding in summary that an individual who had been convicted of unlawfully killing another was precluded on public policy grounds from bringing a claim for damages in negligence
against a person whose act or omission was alleged to have been responsible for bringing about the
claimant's unlawful conduct in carrying out the killing. The decision of the Supreme Court is currently
awaited.

Replace footnote 122 with:

[122] Note the discussion of *Gray v Thames Trains Ltd* [2009] 1 A.C. 1339 by the Supreme Court in **14-034**
Hounga v Allen [2014] UKSC 47; [2014] 1 W.L.R. 2889; *Les Laboratoires Servier v Apotex Inc* [2014]
UKSC 55; [2015] A.C. 430; *Bilta (UK) Ltd (in liquidation) v Nazir* [2015] UKSC 23; [2016] A.C. 1,
and most recently in *Patel v Mirza* [2016] UKSC 42; [2017] A.C. 467, summarised at para.14-002 above.
For a recent case considering *Gray v Thames Trains Ltd* in detail, and also considering *Patel v Mirza*,
see *Henderson v Dorset Healthcare University NHS Foundation Trust* [2018] EWCA Civ 1841; [2018]
3 W.L.R. 1651, summarised at para.14-034A below. For the application of this principle to offences of
strict liability, see *Geddes (D) (Contractors) Ltd v Neil Johnson Health & Safety Services Ltd* [2017]
CSOH 42; [2018] Lloyd's Rep. I.R. 264, in which the Court of Session held that the key concept in
determining whether illegality barred recovery in such circumstances was the claimant's "responsibility" for the offence out of which the penalty arose, not whether the offence was one of mens rea (at [18]).

After the third paragraph, add new paragraph:

The decision in *Gray v Thames Trains Ltd*[123a] was recently considered in detail **14-034A**
by the Court of Appeal in *Henderson v Dorset Healthcare University NHS Foundation Trust*.[123b] The claimant, who had a history of paranoid schizophrenia, killed her
mother by stabbing her during a psychotic episode. At the time of the killing she
was under the care of a community mental health team managed and operated by
the defendant NHS trust (the Trust). She pleaded guilty to manslaughter on the
ground of diminished responsibility and was ordered to be detained in a secure
hospital. The claimant's negligence claim against the Trust (contending that she
would not have killed her mother if it had not been for the Trust's breaches of duty
in failing to respond in an appropriate way to her mental illness) was held by Jay J
to be barred by illegality as a result of her conviction for manslaughter,
notwithstanding that the claimant's personal responsibility for the offence was low.
The Court of Appeal dismissed the appeal, holding in summary that a person who

had been convicted of unlawfully killing another was precluded on public policy grounds from bringing a claim for damages in negligence against a person whose act or omission was alleged to have been responsible for bringing about the claimant's unlawful conduct in carrying out the killing.

[123a] *Gray v Thames Trains Ltd* [2009] 1 A.C. 1339.

[123b] *Henderson v Dorset Healthcare University NHS Foundation Trust* [2018] EWCA Civ 1841; [2018] 3 W.L.R. 1651.

The relevant issue for present purposes was: "(b) What is the ratio of the *Gray* case and in particular were the reservations of Lord Phillips of Worth Matravers approved by the majority of the House of Lords?" The decision in *Gray* was analysed in detail at [48]–[76]. The Court of Appeal helpfully summarised the decision in *Gray* (in relevant part) as follows at [64]:

> "In summary, the majority agreed in the *Gray* case on the following. ... Second, in the context of a criminal conviction for unlawful killing, there is a wider and a narrower form of public policy which precludes a claim by the killer from recovering damages in proceedings for negligence against the person whose act or omission is alleged to have been responsible for bringing about the claimant's unlawful conduct in carrying out the killing. Third, the narrower form is that there can be no recovery for damage which flows from loss of liberty, a fine or other punishment lawfully imposed in consequence of the unlawful act since it is the law, as a matter of penal policy, which causes the damage and it would be inconsistent for the law to require compensation for that damage. Fourth, the wider form is a combination of public policy and causation. If the tortious conduct of the defendant merely provided the occasion or opportunity for the killing, but (in causation terms) the immediate cause of the damage was the criminal act of the claimant, it is offensive to public notions of the fair distribution of resources that a claimant should be compensated (usually out of public funds) for such damage."

The consequence of those principles applied to the facts in the *Henderson* was that all the heads of loss claimed by the claimant were barred as a matter of public policy. Also of importance for present purposes, the Court of Appeal in *Henderson* went on (at [77]–[93]) to consider the effect of the decision of the Supreme Court in *Patel*. At [87], the Court of Appeal noted that in view of the contractual and unjust enrichment issue in the *Patel* case, considerable caution must be taken, in the context of the rules of binding precedent, in determining whether there are any other cases in other areas of the law which the Supreme Court in the *Patel* case held by necessary implication to be overruled or such that they should no longer be followed. Further, at [89], the Court of Appeal concluded that it was impossible to discern in the majority judgments in the *Patel* case any suggestion that the *Gray* case was wrongly decided or to discern that it cannot stand with the reasoning in the *Patel* case. Indeed, as the Court of Appeal continued at [89]:

> "The *Gray* case was referred to in the judgments of Lord Toulson JSC (paras 28–32), Lord Kerr of Tonaghmore JSC (para 129) and Lord Neuberger PSC (paras 153 and 155) but in each case with approval of the way the matter had been approached by Lord Hoffmann in the *Gray* case in identifying the considerations underlying and justifying the rule of public policy. There was no suggestion of any kind that either the approach of Lords Hoffmann, Rodger and Scott or the decision in the *Gray* case was incorrect."

The Court of Appeal therefore concluded that the *Gray* case remained binding on it. However, the Supreme Court granted permission to appeal and the appeal hearing was held in May 2020 (with judgment currently awaited), the issue before the Supreme Court apparently being whether the decision in *Patel* provides a universal test for the operation of the illegality defence across all areas of the law, or whether in tortious claims the courts must apply the illegality defence as articulated in *Gray*.[123c]

[123c] See also *Wallett v Vickers* [2018] EWHC 3088 (QB); [2019] Lloyd's Rep. I.R. 205 at [32]–[34], addressing the decisions in *Gray* and in *Henderson*. The decision in *Wallett* is summarised at para.14-042 below.

Joint criminal enterprise.

Replace footnote 139 with:

[139] See, for example, *Delaney v Pickett* [2011] EWCA Civ 1532; [2012] 1 W.L.R. 2149; *Joyce v O'Brien* [2013] EWCA Civ 546; [2014] 1 W.L.R. 70; *Beaumont and O'Neill v Ferrer* [2014] EWHC 2398 (QB); [2015] P.I.Q.R. P2; *Flint v (1) Tittnesor (2) MIB* [2015] EWHC 466 (QB); [2015] 1 W.L.R. 4370; *Mc-Cracken v Smith* [2015] EWCA Civ 380; [2016] Lloyd's Rep. I.R. 171; and *Smith (by his Mother & Litigation Friend Bonner) v Stratton* [2015] EWCA Civ 1413; *Beaumont v Ferrer* [2016] EWCA Civ 768; [2017] P.I.Q.R. P1 (in which the Court of Appeal considered, amongst others, *Gray v Thames Trains Ltd* [2009] UKHL 33; [2009] 1 A.C. 1339; *Delaney v Pickett* and *Joyce v O'Brien*); *Clark v Farley, MIB, Edmonds* [2018] EWHC 1007 (QB); [2018] Lloyd's Rep. I.R. 645; and *Wallett v Vickers* [2018] EWHC 3088 (QB); [2019] P.I.Q.R. P6, summarised at para.14-042 below.

14-042

Replace footnote 145 with:

[145] See, for example, *Clark v Farley, MIB, Edmonds* [2018] EWHC 1007 (QB); [2018] Lloyd's Rep. I.R. 645, in which Yip J (at [35]) preferred the submission of counsel for the MIB that *Patel v Mirza* did not necessitate any modification or gloss to the approach in *McCracken* and *Joyce v O'Brien*, due to the established line of authority in this area. In any event, Yip J considered that on the facts of that case, the policy considerations in *Patel v Mirza* would not have led to a different result. Much the same approach was taken in *Blake v Croasdale* [2017] EWHC 1336 (QB), in which HHJ Purle QC held (at [14]) that *Joyce v O'Brien* remained binding in a joint enterprise context (albeit noting that the reasoning may need to be revisited in light of *Patel v Mirza*). See also *Wallett v Vickers* [2018] EWHC 3088 (QB); [2019] Lloyd's Rep. I.R. 205 at [56], summarised at para.14-042 below.

After the fourth paragraph, add new paragraph:

For example, in the recent case of *Wallett v Vickers*,[145a] Males J considered the situation where two motorists (without any prior agreement) drove alongside each other on a dual carriageway at speeds approaching twice the speed limit, each determined to be the first to reach the point where the road narrowed to a single lane and refusing to give way to the other (in a form of impromptu race). As the road began to narrow, the motorist in the inner lane lost control of his vehicle and collided with other vehicles on the opposite carriageway, sustaining fatal injuries. His partner brought a claim for damages under the Fatal Accidents Act 1976. In order to succeed it had to be shown that the deceased would himself have been entitled to succeed in a claim for damages for negligence against the other driver. Males J allowed the appeal from the decision of the Recorder in the County Court, who had dismissed the claim on the grounds that the claim was barred by the principle of ex turpi causa because the parties were engaged in the criminal joint enterprise of dangerous driving on a public road. The case was complicated by how the arguments had been put below and on appeal, and only the points of principle are addressed here.

[145a] *Wallett v Vickers* [2018] EWHC 3088 (QB); [2019] P.I.Q.R. P6.

Males J considered the decisions in *Gray*, *Les Laboratoires* and *McCracken* and noted at [40] that the question whether dangerous driving should amount to turpitude for the purpose of the ex turpi causa defence was considered in *McCracken*. At [41], Males J noted that the answer to the question was that the claim was not barred. Viewing the issue in terms of a duty of care, on the facts of the *McCracken* case, "the dangerous driving of the bike had no effect whatsoever on Mr Bell's duty of care or on the standard of care reasonably to be expected of him". Viewing it in terms of causation, there were two causes of the accident, the dangerous driving of the bike and the negligent driving of the minibus. The fact that one of those causes was the criminal conduct of the notional claimant (i.e. Damian, the rider of the bike) was not a sufficient reason to bar the claim. Males J concluded on this issue at [43]:

> "In my judgment *McCracken* is a binding authority that in the absence of a criminal joint enterprise between the claimant and the defendant, dangerous driving by the claimant will not bar a claim pursuant to the *ex turpi causa* principle. Rather, such a claim is to be determined in accordance with principles of causation (has the conduct of the defendant made a material contribution to the claimant's injuries?) and contributory negligence (should the damages be reduced by reason of the claimant's own fault?). These principles are sufficient to give effect to the requirements of justice and public policy".

However, as noted by Males J at [44], the position is materially different in a case where the parties are participants in a criminal joint enterprise. That is because, as the Supreme Court explained in *R. v Jogee*,[145b] each of the parties to such an enterprise is responsible in law for the commission of the offence in question. As summarised by Males J at [45]:

> "Because the accessory or secondary party is equally responsible in law for the crime committed by the principal, an accessory who is injured by the principal's criminal conduct cannot sue the principal to recover compensation for his injuries. As an accessory he stands effectively in the shoes of the principal. If he were allowed to sue the principal, he would be claiming damages for conduct for which in law he is himself responsible. Accordingly he can no more sue the principal than he could sue himself. This is a particular application of the ex turpi causa principle which is established by a series of cases."[145c]

[145b] *R. v Jogee* [2016] UKSC 8; [2017] A.C. 387.

[145c] See [46]–[51] for Males J's further consideration of *McCracken* and of *Clark v Farley* [2018] EWHC 1007 (QB); [2018] Lloyd's Rep. I.R. 645.

No indemnity in respect of punishment for a crime.

Replace footnote 153 with:

14-046 [153] *Colburn v Patmore* (1834) 1 Cr. M. & R. 73; *R Leslie Ltd v Reliable Advertising & Addressing Agency Ltd* [1915] 1 K.B. 652 at 659; *Askey v Golden Wine Co* (1948) 64 T.L.R. 379; *Gray v Thames Trains Ltd* [2009] UKHL 33; [2009] 1 A.C. 1339; *Les Laboratoires Servier v Apotex Inc* [2014] UKSC 55; [2015] A.C. 430. For a recent case considering *Gray v Thames Trains Ltd* in detail, see *Henderson v Dorset Healthcare University NHS Foundation Trust* [2018] EWCA Civ 1841; [2018] 3 W.L.R. 1651, summarised at para.14-034A above.

Replace footnote 157 with:

[157] See now also *Geddes (D) (Contractors) Ltd v Neil Johnson Health & Safety Services Ltd* [2017] CSOH 42; [2018] Lloyd's Rep. I.R. 264. In "Illegality: Indemnification for criminal acts" (2018) 30 I.L.M. 5, it is commented that following *Patel v Mirza* (and in the absence of an express policy exclusion) an assured may be entitled to indemnification for a criminal fine or other financial sanction imposed by a regulator, and that is most likely to be the case where the offence is strict liability and there is no evidence of any intention on the part of the assured to break the law. See also *Wallett v Vickers* [2018] EWHC 3088 (QB); [2019] Lloyd's Rep. I.R. 205 at [32]–[43] for a consideration of the decision in *Les Laboratoires* and, in particular, whether dangerous driving should amount to turpitude for the purpose of the ex turpi causa defence. The *Wallett* case is summarised at para.14-042 above.

Unlawful acts of insured's servant.

Replace footnote 189 with:

14-055

[189] *Bilta (UK) Ltd (in liquidation) v Nazir* [2015] UKSC 23; [2016] A.C. 1 at [41] per Lord Neuberger: "The question is: whose act or knowledge or state of mind is *for the purpose* of the relevant rule to count as the act, knowledge or state of mind of the company?" For a useful application of these principles, see *Singularis Holdings Ltd (in liquidation) v Daiwa Capital Markets Europe Ltd* [2017] EWHC 257 (Ch); [2017] 1 Lloyd's Rep. 226 at [182]–[184] (upheld on appeal—[2018] EWCA Civ 84; [2018] 1 W.L.R. 2777). The order of the judge was also upheld by the Supreme Court: [2019] UKSC 50; [2019] 3 W.L.R. 997. Baroness Hale (giving the judgment of the Supreme Court) held, at [34], that "… in my view, the judge was correct also to say that 'there is no principle of law that in any proceedings where the company is suing a third party for breach of a duty owed to it by that third party, the fraudulent conduct of a director is to be attributed to the company if it is a one-man company'. In her view, what emerged from *Bilta* was that 'the answer to any question whether to attribute the knowledge of the fraudulent director to the company is always to be found in consideration of the context and the purpose for which the attribution is relevant' (para 182). I agree and, if that is the guiding principle, then *Stone & Rolls* can finally be laid to rest".

4. ALIEN ENEMIES

Economic sanctions.

Replace footnote 284 with:

14-102

[284] Footnote 275 to para.14-102 of the 12th edition of this work (and the Second Supplement to the 12th edition) set out a long list of examples of earlier sanctions regimes (now repealed) and current examples. The reader is referred to those passages. By way of brief examples of earlier sanctions regimes (now repealed), see the Southern Rhodesia Act 1965 s.2; the Southern Rhodesia (United Nations Sanctions) (No. 2) Order 1968 (SI 1968/1020); the Iran (Temporary Powers) Act 1980; and the Iran (Trading Sanctions) Order 1980 (SI 1980/737). For examples of current sanction regimes, see the Financial Restrictions (Iran) Order 2009 (SI 2009/2725) and the Syria (European Union Financial Sanctions) Regulations 2012 (as amended by the Syria (European Union Financial Sanctions) (Amendment No. 2) Regulations 2012 (SI 2012/2524). It is not appropriate to list all such measures here. Suffice it to say that the reader must have close regard to which Orders and Regulations have been brought into force, amended and repealed when considering the issues addressed at paras 14-101 and 14-102 above. Although not yet in force (or largely not yet in force), note here, for example, the Syria (Sanctions) (EU Exit) Regulations 2019 (SI 2019/792), the Sanctions (Amendment) (EU Exit) Regulations 2019 (SI 2019/26), the Sanctions (Amendment) (EU Exit) (No 2) Regulations 2019 (SI 2019/380) and the Sanctions (EU Exit) (Miscellaneous Amendments) Regulations 2019 (SI 2019/843).

After the first paragraph, add new paragraph:

In the recent case of *Mamancochet Mining Ltd v Aegis Managing Agency Ltd*,[285] questions arose in respect to both US and EU sanctions.[285a] The claimant was the assignee of the benefit of a marine cargo insurance policy (the Policy) governed by English law and subscribed to by the 11 Defendant underwriters (nine of whom were ultimately owned or controlled by US entities). The Policy protected Metalloyd Ltd against the risk of theft of two cargoes of steel billets carried on board two vessels from Russia to Iran on 23 August 2012 and 25 August 2012, respectively. The policy contained a sanctions clause (on standard wording developed by the Joint Hull Committee of the London market) in the following terms (the Sanctions Clause):

> "No (re)insurer shall be deemed to provide cover and no (re)insurer shall be liable to pay any claim or provide any benefit hereunder to the extent that the provision of such cover, payment of such claim or provision of such benefit would expose that (re)insurer to any sanction, prohibition or restriction under United Nations resolutions or the trade or economic sanctions, laws, or regulations of the European Union, United Kingdom or the United States of America."

[285] *Mamancochet Mining Ltd v Aegis Managing Agency Ltd* [2018] EWHC 2643 (Comm); [2018] 2 Lloyd's Rep. 441.

[285a] For a recent case addressing EU sanctions against Syria, and relevant to reinsurers, see *R. (on the application of Certain Underwriters at Lloyds London) v HM Treasury* [2020] EWHC 2189 (Admin). The sanctions in question were Regulation No.36/2012. The claimants were a consortium of reinsurers who wanted information from the UK Government which the latter said it was powerless to provide. The claimants sought to trace funds, owned by the Syrian state and its agents, which were frozen in accordance with EU law sanctions against Syria. The court explained the purposes of the Regulation and its expectations as to the proper approach to be taken to the provision of sensitive or confidential information to commercial entities.

It was common ground that, on arrival at the port of Bandar-e Anzali in Iran, the cargoes were put in bonded storage. The purchaser, Liberal Resources FZC, did not pay for them and Metalloyd arranged for substitute bills to be issued naming an Iranian national (Mr Fallah) as consignee. The goods were stolen from their bonded storage (by presentation of fraudulent documents) at some time between 22 September 2012 and 7 October 2012. A claim was made under the policy at some time after 8 March 2013.

At the time of the policy and of the loss, there were no sanctions in force under US law against Iranian interests. However, from 9 March 2013 there were sanctions in place and they would have prevented the US entities from paying the claim. The sanctions were, in line with a Joint Comprehensive Plan of Action (JCPOA), modified with effect from 16 January 2016, so that US entities could trade with Iran under licence. A "General License" to that effect was issued. However, on 8 May 2018 President Trump announced the withdrawal of the US from the JCPOA, and the General License was revoked. The revocation was subject to a "wind-down" provision under which transactions were authorised until the end of 4 November 2018, and it was common ground that the claim could not be paid by US entities on or after 5 November 2018. The case (which was heard in October 2018) was therefore determined on an expedited basis.

As to the separate EU sanctions regime, Council Regulation (EU) No 267/2012[286] was amended by Council Regulation (EU) No 1263/2012,[287] and it was common ground that payment of the claim in the period after 21 December 2012 would have been in breach of EU sanctions. However, following the JCPOA, the EU relaxed sanctions against Iran, and it was common ground that payment by the defendants on or after 16 January 2016 would not have been prohibited by EU sanctions.

[286] Council Regulation No 267/2012 of 23 March 2012 concerning restrictive measures against Iran and repealing Regulation (EU) No 961/2010.

[287] Council Regulation No 1263/2012 of 23 December 2012 amending Regulation (EU) No 267/2012 concerning restrictive measures against Iran.

The Defendants relied upon the Sanctions Clause, with two relying solely on EU sanctions as grounding their defence to pay under that clause, and the other nine relying upon both US and EU sanctions. The claimant asserted that the US and EU sanctions did not apply, and if the US sanctions did apply then the claimant could rely upon Council Regulation (EC) No 2271/96 (the Blocking Regulation),[288] under which legal persons incorporated within the EU were to not comply with any requirement or prohibition from specified foreign laws, the list having been amended by Commission Regulation (EU) No 2018/1100[289] to include the US sanctions legislation.

288 Council Regulation No 2271/96 of 22 November 1996 protecting against the effects of the extra-territorial application of legislation adopted by a third country, and actions based thereon or resulting therefrom.

289 Commission Regulation (EU) No 2018/1100 of 6 June 2018 amending the Annex to Council Regulation (EC) No 2271/96 protecting against the effects of extraterritorial application of legislation adopted by a third country, and actions based thereon or resulting therefrom.

Teare J held that the Sanctions Clause did not give the insurers a defence to payment before 5 November 2018. The first issue was: "(i) What is the proper interpretation of the phrase in the policy 'to the extent that … payment of such claim … would expose that insurer to any sanction, prohibition or restriction under … the trade or economic sanctions, laws, or regulations …'?" Teare J held that the proper construction was that an insurer was not liable to pay a claim where payment would be prohibited under one of the named systems of law and thus "would expose" the insurer to a sanction. It did not suffice that there was the risk of a sanction.

The second issue for determination was: "(ii) As a matter of fact, would payment of the claim 'expose' the defendants to US and/or EU sanctions, within the meaning of the sanctions clause in the policy?" After a careful analysis of the facts and of the competing expert evidence on the US law, Teare J held that payment of the claim under the Policy before 23.59 on 4 November 2018 would not expose the Defendants to a sanction (under either US or EU law) within the meaning of the Sanctions Clause. At [76]–[78], Teare J addressed a further construction issue and determined that the Sanctions Clause had suspensory effect, i.e.:

"… that for as long as payment would expose the insurer to sanction, the insurer is not liable to pay. Thus, when, pursuant to General License H (as a matter of US law) and the Repealing Regulation (as a matter of EU law), payment of the claim ceased to be prohibited in 2016, the insurer was again liable to pay the claim under the Policy. In the meantime, that liability was suspended."

Thus, the following third question did not arise for decision: "(iii) If the question above is answered affirmatively, are the defendants prevented from relying on the sanctions clause by virtue of article 5 of Council Regulation (EC) No 2271/96 (as amended by Commission Delegation Regulation (EU) 2018/1100)?" However, Teare J did comment at [82] that:

"Since I have concluded that the US sanctions do not prohibit payment of the claim, this point does not arise for determination. For that reason, and in order not to delay the completion of this judgment, I shall not express a concluded view on this point. I shall merely say that I see considerable force in the defendants' 'short answer' to the point, namely that the Blocking Regulation is not engaged where the insurer's liability to pay a claim is suspended under a sanctions clause such as the one in the Policy. In such a case, the insurer is not 'complying' with a third country's prohibition but is simply relying upon the terms of the policy to resist payment."290

290 For a commentary on *Mamancochet Mining Ltd*, see "Marine Insurance: The effect of sanctions on claims" (2019) 31 I.L.M. 7.

CHAPTER 15

MISTAKE

1. GENERAL PRINCIPLES

Replace paragraph with:

15-001   There are several different categories of case in which a contract may be affected by mistake. Those cases in which no agreement is ever reached because the parties are not *ad idem*, and those in which an error in the written expression of the parties' intention may be rectified, are considered elsewhere.[1] The cases now under consideration are those in which the parties agree, but are both mistaken about a relevant fact. Such cases have been a fruitful source of judicial and academic controversy, for a full account of which the reader is referred to the standard textbooks on the law of contract.[2]

[1] See paras 2-002 and 12-003, above. For a recent and important decision on rectification, see *FSHC Group Holdings Ltd v GLAS Trust Corp Ltd* [2019] EWCA Civ 1361; [2020] Ch. 365.

[2] See *Chitty on Contracts*, edited by H.G. Beale, 33rd edn and First Supplement (London: Sweet & Maxwell, 2019); G.H. Treitel, *Law of Contract*, 15th edn (London: Sweet & Maxwell, 2020).

CHAPTER 16

MISREPRESENTATION

1. INTRODUCTION AND LEGISLATIVE REFORM

After ", there have been no substantive decisions on the 2015 Act", add:
which are relevant to misrepresentation issues.   **16-001**

3. INNOCENT MISREPRESENTATION

Definition.

Replace footnote 35 with:

[35] The authorities on the origins and development of the equitable jurisdiction are collected at the notes   **16-009**
to paras 16-010 to 16-012 of the 9th edition of this work. The grant of a decree of rescission in equity
is subject to the usual bars to rescission—G.H. Treitel, *The Law of Contract*, 14th edn (London: Sweet
& Maxwell, 2015), pp.460–468; and now see G.H. Treitel, *The Law of Contract*, 15th edn (London:
Sweet & Maxwell, 2020).

Marine Insurance Act 1906.

Replace footnote 38 with:

[38] See G.H. Treitel, *The Law of Contract* (2015), pp.449–450; and now see G.H. Treitel, *The Law of*   **16-010**
Contract, 15th edn (2020).

4. CHARACTERISTICS OF ACTIONABLE MISREPRESENTATION

Fact distinguished from opinion.

Replace footnote 58 with:

[58] *Ionides v Pacific Fire & Marine Insurance Co* (1871) L.R. 6 Q.B. 674 at 683; *Irish National Insur-*   **16-014**
ance Co v Oman Insurance Co [1983] 2 Lloyd's Rep. 453 at 461; *Highlands Insurance Co v Continental
Insurance (Note)* [1987] 1 Lloyd's Rep. 109 at 112; *Bank Leumi Le Israel v British National Insurance
Co* [1988] 1 Lloyd's Rep. 71 at 75; *Hill v Citadel Insurance Co Ltd* [1995] Lloyd's Rep. 218 at 227;
[1997] Lloyd's Rep. 167 at 171; *Credit Lyonnais Bank Nederland v E.C.G.D.* [1996] 1 Lloyd's Rep. 200
at 216; *Sirius International Insurance Corp v Oriental Assurance Group* [1999] Lloyd's Rep. I.R. 343
at 351. See also para.16-046 below. Eder J stated (obiter) in *Ted Baker Plc v AXA Insurance UK Plc*
[2012] EWHC 1406 (Comm); [2013] 1 All E.R. (Comm) 129; [2013] Lloyd's Rep. I.R. 174 at [126]
that "... there is no doubt authority to support the general proposition that a statement as to the mean-

ing or effect of a document can amount to an actionable misrepresentation: see *Wauton v Coppard* [1899] 1 Ch. 92; *Kyle Bay v Underwriters Subscribing under Policy No. 019057/08/01* [2007] Lloyd's Rep. I.R. 460". However, regard should be had to the decision in *Kyle Bay Ltd t/a Astons Nightclub v Underwriters Subscribing under Policy No.019057/08/01* [2007] EWCA Civ 57; [2007] Lloyd's Rep. I.R. 460 itself, especially at [33]–[35]. Further, as Popplewell J stated in *Moto Mabanga v Ophir Energy Plc, Ophir Services PTY Ltd* [2012] EWHC 1589 (QB) at [29]: "Statements of opinion are not normally actionable if they consist of no more than contentions or arguments as to the effect of a document whose terms are equally known to both parties." See also *Chitty on Contracts*, 33rd edn and First Supplement (London: Sweet & Maxwell, 2019), paras 7-009 and 7-010.

Materiality of fraudulent statement.

Replace footnote 159 with:

16-040   ¹⁵⁹ *Smith v Kay* (1859) 7 H.L.Cas. 750 at 759, 770; *The Bedouin* [1894] P. 1, 12; *Gordon v Street* [1899] 2 Q.B. 641 at 645–646; *Pan Atlantic Insurance Co v Pine Top Insurance Co* [1995] 1 A.C. 501 at 533. For the elements of actionable fraudulent misstatements, see para.16-002, above. See also G.H. Treitel, *The Law of Contract*, 14th edn (2015), pp.411–412 and pp.420–422; and now see G.H. Treitel, *The Law of Contract*, 15th edn (2020).

Promissory representation.

Replace footnote 166 with:

16-042   ¹⁶⁶ The elements of collateral contracts are outlined in G.H. Treitel, *Law of Contract*, 14th edn (2015), para.9-056; and now see G.H. Treitel, *The Law of Contract*, 15th edn (2020).

Replace footnote 168 with:

¹⁶⁸ The marine cases on promissory representations are discussed very usefully in Arnould: *Law of Marine Insurance*, 17th edn (London: Sweet & Maxwell, 2008, updated by First Supplement to 17th edn, 2010), paras 17–29 to 17–39 and in Arnould: *Law of Marine Insurance and Average*, 18th edn (updated by First Supplement to 18th edn, 2016), paras 17–32 to 17–34. See now, Arnould, *Law of Marine Insurance and Average*, 19th edn and Second Supplement (2020).

Inducement of contract.

After the third paragraph, add new paragraph:

16-047   Although not an insurance case, in *BV Nederlandse Industrie Van Eiprodukten v Rembrandt Enterprises Inc*,¹⁹⁷ᵃ Longmore LJ carefully considered the authorities (in particular the Victorian authorities) on inducement in cases of fraudulent misrepresentation. Longmore LJ noted (at [14] and [15]) that:

"It is … important to know what has to be proved by the party who has the onus of proof. Is it that the representee would/would not have acted differently but for the misrepresentation? Or is it that the representation played a part (or influenced) the decision of the representee? Or is it sufficient that the representee might/might not have acted differently?

It is surprising that these are still controversial questions in English law especially since the test for inducement in cases of innocent or negligent representation appears to be settled in the form that the representee has the burden of showing inducement in the sense that he has to show he would not have entered into the relevant contract had the representation not been made: see *Assicurazioni Generali SpA v Arab Insurance Group* [2003] 1 All ER (Comm) 140, *Pan Atlantic Insurance Co Ltd v Pine Top Insurance Co Ltd* [1995] 1 A.C. 501, *Chitty, Contracts*, 33rd edition, para 7-039."

¹⁹⁷ᵃ *BV Nederlandse Industrie Van Eiprodukten v Rembrandt Enterprises Inc* [2019] EWCA Civ 596; [2019] 1 Lloyd's Rep. 491; [2020] Q.B. 551. Application for permission to appeal to the Supreme Court was refused.

Longmore LJ concluded that if a representor fraudulently intended his words to be taken in a certain sense and the representee understood them in that sense and entered into a contract, it was likely to be inferred that the representee was induced to enter into the contract on the faith of the representor's statement. As Longmore LJ noted (at [25]): "It is fair to call this a presumption of inducement." However, it is a presumption of fact which could be rebutted, not a presumption of law which could not be rebutted or only be rebutted in a particular way. However, the presumption is difficult to rebut. Longmore LJ also concluded that the law at the end of the 19th century had assimilated the requirement of inducement in the tort of deceit and in actions for rescission for fraudulent misrepresentation and could be stated as being that the representee had to prove he had been materially "influenced" by the representations in the sense that it was "actively present to his mind" (at [32]). There was no requirement, as a matter of law, that the representee should state in terms that he would not have made the contract but for the misrepresentation, but the absence of such a statement was part of the overall evidential picture from which the judge had to ascertain whether there was inducement or not (at [32], see also at [43]). As set out above, however, this is not an insurance case and it is noted here for reference and consideration.

Rebuttal of presumption.

Replace footnote 203 with:

[203] See G.H. Treitel, *The Law of Contract*, 14th edn (2015), para.9-028; and now see G.H. Treitel, *The Law of Contract*, 15th edn (2020).   **16-050**

Leaders and followers.

Replace footnote 211 with:

[211] Arnould: *Law of Marine Insurance and Average*, 18th edn (updated by First Supplement to 18th edn, 2016), paras 17–104 to 17–108, and see the citations from the 19th century marine insurance text books in *Grant v Aetna Life Insurance Co* (1860) 11 Low.Can.R. 128 at 136–139. See now, Arnould, *Law of Marine Insurance and Average*, 19th edn and Second Supplement (2020).   **16-054**

5. Miscellaneous

Exclusion of insurers' remedies for misrepresentation.

After the first paragraph, add new paragraph:
    In *UK Acorn Finance Ltd v Markel (UK) Ltd*[238a] HHJ Pelling QC, sitting as a   **16-060**
judge of the High Court, gave a very careful judgment exploring the scope and application of an unintentional non-disclosure (UND) clause providing, as far as material:

> "In the event of non-disclosure or misrepresentation of information to Us, We will waive Our rights to avoid this Insuring Clause provided that …(i) You are able to establish to Our satisfaction that such non-disclosure or misrepresentation was innocent and free from any fraudulent conduct or intent to deceive."

He decided first that as a matter of construction, the clause made it clear that the burden was placed on the insured to establish that any misrepresentation or non-disclosure was "innocent and free from any fraudulent conduct or intent to deceive". That was the effect of the words: "You are able to establish." Further, the language used clearly stated that the decision maker was the insurer. That was the effect of the words: "to Our satisfaction". It followed that it was wrong as a matter of principle to conclude that the court (or, for that matter an arbitrator) could substitute its judgment for that of the insurer. However, following the decision of the Supreme Court in *Braganza v BP Shipping Ltd*,[238b] regarding contract clauses under which one party to the contract is given the power to exercise a discretion, or to form an opinion as to relevant facts, there had to be implied into the clause a term to the effect that the insurer

"will not exercise its decision making powers conferred by the UND Clause arbitrarily, capriciously or irrationally in the sense identified by the Court of Appeal in *Associated Provincial Picture Houses Limited v. Wednesbury Corporation* [1948] 1 KB 223. This requirement imports two elements – namely (i) a requirement that the defendant will not take into account matters that it ought not to take into account and will take into account only matters that it ought to take into account; and (ii) a requirement that it does not come to a conclusion that no reasonable decision maker could ever have come to – see *Braganza* ... per Lady Hale at paragraph 30 and Lord Neuberger at paragraph 103.

In arriving at a conclusion as to whether this latter requirement has been satisfied, it is necessary to bear in mind the often quoted direction in Re H (Minors) (Sexual Abuse: Standard of Proof) (ibid.) that '... the more serious the allegation the less likely it is that the event occurred and, hence, the stronger should be the evidence before the court concludes that the allegation is established on the balance of probabilities ...' - see *Braganza* ... per Lady Hale at paragraph 36. In a case such as this, where contractually the onus has been placed on the insured to prove the misrepresentation or non-disclosure '... was innocent and free from any fraudulent conduct or intent to deceive ...' this principle requires the decision maker to bear in mind that it is inherently more probable that a misrepresentation has been made innocently or negligently rather than dishonestly in arriving at an evaluative conclusion based on the whole of the material that the decision maker ought to take into account."[238c]

[238a] *UK Acorn Finance Ltd v Markel (UK) Ltd* [2020] EWHC 922 (Comm).

[238b] *Braganza v BP Shipping Ltd* [2015] UKSC 17; [2015] 1 W.L.R. 1661.

[238c] *UK Acorn Finance Ltd v Markel (UK) Ltd* [2020] EWHC 922 (Comm) at [64] and [65]. Having then gone carefully through the evidence as to the steps taken by the relatively junior employee of the insurers who had reached the conclusion that the insured has not proved that had acted innocently, the learned judge found that the insurers had not acted in accordance with the implied term.

CHAPTER 17

GOOD FAITH AND THE DUTY OF DISCLOSURE

1. INTRODUCTION AND LEGISLATIVE REFORM

Replace paragraph with:

There have been significant legislative reforms to this area of insurance law. The **17-001** Insurance Act 2015 (the 2015 Act)[1] received Royal Assent on 12 February 2015 and (in relevant parts) came into force on 12 August 2016. The 2015 Act, which is addressed in Ch.20 of this work, followed reasonably soon after the Consumer Insurance (Disclosure and Representations) Act 2012 (the 2012 Act),[2] which is addressed in Ch.19 of this work. The 2012 Act came into force (in relevant parts) on 6 April 2013. The 2015 Act and the 2012 Act are, on any view, major developments in the law of insurance in the UK. It is important for the reader to have regard to the 2015 Act and to the 2012 Act, to the extent that they are relevant, and to read this chapter in light of the 2015 Act and the 2012 Act (insofar as applicable). For the avoidance of doubt, subject to one or two minor references, this chapter does not address the 2015 Act or the 2012 Act. As at the time of writing, there has only been one substantive decision on the 2015 Act.[2a] Further, many current insurance policies and many current disputes remain under the "old" law. For these reasons, the 2015 Act and the 2012 Act are addressed in separate chapters, as above.

[1] The 2015 Act is available online: *http://www.legislation.gov.uk/ukpga/2015/4/contents/enacted* [Accessed 7 June 2018].

[2] The 2012 Act is also available online: *http://www.legislation.gov.uk/ukpga/2012/6/contents/enacted* [Accessed 7 June 2018].

[2a] *Young v Royal and Sun Alliance Plc* [2019] CSOH 32; 2019 S.L.T. 622, discussed at para.20-029A below. The decision in *Young* was affirmed on appeal: [2020] CSIH 25; 2020 S.L.T. 597.

2. DUTY OF UTMOST GOOD FAITH

Replace paragraph with:

Insurance is one of a small number of contracts based upon the principle of **17-002** utmost good faith[4]—uberrimae fidei. Section 17 of the Marine Insurance Act 1906[5] states this principle and, until amended by the Insurance Act 2015, provided that if the utmost good faith be not observed by either party, the contract may be avoided by the other party. It thus appears indirectly to impose on the parties a duty to act in good faith in their mutual dealings. The principle governs all contracts of insurance and reinsurance, and it applies both before a contract is concluded (the pre-formation period) and during the performance of the contract (the post-formation period).[6]

[4] *Bell v Lever Bros Ltd* [1932] A.C. 161 at 227; *Banque Keyser S.A. v Skandia (UK) Insurance Co Ltd* [1990] 1 Q.B. 665 at 769. The expression "uberrimae fidei" was in use in the late eighteenth century— *Wolff v Horncastle* (1789) 1 Bos. & P. 316 at 322 per Buller J. The categories of such contracts are closed—*Bell v Lever Bros Ltd*, above at 227, 231–232. Neither a line slip facility nor a binding authority nor an agreement to indemnify contained in a novating transaction are contracts of utmost good faith, as they are contracts *to insure* and not *of insurance*—*HIH Casualty & General Insurance Ltd v Chase Manhattan Bank* [2001] 1 All E.R. (Comm) 719 at 744 per Aikens J citing earlier authority. See generally P. MacDonald-Eggers and Sir Simon Picken, *Good Faith & Insurance Contracts*, 4th edn (Informa Law, 2018).

[5] Now amended: see para.17-001, above, for the recent legislative developments.

[6] *London Assurance Co v Mansel* (1897) 11 Ch. D. 363 at 367; *Cantieri Meccanico Brindisino v Janson* [1912] 3 K.B. 452; *Manifest Shipping Co Ltd v Uni-Polaris Co Ltd (The Star Sea)* [2001] 1 All E.R. (Comm) 193 at 198, 209–210. As set out above, this section, and this chapter generally, does not address the 2012 Act or the 2015 Act. See para.17-001, above, for the recent legislative developments.

Replace paragraph with:

17-003   In the pre-formation period the principle of utmost good faith creates well-established duties owed by the insured and by his agent effecting the insurance to disclose material facts and to refrain from making untrue statements when negotiating the contract. The law is summarised in ss.18–20 of the 1906 Act, which again apply to all classes of insurance.[7] These sections are not, however, exhaustive of the concept of utmost good faith.[8] During the post-formation period it continues to affect the insurance, but the content and effect of the duty is flexible and varies depending upon the circumstances. If the insured seeks a variation to, or renewal of, the insurance contract, then he again becomes subject to duties similar to those set out in ss.18–20 of the Act.[9] Here a new agreement is being negotiated, and the insurer's sole remedy for breach is avoidance of the particular agreement in respect of which the breach is committed.[10] In contrast both parties are required to act in good faith towards each other in the performance of the contract, although there are few instances in which the courts have held that the duty applies.[10a] One is when a term of the insurance requires the insured to provide the insurer with information in particular circumstances.[11] Another is when a liability insurer exercises his right to conduct his insured's defence to a claim made by a third party.[12] It is said that the party in question must in such cases act in good faith and with regard to the interests of the other party. The duty of good faith can more broadly be seen as a duty supporting the implication of contractual terms in the insurance context when required to achieve the goal of fair dealing between the parties.[13] The irrelevance of the statutory duty as a free-standing obligation is emphasised by the very limited circumstances in which the draconian and often disproportionately severe right of avoidance can be exercised,[14] although it should be noted that the courts in New Zealand seem to be prepared to award damages for breach of the duty by an insurer.[14a] It is available only in cases when the breach of duty occasions such serious prejudice to the innocent party that it permits him to terminate the insurance contract prospectively under the law of contract.[15] Such cases will be extremely rare. It would, with respect, have been simpler to curb the exercise of the remedy of avoidance by interpreting the post-formation duty of good faith as resting on an implied condition of the contract rather than on the separate rule enshrined in s.17 of the Act, but in *The Star Sea* the House of Lords preferred to describe it as a principle independent from contract law and with its own statutory sanction for breach.[16]

[7] *Joel v Law Union & Crown Insurance Co* [1908] 2 K.B. 863 at 878; *Economides v Commercial Union Assurance Co Plc* [1998] Q.B. 587 at 598. For the relevant provisions of the 2012 Act and of the 2015 Act, see Chs 19 and 20, below, as noted at para.17-001 above.

[8] *The Star Sea* [2001] 1 All E.R. (Comm) 193 at 198, 209 and 221.

[9] For the relevant provisions of the 2012 Act and of the 2015 Act, see Chs 19 and 20, below.

[10] *K/S Merc-Scandia XXXXII v Certain Lloyd's Underwriters (The Mercandian Continent)* [2001] 2 Lloyd's Rep. 563 at 573–574; *HIH Casualty & General Insurance Ltd v Chase Manhattan Bank* [2001] 2 Lloyd's Rep. 483 at 494; *Manifest Shipping Co Ltd v Uni-Polaris Shipping Co Ltd (The Star Sea)* [1997] 1 Lloyd's Rep. 360 at 370, not commented upon in the HL.

[10a] It has, though, become a common issue in New Zealand recently in a number of cases arising out of the earthquake in Christchurch in 2010–2011. See the recent decision in *Kilduff v Tower Insurance* [2018] NZHC 704; [2018] Lloyd's Rep. I.R. 621, where Gendall J held at [107]–[108] that there was an implied duty of good faith on an insurer which required, as a bare minimum, to: (a) disclose all material information that the insurer knew or ought to have known, including, but not limited to, the initial formation of the contract and during and after the lodgement of a claim; (b) act reasonably, fairly and transparently, including but not limited to the initial formation of the contract, and during and after the lodgement of a claim; and (c) process the claim in a reasonable time. What was "reasonable" depended on all the relevant circumstances, including the type of insurance, the size and complexity of the claim, compliance with any relevant statutory or regulatory rules or guidance, and factors outside an insurer's control. Further, if the insurer showed that reasonable grounds existed for disputing the claim the insurer did not breach the implied term merely by failing to pay the claim while the dispute was continuing. But the conduct of the insurer in handling a claim might be a relevant factor in deciding whether that good faith duty was breached and, if so, when. In so finding, Gendall J relied on his decision in *Young v Tower Insurance Ltd* [2017] Lloyd's Rep. I.R. 605. See also the decision by the same judge in *Dodds v Southern Response Earthquake Services Limited* [2019] NZHC 2016, which was specifically concerned with the conduct of an insurer in handling a claim and making an offer of settlement. Here, Gendall J would have been prepared, it appears, to award damages for the insurer's breach of the duty although this was not decided as the plaintiffs had damages remedies under specific New Zealand legislation on misrepresentation and under the Fair Trading Act 1973.

[11] *The Mercandian Continent* [2001] 2 Lloyd's Rep. 563 at 571–572, citing *Phoenix General Insurance Co v Halvanon Insurance Co* [1988] Q.B. 216.

[12] *The Mercandian Continent* [2001] 2 Lloyd's Rep. 563 at 571–572; *Cox v Bankside Agency Ltd* [1995] 2 Lloyd's Rep. 437 at 462; *Groom v Crocker* [1939] 1 K.B. 194 at 203; *Beacon Insurance Co v Langdale* [1939] 4 All E.R. 204 at 206. See now also *Ramsook v Crossley* [2018] UKPC 9; [2018] Lloyd's Rep. I.R. 471, in particular at [27]. Other instances may be the duty of the insured to have regard to the interests of the insurer when taking proceedings against a third party who has caused an insured loss— see paras 24-041 to 24-042, below, and the duty of a reinsurer to exercise his powers under a claims control clause in good faith, *Eagle Star & British Dominions Insurance Co v Cresswell* [2004] Lloyd's Rep. I.R. 537 at [55].

[13] *Goshawk v Tyser* [2006] 1 All E.R. (Comm) 501 at [53] per Rix LJ, citing Lord Hobhouse in *The Star Sea* [2001] 1 All E.R. (Comm) 193 at [52]; and *Phoenix General Insurance v Halvanon Insurance Co* [1988] Q.B. 216 at 241.

[14] See Chs 19 and 20 for the legislative amendment to s.17, and its new role.

[14a] See especially *Dodds v Southern Response Earthquake Services Limited* [2019] NZHC 2016. See fn.12 to para.17-003, above.

[15] *The Mercandian Continent* [2001] 2 Lloyd's Rep. 563 at 575; *Agapitos v Agnew* [2003] Q.B. 556 at [44].

[16] It is true that Lord Hobhouse said that a coherent scheme could be achieved by treating the post-formation duty as a contractual implied condition—*The Star Sea* [2001] 1 All E.R. (Comm) 193 at 211, and that Lord Steyn and Lord Hoffmann agreed with his speech. But they also agreed with Lord Scott, who treated the duty as imposed by s.17, and it appears that Lord Hobhouse ultimately abided by the concession of counsel that the continuing duty of good faith was based upon an independent rule of law stated by the Act of 1906: at 210. Lord Clyde did not advert to this point. As set out above, this chapter does not address the 2012 Act or the 2015 Act. See para.17-001 above, for the recent legislative developments.

4. DUTY OF THE ASSURED

Business insurance.

Replace footnote 56 with:

17-015 [56] *Simner v New India Assurance* [1995] L.R.L.R. 240 at 255, applying *Regina Fur Co v Bossom* [1957] 2 Lloyd's Rep. 466 at 484; *ERC Frankona Reinsurance v American National Insurance Co* [2006] Lloyd's Rep. 157 at [122]. But see Arnould: *Law of Marine Insurance and Average*, 18th edn and First Supplement (London: Sweet & Maxwell, 2016), para.16–14. Now see Arnould, *Law of Marine Insurance and Average*, 19th edn and Second Supplement (London: Sweet & Maxwell, 2020).

Change title of paragraph:

Effect of questions in proposal form.[63a]

17-018 [63a] Paragraphs 17-018 to 17-020 (and the same paragraphs in earlier editions of this work) were referred to in argument and by the Judge, with approval, in *Young v Royal and Sun Alliance Plc* [2019] CSOH 32; 2019 S.L.T. 622 at [22], [39], [70], [76] and [86] (affirmed on appeal: [2020] CSIH 25; 2020 S.L.T. 597), the first case to consider the Insurance Act 2015 in any substantive detail. The decision in *Young* is addressed in detail at para.20-029A below. Passages from paras 17-018 to 17-020 were cited with approval by the Court of Session (Inner House, First Division) in *Young v Royal and Sun Alliance Insurance Plc* [2020] CSIH 25; 2020 S.L.T. 597 at [41].

Replace footnote 67 with:

17-019 [67] *Becker v Marshall* (1922) 11 Ll. L. Rep. 114 at 117, affirmed in CA at (1922) 12 Ll. L. Rep. 413; *Glicksman v Lancashire & General Assurance Co* [1925] 2 K.B. 593 at 609; [1927] A.C. 139 at 143; *Insurance Corp of the Channel Islands v Royal Hotel* [1998] Lloyd's Rep. I.R. 151 at 158. The first sentence of para.17-019 was cited with approval by the Court of Session (Inner House, First Division) in *Young v Royal and Sun Alliance Insurance Plc* [2020] CSIH 25; 2020 S.L.T. 597 at [41].

Replace paragraph with:

17-020 It is more likely, however, that the questions asked will limit the duty of disclosure, in that, if questions are asked on particular subjects and the answers to them are warranted, it may be inferred that the insurer has waived his right to information, either on the same matters but outside the scope of the questions, or on matters kindred to the subject-matter of the questions.[68] Thus, if an insurer asks, "[h]ow many accidents have you had in the last three years?" it may well be implied that he does not want to know of accidents before that time, though these would still be material. If an insurer asks whether individual proposers have ever been declared bankrupt, he waives disclosure of the insolvency of companies of which they have been directors.[69] Whether or not such waiver is present depends on a true construction of the proposal form, the test being, would a reasonable man reading the proposal form be justified in thinking that the insurer had restricted his right to receive all material information, and consented to the omission of the particular information in issue?[70]

[68] *Laing v Union Marine Insurance Co* (1895) 1 Com. Cas. 11 at 15; *Schoolman v Hall* [1951] 1 Lloyd's Rep. 139; *Taylor v Eagle Star & British Dominions Insurance Co* (1940) 67 Lloyd's Rep. 136; *Joel v Law Union & Crown Insurance Co* [1908] 2 K.B. 863 at 878; *Roberts v Plaisted* [1989] 2 Lloyd's Rep. 341. Cited with approval by the Court of Session (Inner House, First Division) in *Young v Royal and Sun Alliance Insurance Plc* [2020] CSIH 25; 2020 S.L.T. 597 at [41]. Note the changes to the law in respect to "basis clauses" made by the 2015 Act and the 2012 Act. See para.17-001, above, for the recent legislative developments.

[69] *Doheny v New India Assurance Co* [2005] 1 All E.R. (Comm) 382. See also *R&R Developments Ltd v AXA Insurance UK Plc* [2009] EWHC 2429 (Ch); [2010] Lloyd's Rep. I.R. 521, addressed in more detail at para.16-026, above.

[70] The corresponding paragraph in previous editions of this work was cited with approval by Woolf J in *Hair v Prudential Assurance Co* [1983] 2 Lloyd's Rep. 667 at 673 (see para.17-022 below), by the Supreme Court of Ireland in *Kelleher v Irish Life Assurance Co* [1993] I.L.R.M. 643 (S.C.), by the Commercial Court in *O'Kane v Jones, The Martin P* [2004] 1 Lloyd's Rep. 389 at [238], and by the Court

of Appeal in *Doheny v New India Assurance Co* [2005] 1 All E.R. (Comm) 382 at [19] and [37]; applied in *Noblebright v Sirius International Corp* [2007] Lloyd's Rep. 584 at [9]; and *R&R Developments Ltd v AXA Insurance UK Plc* [2009] EWHC 2429 (Ch); [2010] Lloyd's Rep. I.R. 521 at [40]. See also *Lewis v Norwich Union Healthcare Ltd* [2010] Lloyd's Rep. I.R. 198 at [54]. This test (as set out in this paragraph in the 11th edition of this work) of whether or not a relevant waiver is present was cited with approval by Burton J in *Sugar Hut Group Ltd v Great Lakes Reinsurance (UK) Plc* [2010] EWHC 2636 (Comm); [2011] Lloyd's Rep. I.R. 198 at [2] and the test was also applied by Flaux J in *Synergy Health (UK) Ltd v CGU Insurance Plc* [2010] EWHC 2583 (Comm); [2011] Lloyd's Rep. I.R. 500 at [167]. For some more recent examples, see *Bate v Aviva Insurance UK Ltd* [2013] EWHC 1687 (Comm); [2013] Lloyd's Rep. I.R. 492 at [22]; upheld on appeal (without reference to this specific point): [2014] EWCA Civ 334; and *Cheung Kwan Wah v China Ping An Insurance (Hong Kong) Co Ltd* [2012] HKDC 802 and the *Insurance Law Monthly* (Vol.24, No.9, 23 August 2012) case report on the same. See now also *Young v Royal and Sun Alliance Plc* [2019] CSOH 32; 2019 S.L.T. 622 (affirming the decision of the Outer House) the decision of the Court of Session (Inner House, First Division) in *Young v Royal and Sun Alliance Insurance Plc* [2020] CSIH 25; 2020 S.L.T. 597 at [41], citing with approval the last sentence of para.17-020. In relation to ambiguous questions in the proposal form, see para.16-026 above.

After para.17-021, add new paragraph:

17-021A   In *Young v Royal and Sun Alliance Plc*, addressed in more detail at para.20-029A below, Lady Wolffe held[77a] (in relevant parts) as follows (at [86]):

"It respectfully seems to me that the case law on the construction of proposal forms, including the application of waiver in its second form (ie by limiting questions) may require to be approached with a degree of circumspection in a case such as the present. The observations in the cases and the discussion in *MacGillivray* (at paragraph 17-018ff) cited to the Court are predicated on the use of a conventional proposal form proffered by the insurer and to which an insured responds. By contrast in this case, and in common with *CTI*, the prospective insured initiated the approach in the form of the Market Presentation, the scope of which the prospective insured controlled. In the conventional proposal-type case, there may be greater scope for applying the doctrine of waiver, as the insurer controls the scope of the information it seeks; it signals (via the questions asked) what it regards as material and, by implication, it may be taken as waiving matters outside the scope of the questions posed. The second type of waiver was developed to control unfairness that might flow from an insurer invoking some other matter, beyond the scope of the proposal questions, as material. (Although the law has never been that materiality was confined to the questions on a proposal form). ..."

[77a] *Young v Royal and Sun Alliance Plc* [2019] CSOH 32; 2019 S.L.T. 622; affirmed on appeal: [2020] CSIH 25; 2020 S.L.T. 597.

Declarations in the policy.

Replace footnote 79 with:

17-022   [79] *Economides v Commercial Union Assurance Co* [1998] Q.B. 587. See also *Zeller v British Caymanian Insurance Co Ltd* [2008] UKPC 4; [2008] Lloyd's Rep. I.R. 545 PC at [18]. The *Zeller* case was considered by Akenhead J in *Genesis Housing Association Ltd v Liberty Syndicate Management Ltd for and on behalf of Liberty Syndicate 4472 at Lloyd's* [2012] EWHC 3105 (TCC) at [37]–[38] and referred to by the Court of Appeal, upholding Akenhead J's decision, [2013] EWCA Civ 1173; [2014] Lloyd's Rep. I.R. 318 at [68]–[69]. See now also *Friends Life Ltd v Charles Thomas Miley* [2019] EWCA Civ 261 at [19]: "I consider that this view of the declaration is consistent with the construction of a rather similar declaration made by an insured party to his insurer in *Economides v Commerical Assurance Co Plc* [1998] Q.B. 587. In that case, the declaration was that the statements made were, to the best of the insured's knowledge and belief, true and complete. This court held that such a declaration imported only a requirement of honesty and there was no implied representation that there were objectively reasonable grounds for the belief expressed."

5. MATERIALITY

Opinion of particular insurer.

Replace footnote 175 with:

17-041 [175] *The Bedouin* [1894] P. 1 at 12; *Arnould: Law of Marine Insurance and Average*, 18th edn and First Supplement (2016), paras 17-73 to 17-75. Now see Arnould, *Law of Marine Insurance and Average*, 19th edn and Second Supplement (London: Sweet & Maxwell, 2020).

Insurances on property and chattels: fire.

Replace paragraph with:

17-054   In general, previous losses by the peril insured against are material and ought to be disclosed. In one case a company applied for fire cover on premises where it carried on the business of manufacturing caravans. This business was essentially that of its sole director and major shareholder, who was described as the alter ego of the company. He failed to disclose that, some three years earlier, there had been a loss by fire on premises of another company which he had used as a vehicle for the same business. It was held that this loss was material, and that the insurers were entitled to avoid the contract of insurance.[229] A failure to comply with risk requirements imposed by the insurer in a previous policy period will almost certainly be material.[229a] In liability insurance and reinsurance the insured's loss record is invariably material, being usually a major factor in assessing risk and calculating the premium.[230]

[229] *Arterial Caravans Ltd v Yorkshire Insurance Co Ltd* [1973] 1 Lloyd's Rep. 169, followed in *Marene Knitting Mills Pty Ltd v Greater Pacific General Insurance Ltd* [1976] 2 Lloyd's Rep. 631 (PC). Although factually different, see also *Bate v Aviva Insurance UK Ltd* [2013] EWHC 1687 (Comm); [2013] Lloyd's Rep. I.R. 492; upheld on appeal: [2014] EWCA Civ 334; [2014] Lloyd's Rep I.R. 527, in particular at [32]–[35].

[229a] See, for example, *Niramax Group Ltd v Zurich Insurance Plc* [2020] EWHC 535 (Comm). For a helpful commentary on this case, see "Utmost good faith: the duty of disclosure" (2020) 32 I.L.M. 3.

[230] *New Hampshire Insurance Co v Oil Refineries Ltd* [2003] Lloyd's Rep. I.R. 386.

The Equality Act 2010: race, nationality, religion, sex, disability and age.

After "… since those days and the Equality Act 2010 (the Equality Act)", add new footnote 291a:

17-063 [291a] Although not a non-disclosure / misrepresentation case, see *Re Royal London Mutual Insurance Society Ltd* [2018] EWHC 2215 (Ch), where the court sanctioned the convening of a meeting for certain policyholders of the Royal London Mutual Insurance Society Ltd so that they could vote upon a proposed scheme of arrangement and considered whether the scheme would fall foul of the Equality Act.

6. WHAT THE ASSURED NEED NOT DISCLOSE

Facts as to which the insurer waives information.

Replace footnote 386 with:

17-089 [386] *Mann, Macneal & Steeves v Capital and Counties Insurance Co* [1921] 2 K.B. 300 at 317; *Greenhill v Federal Insurance Co* [1927] 1 K.B. 65 at 89; *CTI Inc v Oceanus Mutual Underwriting Association (Bermuda) Ltd* [1984] 1 Lloyd's Rep. 476 at 511. See also *Bate v Aviva Insurance UK Ltd* [2013] EWHC 1687 (Comm); [2013] Lloyd's Rep. I.R. 492 at [76], where HHJ Mackie QC referred to *Mann, Macneal & Steeves Ltd v Capital and Counties Insurance Co Ltd* [1921] 2 K.B. 300 at 307–308, and stated in relevant part "[m]aterial matters should be the subject of a question in a proposal form: see eg the ABI Statement of General Insurance practice. If there is evidence that insurers in general do not enquire about a particular matter, that indicates that the matter is not material". HHJ Mackie QC's decision was upheld on appeal: [2014] EWCA Civ 334, without specific reference to this point. See now also *Young v Royal* *and Sun Alliance Plc* [2019] CSOH 32; 2019 S.L.T. 622 at [68]: "… waiver is not readily to be inferred (per *MacGillivray* at paragraph 17-089; in *Doheny* Parker LJ stated that an assured must show a 'clear case' (at p 511)) and the person asserting waiver … bears the onus of establishing waiver". The decision in *Young* was affirmed on appeal: [2020] CSIH 25; 2020 S.L.T. 597.

7. THE INSURER'S DUTY OF DISCLOSURE

Replace footnote 406 with:

[406] *Banque Keyser Ullmann SA v Skandia (UK) Insurance Co Ltd* [1990] 1 Q.B. 665 at 772. See also **17-094** *R. (on the application of Critchley) v Financial Ombudsman Service Ltd* [2019] EWHC 3036 (Admin) at [106]–[110].

8. MISCELLANEOUS

Exclusion of duty and remedy for breach.

Replace footnote 439 with:

[439] *Arab Bank Ltd v Zurich Insurance Co* [1999] Lloyd's Rep. 262; *Kumar v AGF Insurance Ltd* [1998] **17-099** 4 All E.R. 788. See, for example, *Mutual Energy Ltd v Starr Underwriting Agents Ltd* [2016] EWHC 590 (TCC); [2016] Lloyd's Rep. I.R. 550, where insurers agreed that the policy could only be avoided for reasons of non-disclosure where that non-disclosure had been deliberate or fraudulent. For an article considering the *Mutual Energy* case, see "Presentation of the risk: interpretation of express presentation clauses" (2016) 28 I.L.M. 10. See also *UK Acorn Finance Ltd v Markel (UK) Ltd* [2020] EWHC 922 (Comm), which is discussed at para.16-060 above. For a helpful article considering the *UK Acorn Finance* case, see "Fair presentation of the risk: unintentional non-disclosure clauses" (2020) 32 I.L.M. 8.

Financial Ombudsman Service.

Replace paragraph with:

The FOS is a statutory body set up under FSMA 2000,[454] replacing the previous **17-109** voluntary scheme. Any private individual insured whose claim is rejected for any reason, including non-disclosure, can make a complaint to it. Small businesses can also complain to the FOS.[455] The rules setting out how the FOS should handle complaints are set out in the *FSA Handbook* under "Dispute Resolution: Complaints". The Ombudsman can order the payment of a monetary award by the insurer to compensate the insured up to a monetary limit (which is £150,000[456] for complaints received from 1 January 2012, or £160,000 in certain circumstances,[456a] and now £350,000 for complaints about actions by firms on or after 1 April 2019), but can also recommend the insurer pay more than this limit if he considers that fair compensation requires payment of a larger amount.[457] The Ombudsman is not bound to follow the law, and is to determine disputes by reference to what is fair and reasonable in the circumstances of the case.[458] The flexibility of the Ombudsman's approach has been outlines by Lewison J in *Bunney v Burns Anderson Plc*[459]:

"In determining what is fair and reasonable in all the circumstances of the case it is common ground that the ombudsman does not have to apply the law. He could for example decide that an insurer had a technical ground on which to repudiate liability under an insurance policy but decide that it was not fair to rely on it; or override a limitation defence to which the court would have to give effect if he thought that it was unfair to rely on limitation."[460]

[454] Note the significant regulatory changes set out in the Financial Services Act 2012, addressed briefly at para.17-108 above, and more fully in Ch.36. Note, however, that Pt XVI of and Sch.17 to the Financial Services and Markets Act 2000 remain in force and in relation to the FOS. For recent cases considering the role and functioning of the FOS, see *R. (on the application of Calland) v Financial Ombudsman Service Ltd* [2013] EWHC 1327 (Admin) and *Clark v In Focus Asset Management & Tax Solu-*

tions Ltd [2014] EWCA Civ 118; [2014] 1 W.L.R. 2502; and *R. (on the application of Aviva Life and Pensions (UK) Ltd) v Financial Ombudsman Service* [2017] EWHC 352 (Admin); [2017] A.C.D. 53.

[455] From 1 November 2009 such businesses are those which fall within the definition of "micro enterprise" following recommendation 2003/361 of the EC Commission. The key characteristics of a micro enterprise are that it employs fewer than 10 people and has an annual turnover not exceeding €2 million. From 1 April 2019, the FOS service was extended to larger small and medium-sized enterprises (SMEs). These are firms with an annual turnover of under £6.5 million, an annual balance sheet total of under £5 million, or fewer than 50 employees.

[456] The previous limit was £100,000 and it was held in *Bunney v Burns Anderson Plc* [2007] EWHC 1240 (Ch); [2008] Lloyd's Rep. I.R. 198 that the Ombudsman had no jurisdiction to award or direct the payment of more than £100,000. Note the relevance of the recent decision of the Court of Appeal in *Clark v In Focus Asset Management & Tax Solutions Ltd* [2014] EWCA Civ 118; [2014] 1 W.L.R. 2502, referred to more fully in the final footnote at para.17-110 below.

[456a] For complaints about actions before 1 April 2019 that are referred to the Financial Ombudsman Service after that date, the limit has been raised to £160,000.

[457] Financial Services and Markets Act 2000 s.229. Also see *Clark v In Focus Asset Management & Tax Solutions Ltd* [2014] EWCA Civ 118; [2014] 1 W.L.R. 2502, referred to more fully in the final footnote at para.17-110 below.

[458] Financial Services and Markets Act 2000 s.228(2). See, for example, *R. (on the application of Heather Moor & Edgecomb Ltd) v FOS* [2008] EWCA Civ 642; [2008] Bus L.R. 1486 at [36] and [80]. See the decision of Males J in *R. (on the application of Calland) v Financial Ombudsman Service Ltd* [2013] EWHC 1327 (Admin), considering the role and functioning of the FOS in some detail, and a commentary on the case by Dr Judith P Summer, "Regulation: Financial Ombudsman Service" (2014) 26 I.L.M. 4. See also the decision of the Court of Appeal in *Clark v In Focus Asset Management & Tax Solutions Ltd* [2014] EWCA Civ 118; [2014] 1 W.L.R. 2502 at [1] and [17]–[28]. In the recent decision of *R. (on the application of Aviva Life and Pensions (UK) Ltd) v Financial Ombudsman Service* [2017] EWHC 352 (Admin); [2017] EWHC 352 (Admin), Jay J set out a helpful account of the relevant principles and authorities at [33]–[47]. Jay J emphasised a passage from the decision of Stanley Burnton LJ in *R. (Heather Moor & Edgecomb) v FOS* (above) at [49], which was that "[the Ombudsman] is free to depart from the relevant law, but if he does so he should say so in his decision and explain why". At [73], Jay J expressed some concerns about the nature of this jurisdiction and the relationship between what is fair and reasonable and what the law lays down. See also *R. (on the application of Critchley) v Financial Ombudsman Service Ltd* [2019] EWHC 3036 (Admin) on the correct approach to the resolution of disputes by the FOS.

[459] *Bunney v Burns Anderson Plc* [2007] EWHC 1240 (Ch); [2008] Lloyd's Rep. I.R. 198 at [22]. See also *R. (on the application of Aviva Life and Pensions (UK) Ltd) v Financial Ombudsman Service* [2017] EWHC 352 (Admin) at [33]–[47].

[460] Cited with approval by the Court of Session (Outer House) in *David Clark v Argyle Consulting Ltd* [2010] CSOH 154; 2011 S.L.T. 180 at [20].

CHAPTER 18

FRAUD, MISREPRESENTATION AND NON-DISCLOSURE BY THIRD PARTIES

1. GENERAL PRINCIPLES

Introduction and legislative reform.

Replace first paragraph with:

There have been significant legislative reforms to this area of insurance law. The **18-001** Insurance Act 2015 (the 2015 Act)[1] received Royal Assent on 12 February 2015 and (in relevant parts) came into force on 12 August 2016. The 2015 Act, which is addressed in Ch.20 of this work, followed reasonably soon after the Consumer Insurance (Disclosure and Representations) Act 2012 (the 2012 Act),[2] which is addressed in Ch.19 of this work. The 2012 Act came into force (in relevant parts) on 6 April 2013. The 2015 Act and the 2012 Act are, on any view, major developments in the law of insurance in the UK. It is important for the reader to have regard to the 2015 Act and to the 2012 Act, to the extent that they are relevant, and to read this chapter in light of the 2015 Act and the 2012 Act (insofar as applicable). For the avoidance of doubt, subject to one or two minor references, this chapter does not address the 2015 Act or the 2012 Act. As at the time of writing, there has only been only one substantive decision on the 2015 Act.[2a] Further, many current insurance policies and many current disputes remain under the "old" law. For these reasons, the 2015 Act and the 2012 Act are addressed in separate chapters, as above.

[1] The 2015 Act is available online: *https://www.legislation.gov.uk/ukpga/2015/4/contents* [Accessed 22 September 2020].

[2] The 2012 Act is also available online: *https://www.legislation.gov.uk/ukpga/2012/6/contents/enacted* [Accessed 22 September 2020].

[2a] *Young v Royal and Sun Alliance Plc* [2019] CSOH 32; 2019 S.L.T. 622, discussed at para.20-029A below. The decision in *Young* was affirmed on appeal: [2020] CSIH 25; 2020 S.L.T. 597.

2. AGENTS OF THE INSURED

After "... which are now", add new footnote 19a:

[19a] Of course, subject to the 2012 Act and the 2015 Act: see Chs 19 and 20, below, and see para.18-001 **18-009** above, for these recent legislative developments.

Non-disclosure of partial loss.

Replace footnote 42 with:

18-017   [42]   *Blackburn, Low & Co v Vigors* (1887) 12 App. Cas. 531 at 540 per Lord Watson; J. Arnould, *Law of Marine Insurance and Average*, 18th edn (London: Sweet & Maxwell, 2013, updated by First Supplement, 2016), paras 16-29 to 16-31. Now see Arnould, *Law of Marine Insurance and Average*, 19th edn and Second Supplement (London: Sweet & Maxwell, 2020).

Agent acting to defraud principal.

Replace footnote 44 with:

18-018   [44]   *PCW Syndicates v PCW Reinsurers* [1996] 1 Lloyd's Rep. 241 at 255, 257, applying *Re Hampshire Land Co* [1896] 2 Ch. 743; *Houghton v Nothard, Lowe & Wills* [1928] A.C. 1. *Newsholme Bros v Road Transport & General Insurance Co* [1929] 2 K.B. 356 at 374; *Société Anonyme d'Intermédiaires Luxembourgeois v Farex Gie* [1995] L.R.L.R. 116 at 143; *Arab Bank Plc v Zurich Insurance Co* [1999] 1 Lloyd's Rep. 262 at 282–283; *Australia & New Zealand Bank v Colonial & Eagle Wharves* [1960] 2 Lloyd's Rep. 241; *Kingscroft Insurance Co v Nissan Fire & Marine Insurance Co* [1999] Lloyd's Rep. I.R. 371 at 375; *Moore Stephens v Stone & Rolls Ltd* [2008] 2 Lloyd's Rep. 319 (and on appeal to the House of Lords: [2009] UKHL 39; [2009] 1 A.C. 1391). See also, generally, *Bilta (UK) Ltd (In Liquidation) v Nazir* [2015] UKSC 23; [2016] A.C. 1; and *Singularis Holdings Ltd (In Liquidation) v Daiwa Capital Markets Europe Ltd* [2019] UKSC 50; [2019] 3 W.L.R. 997.

3.   AGENT OF INSURERS

Introduction.

Replace footnote 70 with:

18-027   [70]   In general see *Bowstead & Reynolds on Agency*, 21st edn (London: Sweet & Maxwell, 2017), art.95; and now see *Bowstead & Reynolds on Agency*, 21st edn and Second Supplement (London: Sweet & Maxwell, 2019).

Acquisition of knowledge in ordinary course of duty.

Replace footnote 78 with:

18-030   [78]   *Bowstead & Reynolds on Agency*, 21st edn (London: Sweet & Maxwell, 2017), art.72; and now see *Bowstead & Reynolds on Agency*, 21st edn and Second Supplement (2019).

4.   LAW REFORM

Reform of the law.

After the sixth paragraph, add new paragraph:

18-052   On 6 July 2018, the FCA and Legal Services Board approved the Solicitors Regulation Authority's (SRA) approach to dealing with Directive 2016/97 (European Insurance Distribution Directive). As set out above, the Directive, which came into effect from 1 October 2018, aims to strengthen protections in place for clients. At the time of the above approval, it was said that the Handbook would be amended to cater for the new requirements and guidance on the new Directive would also be made available. On 1 October 2018, the SRA published rules for dealing with the new Directive. The FCA guidance on the IDD was updated on 20 May 2020.

CHAPTER 19

CONSUMER INSURANCE (DISCLOSURE AND REPRESENTATIONS) ACT 2012

1. INTRODUCTION

Overview and introduction.

Replace paragraph with:

The Consumer Insurance (Disclosure and Representations) Act 2012 (the Act)[1]   **19-001**
received Royal Assent on 8 March 2012. Pursuant to s.2 of the Consumer Insurance (Disclosure and Representations) Act 2012 (Commencement) Order 2013 (2013/450) ss.2–11 of, and Schs 1 and 2 to, the Act came into force on 6 April 2013.[2] The Insurance Act 2015 (the 2015 Act)[3] received Royal Assent on 12 February 2015 and (in relevant part) came into force on 12 August 2016, and certain amendments came into force on 4 May 2017 (see Ch.20 below). The 2015 Act amends the Act in the manner set out at paras 19-021 and 19-041, below. The 2015 Act is addressed in Ch.20 of this work and Ch.19 should be read in light of the fact that the 2015 Act is now in force. Further, references in this chapter to the "current" law (including, unless otherwise indicated, references to the Marine Insurance Act 1906 (the 1906 Act)) should, unless otherwise indicated, be read as being references to the pre-Act law and the pre-2015 Act law.

[1] The Act is available online: *https://www.legislation.gov.uk/ukpga/2012/6/contents/enacted* [Accessed 22 September 2020].

[2] For general reference and for detailed discussion of particular issues, the reader is referred to P. MacDonald-Eggers and Sir Simon Picken, *Good Faith & Insurance Contracts*, 4th edn (Informa Law, 2018); *Colinvaux & Merkin's Insurance Contract Law*; Malcolm A. Clarke, *The Law of Insurance Contracts*; *Arnould: Law of Marine Insurance and Average*, 18th edn (London: Sweet & Maxwell, 2013, updated by First Supplement to 18th edn, 2016), paras 15–217 to 15–240; now Arnould, *Law of Marine Insurance and Average*, 19th edn and Second Supplement (London: Sweet & Maxwell, 2020); Peter J. Tyldesley, *Consumer Insurance Law: Disclosure, Representation and Basis of the Contract Clauses* (Bloomsbury Professional, 2013), Chs 2 and 6, in particular; Peter MacDonald Eggers, "The past and future of English insurance law: good faith and warranties" (2012) 1(2) *UCL Journal of Law and Jurisprudence*; Graham Charkham, "Reform of insurance law: the Consumer Insurance (Disclosure and Representations) Act 2012" (2013) 25 I.L.M. 41; David Hertzell and Laura Burgoyne, "The Law Commissions and insurance contract law reform: an update" (2013) 19 J.I.M.L. 105; and Paul Jaffe, "Reform of the Insurance Law of England and Wales—Separate Laws for the Different needs of Businesses and Consumers" (2013) 126 *BILA Journal* 18. There have been various FOS ombudsman decisions applying the Act, which decisions are available on the FOS website. There is also a "misrepresentation and non-disclosure" technical note available on the FOS website.

Replace footnote 4 with:

19-002   ⁴ At the time of writing, there have been only a small number of reported cases addressing the Act in any detail. The Court of Session (Outer House) recently considered the Act in *Southern Rock Insurance Co Ltd v Hafeez* [2017] CSOH 127; [2018] Lloyd's Rep. I.R. 207, as did HHJ Cotter QC in *Ageas Insurance Ltd v Stoodley* [2019] Lloyd's Rep. I.R. 1; and HHJ Simpkiss in *Tesco Underwriting Ltd v Achunche* [2016] EWHC 3869 (QB). The decision of the Court of Appeal in *Ashfaq v International Insurance Co of Hannover Plc* [2017] EWCA Civ 357; [2018] Lloyd's Rep. I.R. 228 briefly referred to the Act (see para.19-042 below), as did the Court of Session (Outer House) in *Young v Royal and Sun Alliance Plc* [2019] CSOH 32 (see Ch.20); and Jay J in *R. (on the application of Aviva Life and Pensions (UK) Ltd) v Financial Ombudsman Service* [2017] EWHC 352 (Admin); [2017] Lloyd's Rep. I.R. 404 (see para.19-026 below). Akenhead J briefly referred to the Act (without deciding any issues relating to the same) at [35] and [38] in *Genesis Housing Association Ltd v Liberty Syndicate Management Ltd* [2012] EWHC 3105 (TCC). The Act was also briefly mentioned by the Supreme Court in *Versloot Dredging BV v HDI Gerling Industrie Versicherung AG* [2016] UKSC 45; [2017] A.C. 1 at [102].

3.   Commentary on the Act

Replace footnote 9 with:

19-015   ⁹ This structure is followed for ease of reference and also for ease of exposition of the content of the Act. The correct approach to the proper interpretation of the Act (and, in particular, whether or not the Report and/or the Explanatory Notes are referred to in this regard) is beyond the scope of this work and will, of course, be a matter for submission and ultimately for determination by the courts. For example, in G. Charkham, "Reform of insurance law: the Consumer Insurance (Disclosure and Representations) Act 2012" (2013) 25 I.L.M. 41 it is stated (under the heading "Mixed purposes") that: "The Law Commission's Report, upon which the Act is based but which is not admissible as an aid to construction". However, see also (for example) *Aswan Engineering Establishment v Lupdine Ltd* [1987] 1 W.L.R. 1 at 14; *R. v Horseferry Road Metropolitan Stipendiary Magistrate Ex p. Siadatan* [1991] 1 Q.B. 260 at 267–268 and other textbooks such as, for example, *Bennion on Statutory Interpretation*, 7th edn and First Supplement (Butterworths: LexisNexis, 2019).

Main definitions.

Replace footnote 12 with:

19-017   ¹² What amounts to a "consumer insurance contract" is, of course, critically important. Whilst the approach taken in the Act to what is a consumer broadly follows the general approach of European law, as imported into UK consumer legislation by EU directives, this is not entirely the case because the Act provides (as above) for "mixed use" contracts: see paras 5.5 to 5.19 of the Report. Understandably, given the importance of these core definitions, commentators have expressed various views: see, for example, para.6.7 of *Consumer Insurance Law: Disclosure, Representation and Basis of the Contract Clauses* (Peter J. Tyldesley, 2013), *Arnould: Law of Marine Insurance and Average*, 18th edn (updated by First Supplement to 18th edn, 2016), paras 15–219 to 15–220; now Arnould, *Law of Marine Insurance and Average*, 19th edn and Second Supplement (London: Sweet & Maxwell, 2020); and "Reform of insurance law: the Consumer Insurance (Disclosure and Representations) Act 2012" (Graham Charkham (2013) 25 I.L.M. 41, under the headings "The definition of 'consumer insurance contract'" and "Mixed purposes"). For a recent case considering the definition of "consumer" in the Unfair Terms in Consumer Contracts Regulations 1999 (UTCCR) and the Insurance Conduct of Business Sourcebook (ICOBS), see *Ashfaq v International Insurance Co of Hannover Plc* [2017] EWCA Civ 357; [2018] Lloyd's Rep. I.R. 228. Note, however, that the definitions of "consumer" in the UTCCR and ICOBS differ from the equivalent definition ("consumer insurance contract") in the Act. Note also that the UTCCR were repealed and replaced by the Consumer Rights Act 2015 from 1 October 2015.

Qualifying misrepresentations: classification and presumptions.

Replace the first paragraph with:

19-030   Subsection 5(1) provides for qualifying misrepresentations to be classified under the Act as either: (a) deliberate or reckless²⁷; or (b) careless. Pursuant to Subsection 5(2), a qualifying misrepresentation is "deliberate or reckless" if the consumer: (a) knew that it was untrue or misleading, or did not care whether or not it was untrue or misleading; and (b) knew that the matter to which the misrepresentation related was relevant to the insurer, or did not care whether or not it was relevant to the insurer.[28] As set out at para.39 of the Explanatory Notes, a consumer acts "deliberately" if they act with knowledge. As established in the case of *Derry v Peek*,[29] a consumer acts recklessly if they act without care and regard for the truth of an answer. This can be distinguished from making a statement which one genuinely believes to be true but without sufficient care to check the facts. This would potentially be a careless misrepresentation.

[27] See the summary of the decision in *Tesco Underwriting Ltd v Achunche* [2016] EWHC 3869 (QB), in the second footnote to para.19-031 below. See also the decision of HHJ Cotter QC in *Ageas Insurance Ltd v Stoodley* [2019] Lloyd's Rep. I.R. 1, where there was an objectively straightforward, clear and specific question which was answered inaccurately by a person (the consumer insured) who clearly knew what was required and why. For a commentary on the *Ageas* case, see "Consumer Insurance: Misrepresentation" (2018) 30 I.L.M. 12. In *Southern Rock Insurance Co Ltd v Hafeez* [2017] CSOH 127; [2018] Lloyd's Rep. I.R. 207 the insurers failed to prove that there had been a deliberate or reckless misrepresentation. Lady Paton held at [73] that when assessing whether a representation was made deliberately or recklessly, all the circumstances must be taken into account, including the type of communication used, the terms of any question put and the opportunity given to the consumer to qualify or particularise any response, or to provide non-standard information.

[28] See para.6.33 of the Report.

[29] *Derry v Peek* (1889) 14 App. Cas. 337. See also, *Arnould: Law of Marine Insurance and Average*, 18th edn (updated by First Supplement to 18th edn, 2016), para.15-225; now Arnould, *Law of Marine Insurance and Average*, 19th edn and Second Supplement (London: Sweet & Maxwell, 2020).

Replace the first paragraph with:

Under subs.5(4), the onus is on the insurer to show that a misrepresentation was **19-031** deliberate or reckless.[32] There are, however, two presumptions set out in subs.5(5). Subsection 5(5) provides that it is to be presumed, unless the contrary is shown: (a) that the consumer had the knowledge of a reasonable consumer; and (b) that the consumer knew that a matter about which the insurer asked a clear and specific question was relevant to the insurer.[33] Where the presumptions apply, the burden of proof is reversed.[34] The Law Commissions state at para.4.23 of the Report that:

> "The insurer's task of proving that a misrepresentation was made deliberately or recklessly should not be unduly onerous or require an exceptionally high standard of proof. In the consultation paper we suggested that the insurer's task of proving fraud might be helped by two presumptions, namely that the consumer knew: (1) what someone in their position would normally be expected to know; and (2) that where the insurer asked a clear question, the issue was relevant to the insurer."

[32] See, for example, *Southern Rock Insurance Co Ltd v Hafeez* [2017] CSOH 127; [2018] Lloyd's Rep. I.R. 207 at [73].

[33] In *Tesco Underwriting Ltd v Achunche* [2016] EWHC 3869 (QB), the claimant insurer sought to avoid the defendant insured's insurance, alleging that the insured had made a positive statement (when applying for insurance) that he did not have any motoring convictions when in fact he had had one within the past five years. The decision turned on the finding that under s.5 of the Act there was a presumption that the policyholder knew that previous motoring convictions were relevant to the insurer, and that the documents made it clear that disclosing convictions was necessary. HHJ Simpkiss was satisfied that failure to disclose the conviction was a deliberate or reckless omission. See also the decision of HHJ Cotter QC in *Ageas Insurance Ltd v Stoodley* [2019] Lloyd's Rep. I.R. 1 at [74] where it was held that the statutory presumptions under s.5(5) operated on the facts that case—i.e. there was a statutory presumption in s.5(5) that the consumer knew that a matter about which the insurer asked a clear and specific question was relevant to the insurer. For a commentary on the *Ageas* case, see "Consumer Insurance: Misrepresentation" (2018) 30 I.L.M. 12.

[34] At para.15–226 of *Arnould: Law of Marine Insurance and Average*, 18th edn (updated by First Supplement to 18th edn, 2016) it is stated, in relevant part, that: "This is a significant change in the law and will likely prove a powerful weapon in the hands of insurers." Now see Arnould, *Law of Marine Insurance and Average*, 19th edn and Second Supplement (London: Sweet & Maxwell, 2020).

Schedule 1, Pt 4: supplementary.

Replace footnote 58 with:

19-052 [58] See *Arnould: Law of Marine Insurance and Average*, 18th edn (updated by First Supplement to 18th edn, 2016), para.15-234. Now see Arnould, *Law of Marine Insurance and Average*, 19th edn and Second Supplement (London: Sweet & Maxwell, 2020).

Further commentary.

Replace paragraph with:

19-057 A link to the full wording of the Act is set out at in the first footnote above. For academic commentary on the Bill, Act and/or related matters, see Andrew Ross and David McCarthy, "Consumer bill first step to overhaul of insurance law" (27 May 2011) L.L.I.D. 6; Peter Tyldesley, "Reform at last?" (2011) 161(7470) N.L.J. 843–844 and "Consumer insurance and the duty of disclosure" (2011) 123 B.I.L.A.J. 38–49; P. MacDonald-Eggers and Sir Simon Picken, *Good Faith & Insurance Contracts*, 4th edn (Informa Law, 2018); *Colinvaux & Merkin's Insurance Contract Law*; Malcolm A. Clarke; *The Law of Insurance Contracts*; *Arnould: Law of Marine Insurance and Average*, 18th edn (London: Sweet & Maxwell, updated by First Supplement to 18th edn, 2016), paras 15-217 to 15-240; now Arnould, *Law of Marine Insurance and Average*, 19th edn and Second Supplement (London: Sweet & Maxwell, 2020); Peter J. Tyldesley, *Consumer Insurance Law: Disclosure, Representation and Basis of the Contract Clauses* (London: Bloomsbury Professional, 2013), Chs 2, 6, 7A and 7D; Peter MacDonald Eggers, "The past and future of English insurance law: good faith and warranties" (2012) 1 *UCL Journal of Law and Jurisprudence* 211–244; Graham Charkham, "Reform of insurance law: the Consumer Insurance (Disclosure and Representations) Act 2012" (2013) 25 I.L.M. 41; David Hertzell and Laura Burgoyne, "The Law Commissions and insurance contract law reform: an update" (2013) 19 JIML 105; and Paul Jaffe, "Reform of the Insurance Law of England and Wales—Separate Laws for the Different needs of Businesses and Consumers" (2013) 126 *BILA Journal* 18.

CHAPTER 20

THE INSURANCE ACT 2015

1. INTRODUCTION

Overview and introduction.

Replace footnote 2 with:

[2] The 2015 Act is available online: *https://www.legislation.gov.uk/ukpga/2015/4/contents* [Accessed 22 September 2020].

20-001

Replace footnote 3 with:

[3] *https://www.legislation.gov.uk/ukpga/2015/4/notes/contents* [Accessed 22 September 2020].

20-004

Replace footnote 4 with:

[4] For example, in relation to the CIDRA, in Graham Charkham, "Reform of insurance law: the Consumer Insurance (Disclosure and Representations) Act 2012" (2013) 25 I.L.M. 41 it was commented (under the heading "Mixed purposes") that: "The Law Commission's Report, upon which the Act is based but which is not admissible as an aid to construction …". It has also been commented that what the 2015 Act means and what the Law Commissions said that they wanted it to mean may at times be two different things. However, see also (for example) *Aswan Engineering Establishment Co v Lupdine Ltd* [1987] 1 W.L.R. 1 at 14; *R. v Horseferry Road Metropolitan Stipendiary Magistrate Ex p. Siadatan*

20-005

[1991] 1 Q.B. 260 at 267–26 and other textbooks such as, for example, *Bennion on Statutory Interpretation*, 7th edn and First Supplement (Butterworths: LexisNexis, 2019).

2. Law Reform and the Law Commissions' Reports

The duty of fair presentation: the case for reform.

After "... there were five criticisms of the then-current law", add new footnote 8a:

20-018 8a See *Young v Royal and Sun Alliance Plc* [2019] CSOH 32; 2019 S.L.T. 622 at [61]. The decision in *Young* was affirmed on appeal: [2020] CSIH 25; 2020 S.L.T. 597.

3. Commentary on the Act

(b) Part 2: The Duty of Fair Presentation

(i) The duty of fair presentation

The duty of fair presentation: introduction.

After "... and it would be wrong to understate the significance of such changes.", add new footnote 13a:

20-025 13a See for example, *Young v Royal and Sun Alliance Plc* [2019] CSOH 32; 2019 S.L.T. 622 at [59]. The decision in *Young* was affirmed on appeal: [2020] CSIH 25; 2020 S.L.T. 597.

The duty of fair presentation: subs.3(3).

After "Subsection 3(3) provides that a fair presentation of the risk is one", add new footnote 13b:

20-027 13b The elements of the fair presentation duty were summarised by the court in *Young v Royal and Sun Alliance Plc* [2019] CSOH 32; 2019 S.L.T. 622 at [63]. The decision in *Young* was affirmed on appeal: [2020] CSIH 25; 2020 S.L.T. 597.

The duty of fair presentation: subs.3(4).

After "Garnat Trading & Shipping (Singapore) Pte Ltd v Baominh Insurance Corporation [2011] EWCA Civ 773; [2011] 2 Lloyd's Rep. 492", add new footnote 13c:

20-028 13c See *Young v Royal and Sun Alliance Plc* [2019] CSOH 32; 2019 S.L.T. 622 at [60]. The decision in *Young* was affirmed on appeal: [2020] CSIH 25; 2020 S.L.T. 597.

The duty of fair presentation: subss.3(5) and 3(6).

After "... or (e) it is something as to which the insurer waives information.", add new footnote 15a:

20-029 15a See *Young v Royal and Sun Alliance Plc* [2019] CSOH 32; 2019 S.L.T. 622 generally, and at [66] onwards, in particular. As addressed more fully at para.20-029A, it was not suggested by either party in that case that the 2015 Act altered the prior law on waiver. As to the court's conclusions, see para.20-029A below. The decision in *Young* was affirmed on appeal: [2020] CSIH 25; 2020 S.L.T. 597.

After para.20-029, add new paragraph:

20-029A In *Young v Royal and Sun Alliance Plc*,[15b] the Court of Session (Outer House) considered the duty to make fair presentation and, in particular, the issue of waiver. As this is the first case to consider the Insurance Act 2015 in any substantive detail, it is addressed more fully here than might otherwise be the case.

[15b] *Young v Royal and Sun Alliance Plc* [2019] CSOH 32; 2019 S.L.T. 622; affirmed on appeal: [2020] CSIH 25; 2020 S.L.T. 597.

The insured under an insurance policy in respect of commercial premises sought declarator that the insurer was obliged to indemnify him following extensive fire damage to the premises. The defender declined to make payment and sought to avoid the policy by reason of nondisclosure on the pursuer's part. As noted at [3], the non-disclosure was said to be the fact that the pursuer had been a director of four companies which had been dissolved after an insolvent liquidation or had been placed into insolvent liquidation within the five-year period immediately preceding commencement of the policy ("the undisclosed information"). The pursuer's case was that the defender had waived disclosure of the undisclosed information.

As set out at [57], the principal issue in the case was whether the pursuer had breached the duty under s.3(1) of the 2015 Act to make a fair presentation of the risk and, as a subsidiary issue, in the event that the undisclosed information was material, whether the defender insurer nonetheless waived disclosure of that information. Lady Wolffe considered the 2015 Act, and the relevant Law Commissions' papers, from [59] onwards. The majority of the discussion in the judgment addressed the issue of waiver. At [67], Lady Wolffe noted that it was not suggested by either party that the 2015 Act altered the prior law on waiver and that, under the pre-2015 Act law, waiver typically arose in an insurance context in two ways:

(1) The first was where the prospective insured submitted information which contained something that would prompt a reasonably careful insurer to make further enquiries, and the insurer fails to do so. The case of *WISE (Underwriting Agency) Ltd v Grupo Nacional Provincial SA*[15c] was an example of this. Lady Wolffe noted that s.3(4)(b) of the 2015 Act provides for this form of waiver.

(2) The second was where the insurer asks a "limiting" question, i.e. one from which a prospective insured may reasonable infer that the insurer has no interest in knowing, and has waived, information falling outside the scope of the question or questions, even if that information was otherwise material. The classic example was said to be where the proposal form asks about convictions within the last five years and which can instruct waiver of information about convictions more than five years ago. The case of *Doheny v New India Assurance Co Ltd*[15d] was one of the cases cited by the parties for its discussion (albeit obiter) of this second form of waiver.

[15c] *WISE (Underwriting Agency) Ltd v Grupo Nacional Provincial SA* [2004] EWCA Civ 962; [2004] 2 Lloyd's Rep. 483.

[15d] *Doheny v New India Assurance Co Ltd* [2004] EWCA Civ 1705; [2005] Lloyd's Rep. I.R. 251.

The *Young* case (allegedly) involved the second kind of waiver. From [69] onwards, the court considered the decision in *Doheny* in detail, noting the formulation (at [17]) in *Doheny* that:

"There can be no doubt that, when a proposal form is submitted to the insured who answers the relevant questions, authority has laid down that an insurer as a result of asking certain questions may show that he is not interested in certain other matters and can, therefore, be said to have waived disclosure of them",

and the reference by the Court of Appeal to an earlier edition of this work at paras

17-17 to 17-19 (now paras 17-018 to 17-020 of the current edition), which the Court of Appeal felt accurately summarised the relevant authorities.

At [76] Lady Wolffe summarised the test to be applied to this "second type" of waiver as follows:

"[T]he test to be applied in construing an insurers' questions is to ask: would a reasonable person reading the proposal form be justified in thinking that the insurer had restricted its right to receive all material information and consented to omission of the particular information not disclosed? (per *Dohney* at paragraph 19, *R&R Developments Ltd* at paragraph 40, and *MacGillivray* at paragraph 17-020)."

At [72], Lady Wolffe made the following important statement in respect to the issue of waiver under the 2015 Act:

"Neither party addressed me on whether this formulation (at para 17 of *Doheny*) was consistent with the statutory expression of waiver in the 2015 Act. For my own part, in the context of insurance, and as distinct from waiver or personal bar as it arises in Scots law in other contexts, I am inclined to approach this on the basis that the 2015 Act did not seek to innovate on or alter the existing law on what constitutes waiver in the context of insurance contracts and the test affirmed by the Court of Appeal remains good law (even if it potentially falls to be applied to other communications (beside proposal forms) from an insurer)."

On the facts of the *Young* case, the court ultimately held that on the documentation proffered, namely the market presentation, which was intended to be the totality of the information placed in fulfilment of the duty to make fair presentation, and the defender's responding email which introduced a number of contingencies, including that the terms were subject to matters going to moral hazard, no reasonable reader of the said stipulation would understand it as waiving that part of the moral hazard declaration relating to "any other business capacity" in which the pursuer might have acted. Lady Wolffe also commented as follows (at [86]), which would be of potentially wider application, at least in cases arising out of similar factual circumstances:

"It respectfully seems to me that the case law on the construction of proposal forms, including the application of waiver in its second form (ie by limiting questions) may require to be approached with a degree of circumspection in a case such as the present. The observations in the cases and the discussion in *MacGillivray* (at paragraph 17-018ff) cited to the Court are predicated on the use of a conventional proposal form proffered by the insurer and to which an insured responds. By contrast in this case, and in common with *CTI*, the prospective insured initiated the approach in the form of the Market Presentation, the scope of which the prospective insured controlled. In the conventional proposal-type case, there may be greater scope for applying the doctrine of waiver, as the insurer controls the scope of the information it seeks; it signals (via the questions asked) what it regards as material and, by implication, it *may* be taken as waiving matters outside the scope of the questions posed. The second type of waiver was developed to control unfairness that might flow from an insurer invoking some other matter, beyond the scope of the proposal questions, as material. (Although the law has never been that materiality was confined to the questions on a proposal form). The 2015 Act shifted the burden of identifying what is material to the insured in the form of the duty to make a fair presentation of the risk. One consequence is that that may affect the application of this second type of waiver, not least because there is no longer a proposal form ('the extended enquiry') that falls to be construed (and which is the context in which this form of waiver arises). There is, therefore, no *in limine* identification by the insurer of the scope of what it considers material and which could form the basis of this form of waiver."

Lady Wolffe's comments (at [87]) are also helpful to note here, and also of potentially broader application:

"While proposal forms were characterised as an 'enquiry', no like presumption operates in respect of an insurer's response to a proposer's initial presentation. Accordingly, consideration requires to be given to what is the form or purpose of an insurer's response to a proposer's market presentation. An insurer's response may take a variety of forms. It may be a question eliciting further information; it may be a limiting question waiving matters outwith the scope of that question. It may, however, be confirming or clarifying the particular information presented. It may be a stipulation as to a state of affairs to exist at inception or to be maintained during the policy term. If such responses are uncritically construed as 'enquiries' defining or limiting the scope of what the insurer considers is material, then one of the aims underlying the reforms of simplifying the process of presenting and assessing any risk would be defeated, if it required insurers, faced with a brief presentation, defensively to ask a large number of questions lest it be argued that it waived any matter on which it did not seek a specific assurance."

The decision of the Inner House was affirmed on appeal.[15e] The Court of Session (Inner House, First Division) noted, at [7], that on appeal the sole issue was a narrow one: did the defender waive its entitlement to be provided with the undisclosed information? At [37]–[40], the court helpfully summarised the duty to make a fair presentation of the risk and the exception at s.3(5)(e) of the 2015 Act. The court noted that the pursuer did not say that the defender expressly communicated that it was not concerned to know the undisclosed information. The pursuer contended that it did so by implication; by showing that it was interested in one aspect of the pursuer's experience of insolvency, the defender was impliedly showing that it was not interested in others and thereby restricted the pursuer's duty of disclosure. At [41]–[42], the court referred to *Economides v Commercial Union Insurance Co Plc*,[15f] stating, at [41], that it is clear than an insurer can impliedly waive an insured's duty to disclose certain information by virtue of the questions it asks. The court concluded at [42]–[44] (in relevant parts) as follows:

"[42] ... where it is contended, as here, that the insurer impliedly waived its entitlement to disclosure of material information by reason of the terms in which parties communicated with each other, the expectation will be that there will be something in the nature of an enquiry by the insurer directing the insured to provide certain information but no other information. We took Mr Dunlop to accept that. He submitted that by including the text 'Insured has never Been declared bankrupt or insolvent Had a liquidator appointed' the defender was inviting the pursuer to confirm the accuracy of that statement and by restricting itself to that question demonstrating that it was not concerned to know about the pursuer's wider experience of insolvency including the undisclosed information.

[43] ... The email indicates that the defender considers that the presentation of the risk has been sufficient and that the defender has assessed and priced it, as the risk is further defined by the stated terms, conditions and limitations. For the pursuer to succeed with his plea of waiver he has to establish that the defender, which had an entitlement to disclosure of information which included the pursuer's more general experience of insolvency, is to be held to have (inadvertently, because the no inducement line of argument has been abandoned by the pursuer) waived that entitlement by confirming that there would be no cover in the event that the policy-holders had a direct experience of insolvency. We do not accept that contention. It is simply not a reasonable interpretation of the communications between the parties. ...

[44] ... it is sufficient for a determination of the reclaiming motion that we find that a reasonable reader of the email would not have understood it as containing an enquiry that was to be construed as an expression of limited concern about the pursuer's past experience of insolvency such as to exclude the undisclosed information from what was required

[65]

to be disclosed for a fair presentation of the risk. In all the circumstances as admitted by the pursuer, the defender was therefore entitled to avoid the policy."

[15e] *Young v Royal and Sun Alliance Insurance Plc* [2020] CSIH 25; 2020 S.L.T. 597.

[15f] *Economides v Commercial Union Insurance Co Plc* [1998] Q.B. 587; [1997] 3 W.L.R. 1066; and *Chitty on Contracts*, 33rd edn (2018), para.42-036; and extracts from this work at paras 17-018 to 17-020.

(e)   Part 4A: Late Payment of Claims

Late Payment of Claims.

Replace paragraph with:

20-056   On 4 May 2017, a new "Part 4A" of the 2015 Act came into force and was added after s.13 of the 2015 Act. Part 4A is titled "Late Payment of Claims" and is addressed in more detail at para.21-082. By s.13A(1) of the 2015 Act, it is an implied term of every contract of insurance that if the insured makes a claim under the contract, the insurer must pay any sums due in respect of the claim within a reasonable time. Section 16A (which also came into force on 4 May 2017) addresses contracting out of the implied term about payment of claims (both in respect to consumer and non-consumer contracts). See the New Zealand decision in *Kilduff v Tower Insurance Ltd*[28a] by way of helpful comparison on the law on late payment in New Zealand. For a commentary on the *Kilduff* case, see "Property insurance: Measure of damages and late payment" (2019) 31 I.L.M. 3.

[28a] *Kilduff v Tower Insurance Ltd* [2018] NZHC 704.

CHAPTER 21

THE LOSS

1. CAUSATION

General rule.

Replace footnote 1 with:

¹ The identification of the proximate cause is not to be confused with the "but for" test for factual causa- **21-001**
tion in tort. In *Orient-Express Hotels Ltd v Assucurazioni Generali S.A.* [2010] Lloyd's Rep. I.R. 531,
Hamblen J heard an appeal from an arbitration award under s.69 of the Arbitration Act 1996, in respect
of a claim for business interruption losses arising from hurricane damage to a hotel in New Orleans. In
addressing the question of what losses were recoverable as a result of the business interruption, the
arbitral tribunal had concluded that, applying the "but for" test, the correct counterfactual for assessing
recoverable business insurance losses was one in which the hotel was undamaged but the city of New
Orleans had nonetheless been devastated by the hurricanes. As in those circumstances the business of
the hotel would have been severely reduced due to the damage to the city even if the hotel itself had
not been physically damaged, the recoverable business interruption losses were significantly reduced.
On appeal, Hamblen J considered that the critical question was whether the arbitral tribunal had erred
in applying a test of "but for" causation, or whether the case was a rare one in which that test fell to be
relaxed on grounds of fairness and reasonableness. Hamblen J held that whilst there might be cases in
which it was appropriate to relax the but for test on such grounds, it was not open to the Court to make
findings on that issue on an appeal on a point of law from an arbitral award, and had he been able to do
so, he would not have found that this was a case in which the "but for" test fell to be relaxed in any event.
   Orient Express was considered in *Financial Conduct Authority v Arch Insurance (UK) Ltd* [2020]
EWHC 2448 (Comm), a test case brought to determine a number of issues of principle relating to cover
provided under business interruption policies consequent on interruption to business caused by the
Covid-19 pandemic (see further para.33-001A below). Although the High Court (Flaux LJ and Butcher
J) held (at [503]) that the issues of causation in the test case were resolved by the proper construction
of the policies, and that *Orient Express* was distinguishable due to the different nature of the policy in
that case, the judges nonetheless gave a detailed obiter consideration to *Orient Express*, upon which
significant reliance had been placed in argument. At [523]–[529], the judges criticised the reasoning in

Orient Express and held that they would have declined to follow it, primarily because of what they held to be a confusion in the judge's reasoning between the proper identification of the insured peril, that arose from a focus on the "but for" test, rather than the question of proximate causation (see in particular [523]–[525]). The proximate cause of the loss was not business interruption arising from damage to the hotel per se, but business interruption arising from damage caused by a covered fortuity, in this case hurricanes. That being the position, there was no need to consider whether the hurricanes and the damage to the hotel were separate causes of the loss, each of which passed the "but for" test, as both the hurricane and damage to the hotel were each necessary components of the insured peril, and the relevant question was what losses were proximately caused by that insured peril.

Two effective causes.

Replace footnote 27 with:

21-005   27 The equivalent paragraph in the 11th edition of this work was described by Lord Philips of Worth Matrevers PSC as correctly summarising the relevant principles where there are two proximate causes of the loss, in *ENE 1 Kos Ltd v Petroleo Brasileiro SA (No.2) (The Kos)* [2012] UKSC 17; [2012] 2 A.C. 164 at [74]. This situation must be distinguished from the situation in which there are two concurrent but *independent* causes, each of which would alone have been sufficient to cause the loss. In that situation, the "but for" test for causation will not be met in respect of either cause: see *Orient-Express Hotels Ltd v Assucurazioni Generali S.A.* [2010] Lloyd's Rep. I.R. 531 at 538, considered in the first footnote to para.21-001 above. But see also the criticisms of *Orient Express* in *Financial Conduct Authority v Arch Insurance (UK) Ltd* [2020] EWHC 2448 (Comm) at [503]–[529].

  For a recent case applying the relevant principles in the context of a claims made liability policy, see *Cultural Foundation v Beazley Furlonge Ltd* [2018] EWHC 1083 (Comm); [2018] Bus. L.R. 2174 at [171]–[176] per Andrew Henshaw QC (sitting as a Deputy High Court Judge). A further distinction must be made between cases where there is a unitary loss with two proximate causes, and cases where there are two discrete losses, each of which may have its own proximate cause—see *Cultural Foundation* [2018] Bus. L.R. 2174 at [214]–[217].

2.   BURDEN OF PROOF

Generally on the insured.

Replace footnote 39 with:

21-006   39 *Austin v Drewe* (1815) 4 Camp. 360; (1816) 6 Taunt. 436; *Everett v London Assurance Co* (1865) 19 C.B.(N.S.) 126; *Marsden v City and County Assurance Co* (1865) L.R. 1 C.P. 232. For a recent summary of this principle, see *Contact (Print and Packaging) Ltd v Travelers Insurance Co Ltd* [2018] EWHC 83 (TCC); [2018] Lloyd's Rep. I.R. 295 at [143]–[144].

Exceptions.

Replace third paragraph with:

21-007   However, in *Impact Funding Solutions Ltd v Barrington*[43] the Supreme Court declined to construe an exclusion clause *contra proferentem*, on the basis that the clause was not ambiguous, and it did not operate to exclude or limit a liability which arises by operation of law. The correct approach to the construction of the clause in that case was to construe it having regard to all the policy terms, and in a manner which was consistent with, and not repugnant to, the purpose of the insurance contract.[44] It is therefore doubtful whether the doctrine of *contra proferentem* will play a significant role in the construction of contracts of insurance, absent genuine ambiguity, or cases in which it is clear that the exclusion clause operates to exclude primary liability rather than define the scope of the cover.[45]

43 *Impact Funding Solutions Ltd v Barrington Support Services Ltd (formerly Lawyers At Work Ltd)* [2016] UKSC 57; [2017] A.C. 73. See also *Financial Conduct Authority v Arch Insurance (UK) Ltd* [2020] EWHC 2448 (Comm) at [71]–[74].

44 At [6]–[7] per Lord Hodge JSC (with whom Lord Mance, Lord Sumption and Lord Toulson JJSC agreed). To similar effect, Lord Toulson JSC (with whom Lord Mance, Lord Sumption and Lord Hodge JJSC agreed) held at [35] that the fact that the provision was expressed as an exception did not neces-

sarily mean that it should be approached "with a pre-disposition to construe it narrowly", and that words of exception may simply be a way of defining the scope of the primary obligation.

45 See *Crowden v QBE Insurance (Europe) Ltd* [2017] EWHC 2597 (Comm); [2018] P.N.L.R. 9 at [61]–[65]; *Financial Conduct Authority v Arch Insurance (UK) Ltd* [2020] EWHC 2448 (Comm) at [74] (approving *Crowden v QBE* at [65]). See also *Spire Healthcare Ltd v Royal & Sun Alliance Insurance Plc* [2018] EWCA Civ 317 at [28]; *Zagora Management Ltd & Ors v Zurich Insurance Plc & Ors* [2019] EWHC 140 (TCC) at [350]. For a case, however, in which there was "real doubt" as to meaning such that the principle was applied, see *Manchikalapati v Zurich Insurance Plc* [2019] EWCA Civ 2163 at [68].

Wilful act of the insured.

Replace footnote 62 with:

62 *Astrovlanis Compania Naviera SA v Linard* [1972] 2 Q.B. 611 and [1972] 2 Lloyd's Rep. 187; **21-010**
Palamisto General Enterprises SA v Ocean Marine Insurance Ltd [1972] 2 Q.B. 625; *Lambhead Shipping Co v Jennings* [1994] 1 Lloyd's Rep. 624. For a recent Scottish case in which that was the result (in a claim under a fire policy), see *T & G Grampian Limited v Allianz Insurance Plc* [2018] SAC (Civ) 23.

Replace footnote 63 with:

63 *Slattery v Mance* [1962] 1 Q.B. 676 at 681; *The Alexion Hope* [1987] 1 Lloyd's Rep. 60 at 67; [1988] 1 Lloyd's Rep. 311 at 317. The standard of proof is not proof beyond a reasonable doubt. It is proof on the balance of probabilities that the insured wilfully caused the loss. There is a line of authority to the effect that the degree of probability varies with the degree of fraud or criminality alleged, amounting to "a standard falling not far short of the rigorous criminal standard"—*The Zinovia* [1984] 2 Lloyd's Rep. 264 at 272. Those cases include *Grunther v Federated Employers' Insurance Association* [1976] 2 Lloyd's Rep. 259; *S. & M. Carpets (London) Ltd v Cornhill Insurance Co* [1982] 1 Lloyd's Rep. 423; *Continental Illinois v Alliance Assurance Co* [1989] 1 Lloyd's Rep. 33; *Polivette v Commercial Union Assurance Co* [1987] 1 Lloyd's Rep. 379. This is an imprecise formulation, difficult to apply in practice. A better formulation is that the standard of proof required is the mere balance of probabilities but the gravity of the plea and implausibility of respectable persons (where appropriate) committing frauds are taken into account as weighting the balance in favour of the insured—*The Filiatra Legacy* [1991] 2 Lloyd's Rep. 337 at 365–366; *The Ikarian Reefer* [1995] 1 Lloyd's Rep. 455 at 459, followed in *Patel v Windsor Life Assurance Co* [2008] Lloyd's Rep. I.R. 359; also followed in *Markel International Insurance Co Ltd v Surety Guarantee Consultants Ltd* [2009] EWCA Civ 790 per Rix LJ at [50]; and in *AC Ward & Son Ltd v Catlin (Five) Ltd* [2010] Lloyd's Rep. I.R. 695 per Flaux J at [157]. See [1995] L.M.C.L.Q. 305. See also *T & G Grampian Limited v Allianz Insurance Plc* [2018] SAC (Civ) 23, where the claim failed notwithstanding that the insurer did not establish that the fire was caused by the insured's wilful act, in circumstances where there was no evidence of a credible accidental cause for the fire (at [16]).

3.   AMOUNT OF LOSS PAYABLE

(a)   General Rules

Assessment of loss.

Replace footnote 81 with:

81 *McLean Enterprises v Ecclesiastical Insurance Office* [1986] 2 Lloyd's Rep. 416. For a recent case **21-015**
containing a detailed analysis of the principles applicable to the assessment of loss on a reinstatement basis, see *Endurance Corporate Capital Ltd v Sartex Quilts and Textiles Ltd* [2020] EWCA Civ 308 at [34]–[38] per Leggatt LJ, and see further para.21-019A below.

Value of property before the loss.

Replace footnote 82 with:

82 *Leppard v Excess Insurance Co Ltd* [1979] 1 W.L.R. 512 and cases cited in fn.47 to para.21-007, **21-016**
above; *Equitable Fire Insurance Co v Quinn* (1861) 11 Low.Can.R. 170. In *Endurance Corporate Capital Ltd v Sartex Quilts and Textiles Ltd* [2020] EWCA Civ 308 at [38] per Leggatt LJ, the Court of Appeal held that assessment on a market value basis is appropriate where the insured was intending to sell the building at the time when the damage occurred. In some cases the market value of the insured's interest may not afford a true indemnity, especially where the insured has a limited interest in real

property, *Castellain v Preston* (1883) 11 Q.B.D. 380 at 400–401 per Bowen LJ. In such cases the insured is still entitled to a full indemnity, cf. *Westminster Fire Office v Glasgow Provident Investment Society* (1888) 13 App. Cas. 699 at 713 per Lord Selborne. In *Prattley Enterprises Ltd v Vero Insurance New Zealand Ltd* [2016] NZSC 158, the New Zealand Supreme Court held that market value is likely to be the most obvious basis for calculating indemnity in a property held for investment purposes that is not to be reinstated, as the insured will be able to replace the property with a similarly performing investment (at [40]).

Value of property after loss.

Replace footnote 92 with:

21-018   [92] *Pleasurama v Sun Alliance* [1979] 1 Lloyd's Rep. 389 at 393 per Parker J; cf. *Quorum A/S v Schramm (No.2)* [2002] 1 Lloyd's Rep. 249, where the measure of indemnity for fire damage to a work of art under an unvalued policy was taken as the cost of restoration plus its depreciation in value thereafter compared to before the fire, assuming that the picture had been sold as soon as a reasonable time for restoration and assessment had elapsed. See also *Prattley Enterprises Ltd v Vero Insurance New Zealand Ltd* [2016] NZSC 158 at [41]; *Sartex Quilts and Textiles Ltd v Endurance Corporate Capital Ltd* [2020] EWCA Civ 308.

Replace paragraph with:

21-019   Difficulties will arise if the cost of repair is greater than the value of the property before loss or greater than the cost of replacement.[94a] In such cases courts will usually only allow the cost of repair if: (a) the insured genuinely intends to repair; and (b) such a course is not eccentric or absurd. In *Reynolds v Phoenix Assurance Co*,[95] the plaintiff acquired some old maltings in Suffolk for the storage and milling of grain and insured them for £550,000. There was a serious fire in November 1973 which destroyed about seven-tenths of the buildings. The cost of reinstatement was held to be £246,583 but the money required to buy and erect a suitable building of modern steel and asbestos construction together with the land on which to erect it was no more than £50,000. Forbes J held that the plaintiff genuinely intended to repair if he got sufficient money for the purpose and that, although a sensible commercial concern might well not choose to reinstate if using its own money, the plaintiff's intention was not a mere eccentricity but arose from the fact that he would not be properly indemnified unless he was given the means to reinstate the buildings substantially as they were before the fire.

[94a] For a recent case considering the relevance of events after the date of the loss in determining the measure of indemnity, see *Sartex Quilts and Textiles Ltd v Endurance Corporate Capital Ltd* [2019] EWHC 1103 (Comm), in which it was held (at [76]) that events up to the date of the trial may be relevant insofar as they demonstrate that a particular measure of indemnity may lead to over-compensation.

[95] *Reynolds v Phoenix Assurance Co* [1978] 2 Lloyd's Rep. 440. If no claim is made for the cost of repair as such, it will usually be appropriate to award the cost of replacement: *Exchange Theatre v Iron Trades Mutual* [1983] 1 Lloyd's Rep. 674, reversed on other points: [1984] 2 Lloyd's Rep. 169.

After para.21-019, add new paragraph:

21-019A **Intention to reinstate.**   Two recent authorities of the Court of Appeal have considered the question of whether and in what circumstances an insured is required to demonstrate a genuine intention to reinstate, in order to recover its losses under a policy on the reinstatement basis.

Western Trading Ltd v Great Lakes Reinsurance (UK) Plc[95a] concerned a situation in which two disused buildings were destroyed by fire. The insured sought to recover the cost of reinstating the property up to the policy's limit of indemnity of £2,121,800, in circumstances where the market value of the property had been only approximately £75,000 prior to the fire, but had increased to approximately £500,000 thereafter, as a result of the removal of listed building status, which rendered a development plan feasible. The Court of Appeal (per Christopher Clarke

LJ, with whom Laws and Lewison LJJ agreed) doubted (at [72]) whether a claimant who had no intention of using the insurance money to reinstate, and whose property has increased in value on account of the fire, is entitled to claim the cost of reinstatement as the measure of indemnity unless the policy so provides. At [75], Christopher Clarke LJ considered the "requisite degree of intention" required and stated:

> "[I]t seems to me that the insured's intention needs to be not only genuine, but also fixed and settled, and that what he intends must be at least something which there is a reasonable prospect of him bringing about (at any rate if the insurance money is paid)."

In *Endurance Corporate Capital Ltd v Sartex Quilts and Textiles Ltd*,[95b] the Court of Appeal (per Leggatt LJ, with whom McCombe and Dingemans LJJ agreed) rejected the submission that *Western Trading Ltd v Great Lakes Reinsurance (UK) Plc* was authority for the general proposition that in order to recover on the reinstatement basis, it is necessary for the insured to demonstrate an intention to reinstate that is "not only genuine, but also fixed and settled". Leggatt LJ held that that aspect of Christopher Clarke LJ's judgment in *Great Lakes* was limited to circumstances in which the value of the property increased on account of the fire (i.e. the situation in *Great Lakes*) and in any event was obiter dicta (at [57]–[59]).

Leggatt LJ then went on to consider the issue as a matter of principle and held, in accordance with general principles of contractual damages, that an insured's intention as to how it will deal with the insurance proceeds is only relevant to the measure of loss in limited circumstances, typically where there is some feature of the property that it would be expensive to reinstate, but which has some subjective value to the insured. In those circumstances, the insured's intention will be relevant as evidence as to whether: (1) the feature does in fact have such subjective value; or (2) it is unreasonable to expect the defendant to pay the cost of reinstating a feature which is only of subjective value, if the insured does not actually intend to incur that cost. This is unlikely to be the case in most instances in which buildings are used for commercial purposes, however the result in *Reynolds v Phoenix* can be explained on that basis.

[95a] *Western Trading Ltd v Great Lakes Reinsurance (UK) Plc* [2016] EWCA Civ 1003; [2016] 2 C.L.C. 478.

[95b] *Endurance Corporate Capital Ltd v Sartex Quilts and Textiles Ltd* [2020] EWCA Civ 308, upholding the decision of David Railton QC (sitting as a Deputy High Court Judge) in *Sartex Quilts and Textiles Ltd v Endurance Corporate Capital Ltd* [2019] EWHC 1103 (Comm). See also *Hodgson v National House Building Council* [2018] EWHC 2226 (TCC); [2018] B.L.R. 663 at [36]–[37], considering the dicta of Christopher Clarke LJ in *Great Lakes* in the context of a summary judgment application; *Zagora Management Ltd v Zagora Insurance Plc* [2019] EWHC 140 (TCC) at [379]–[387]; *Manchikalapati v Zurich Insurance Plc* [2019] EWCA Civ 2163 at [96]–[109] (per Coulson LJ, with whom McCombe LJ and Sir Rupert Jackson agreed).

Betterment.

Replace footnote 99 with:

[99] *Vance v Forster* (1841) Ir.Circ.Rep. 47; *Hercules Insurance v Hunter* (1836) 14S. (Ct. Sess.) 1137 **21-020** at 1141; *Brinley v National Insurance Co* 52 Mass. 195 (1864); *Reynolds and Anderson v Phoenix Insurance Co* [1978] 2 Lloyd's Rep. 440. However, it should be noted that, unless the policy provides otherwise, the insurer bears the burden of proving the quantum of any deduction for betterment, and in the absence of sufficient evidence a deduction may be refused altogether—see *Sartex Quilts and Textiles Ltd v Endurance Corporate Capital Ltd* [2019] EWHC 1103 (Comm) at [121].

Replace footnote 101 with:

[101] *Reynolds and Anderson v Phoenix Insurance Co* [1978] 2 Lloyd's Rep. 440 at 453. The principle of betterment was upheld in *Fire & All Risks Insurance Co v Rousianos* (1989) 19 N.S.W.L.R. 57 by the New South Wales Court of Appeal, followed in *Vintix v Lumley General Insurance LH* (1991) 24 N.S.W.L.R. 627 at 636–637, refusing to follow the English decisions in tort law. See also *Prattley Enterprises Ltd v Vero Insurance New Zealand Ltd* [2016] NZSC 158 at [41] referring to this paragraph of the 13th edition of this work, and *Western Trading Limited v Great Lakes Reinsurance (UK) Plc* [2016] EWCA Civ 1003 at [80], in which Christopher Clarke LJ (referring to this paragraph of the 13th edition of this work) described the justification for a deduction for betterment as "open to question". In *Sartex Quilts and Textiles Ltd v Endurance Corporate Capital Ltd* [2019] EWHC 1103 (Comm), David Railton QC held (at [115]–[116]) that whilst there was "considerable force" in the submission that the law of betterment in insurance law should reflect the position in the law of damages in contract and tort, the principle remained well-established, notwithstanding the obiter criticisms of Christopher Clarke LJ in *Western Trading Limited*.

After the second paragraph, add new paragraph:

In *Endurance Corporate Capital Ltd v Sartex Quilts and Textiles Ltd*,[101a] Leggatt LJ gave detailed consideration to the principles applicable to deductions for betterment, distinguishing between three different senses in which the term is used. The first sense is where the insured, instead of seeking simply to reinstate the property to the condition it was in before the damage, chooses to make improvements to the property at an additional cost. Unless covered under an express term in the policy, such additional costs are not recoverable as part of the cost of reinstatement. The second sense in which the term is used is where the insured derives a benefit as an incidental consequence of adopting a reasonable reinstatement scheme, for example where modern building materials are used that are less expensive than those originally used, but which have benefits such as insulation or similar, or where the only reasonable replacement for an old machine is to purchase a new one because the old can no longer be found. In neither case should any deduction be made for betterment, as in the first case there is no additional cost, whereas in the second any additional cost is unavoidable.

[101a] *Endurance Corporate Capital Ltd v Sartex Quilts and Textiles Ltd* [2020] EWCA Civ 308 at [90]–[98] per Leggatt LJ (with whom McCombe and Dingemans LJJ agreed).

A further distinction is to be drawn in such circumstances between "pecuniary" incidental benefits (or benefits easily converted to money) and "non-pecuniary" incidental benefits. A deduction for betterment should only be made where the benefit is pecuniary (or easily convertible to money, such as a benefit conferring a business advantage). Where the benefit is non-pecuniary, any deduction for betterment would be unjust as "it would force the claimant to pay for an advantage which it has not chosen and which makes it no better off in money terms". The burden of proving that any deduction for betterment should be made rests on the insurer.

Reinstatement clauses.

Replace footnote 102 with:

21-022   [102] *McLean Enterprises v Ecclesiastical Insurance Office* [1986] 2 Lloyds Rep. 416, where the policy was, after some hesitation, construed to mean that the cost of reinstatement was to be the measure of indemnity; *Lonsdale & Thompson v Black Arrow Group* [1993] Ch. 361 at 365. By contrast, for an example of a clause that was construed without much hesitation to provide an express right to be indemnified for the cost of reinstatement, see *Western Trading Ltd v Great Lakes Reinsurance (UK) Plc* [2015] EWHC 103 (QB); [2015] Lloyd's Rep. I.R. 561. The New Zealand Supreme Court has held that a right to reinstate and claim the reinstatement costs is personal to the insured and not assignable—see *Xu v IAG* [2019] NZSC 68, considered further in the first footnote to para.22-017 below.

(b)   Particular Cases

Salvage.

Replace footnote 110 with:

110   See J. Arnould, *Marine Insurance*, 18th edn (London: Sweet & Maxwell, 2013), Ch.29. For a recent **21-024**
case discussing the distinction and the differing evidential requirements for actual total loss and constructive total loss (in the context of a marine policy albeit one insuring a non-marine adventure) see *Cloth-
ing Management Technology Ltd v Beazley Solutions Ltd* [2012] Lloyd's Rep. I.R. 329. For a recent case
considering the application of the relevant provisions of the Marine Insurance Act 1906 and the
consequences of a failure to give notice of abandonment promptly, see *Involnert v Aprilgrange* [2015]
EWHC 2225 (Comm) at [257]–[268]. In that case, Leggatt J held that the purpose of a notice of abandonment is not to enable insurers to investigate the casualty, but "to enable them, if they choose to accept
the abandonment, to take over the assured's interest in the vessel and any rights incidental to it" (at
[265]). See also *Sveriges Angfartygs Assurans Forening (The Swedish Club) v Connect Shipping Inc*
[2019] Bus. L.R. 1584 (holding that expenditure already incurred before service of the notice of abandonment is to be taken into account in determining whether there is a constructive total loss).

4.   NOTICE OF LOSS

Condition precedent.

Replace footnote 145 with:

145   There is no requirement for the insurer to show prejudice in order to invoke a notice clause construed **21-037**
as a condition precedent, *Pioneer Concrete (UK) Ltd v National Employers Assurance Ltd* [1985] 1
Lloyd's Rep. 274; *Motor and General Insurance v Pavey* [1994] 1 W.L.R. 462 at 469; *Shinedean v
Alldown Demolition* [2006] 2 All E.R. (Comm) 982 at [16]. For a case in which damages were awarded
for breach of an obligation to give immediate notice of an incident which could result in a claim, see
Milton Keynes Borough Council v Nulty [2011] EWHC 2847 (TCC). In Australia, an insurer is required
by statute to show prejudice before it can rely on a late notification defence to defeat a claim—see *Weir
Services Australia Pty Ltd v AXA Corporate Solutions Assurance SA* [2017] NSWSC 259 at [181]. On
the question of whether there is a general "principle of futility" in the construction of contracts such that
if the fulfilment of a precondition to the accrual of a contractual right becomes futile or unnecessary the
courts do not insist upon its performance see *Astor Management AG (formerly MRI Holdings AG) &
Anor v Atalaya Mining plc (formerly Emed Mining Public Ltd)* [2018] EWCA Civ 2407; [2019] Bus.
L.R. 106 (not an insurance case). In that case Simon LJ and Dame Elizabeth Gloster (with whom Macur
LJ agreed) held that the expression "principle of futility" was misleading and in that context reflected
an approach to construction whereby in certain circumstances (depending on the terms of the contract)
a condition precedent may, as a matter of construction and in light of subsequent events, no longer apply or may cease to have effect (at [33]).

Impossibility of performance.

Replace paragraph with:

The fact that it may have been impossible for the claimant to give notice within **21-038**
the prescribed time—e.g. because he did not know of the facts giving rise to his
right to claim[153] or because an injury only became apparent after the time for notice
had expired[154]—will sometimes prevent a court from denying the right to recover
under the policy, however this is always a matter of construction of the particular
clause.[154a] An accident may result in instantaneous death and those having the right
to claim may not know of the death of the insured or even that he was insured.[155]
There are, however, cases in which the courts have mitigated the harshness of this
doctrine. In *Re Coleman's Depositories Ltd and Life and Health Assurance Association*[156] the accident occurred before the policy containing a notice clause was
delivered to the insured; meanwhile he had been covered by a cover note which
neither contained a condition as to notice nor referred to the conditions in the policy.
It was held by the Court of Appeal that the insurers could not rely on the clause
requiring notice in the policy. It has also been suggested that in cases of liability

insurance, time for giving notice will only run when it is clear that insurers will be concerned in the case,[157] but this must be regarded as doubtful.[158] Sometimes the notice clause can be construed so as to excuse the delay which has occurred, as in *Ward v Law Property Assurance and Trust Society*[159] where, in a guarantee policy, the insured was obliged to give notice "within six days of any liability being incurred". It was held that this meant notice of any criminal misconduct whereby it was clear that a liability had been incurred and that the insured was not therefore bound to give notice until he had ascertained that a liability had actually been incurred.[160]

[153] *Verelst's Administratrix v Motor Union Insurance Co* [1925] 2 K.B. 137.

[154] *Cassel v Lancashire and Yorkshire Accident Insurance Co* (1885) 1 T.L.R. 495. See also *Denso Manufacturing UK Ltd v Great Lakes Reinsurance (UK) Plc* [2017] EWHC 391 (Comm) at [30] referring to this paragraph of this work.

[154a] Recent authority tends to support the view that the insured is not in general required to notify circumstances of which he is unaware: see e.g. *Aspen v Pectel Insurance UK Ltd* [2009] Lloyd's Rep. I.R. 440 at [9]. However, where the wording of a policy imposes a strict cut-off for notification irrespective of the insured's state of knowledge during the relevant period, then this will be given effect to— see, for example, *TH Adamson & Sons v Liverpool and London and Globe Insurance Co Ltd* [1953] 2 Lloyd's Rep. 355. For a recent case in which the relevance of the insured's lack of knowledge was considered, see *Maccaferri Ltd v Zurich Insurance Plc* [2016] EWCA Civ 1302; [2018] 1 All E.R. (Comm) 112. In that case, a condition precedent requiring notification of any event likely to give rise to a claim fell to be assessed in the light of the insured's actual knowledge, such that the condition was not breached if a reasonable person in the insured's position would not have thought it at least 50% likely that a claim would have been made (at [34]). See also, in the context of a claims made policy, *Euro Pools Plc (In Administration) v Royal and Sun Alliance Insurance Plc* [2019] EWCA Civ 808 at [95] per Males LJ (with whom Hamblen LJ agreed): "In order to give a valid notice, the insured must be aware of the circumstances in question. You cannot notify something of which you are not aware."; see further *Cultural Foundation v Beazley Furlonge Ltd* [2018] Bus. L.R. 2174 at [154].

[155] *Gamble v Accident Insurance Co Ltd* (1869) I.R. 4 C.L. 204, followed in *Patton v Employers' Liability Assurance Corp* (1887) 20 L.R.Ir. 93 and *Evans v Railway Passengers' Assurance Co* (1912) 3 D.L.R. 61. See also *Accident Insurance Co of North America v Young* (1892) 20 S.C.R. 280.

[156] *Re Coleman's Depositories Ltd and Life and Health Assurance Association* [1907] 2 K.B. 798.

[157] *Smellie v British General Insurance Co* 1918 2 S.L.T. 58; W.C. & Ins.Rep. 233.

[158] See *Re Williams and Lancashire and Yorkshire Accident Insurance Co's Arbitration* (1902) 19 T.L.R. 82; 51 W.R. 222; and *General Motors Ltd v Crowder* (1931) 40 Lloyd's Rep. 87.

[159] *Ward v Law Property Assurance and Trust Society* (1856) 27 L.T.(O.S.) 155; 4 W.R. 605.

[160] A further complication arises where the insured was not aware of the contractual notification requirement until it was too late to comply with it, for example where the notification requirement is contained in a set of policy conditions which are sent out to the insured some time after the insurance contract is concluded by means of a cover note. This was the position in *China Ping An Assurance (Hong Kong) Co Ltd v Tsang Fu Yin* [2012] Lloyd's Rep. I.R. 493 (Hong Kong High Court). To J held that the notification in question had been incorporated from the outset by reference into the contract concluded through the cover note, but that it was "suspended until such time when the policy has been brought to the notice of the assured, or at least has been delivered to the assured" (at [51]). It is submitted that an English court would not necessarily follow this approach. If there had been sufficient notice in the cover note to incorporate the notification requirement as a term of the contract (cf. *Interfoto Picture Library v Stiletto Visual Programmes Ltd* [1989] Q.B. 433), it is not easy to see why the parties would objectively intend the term to be suspended pending a greater degree of notification being given.

By whom notice can be given.

Replace footnote 186 with:

21-045   [186] *Barrett Bros (Taxis) Ltd v Davies* [1966] 1 W.L.R. 1334. This ground for the decision was followed in *M.V. Mozart (Owner) v Ferrum GmbH* [1985] 1 Lloyd's Rep. 239; and *Valla Giovanni & C. S.p.A. v Gebr. Van Weelde (The Chanda)* [1985] 1 Lloyd's Rep. 563. In *Bass Brewers v Independent Insurance Co Ltd*, 2002 S.L.T. 512 it was held that failure by one insured under a composite policy to notify an occurrence likely to rise to a claim was a breach of a notice clause in the form of a condition precedent even when the other co-insured had given the relevant notice. The English authorities were not cited.

The wider observation by Lord Denning MR in *Barrett Bros* that insurers can never rely on a breach of a notice clause in the form of a condition precedent unless they can show that it has caused them prejudice has been doubted and cannot now be regarded as good law—*Pioneer Concrete (UK) Ltd v National Employers Mutual Insurance Association Ltd* [1985] 2 All E.R. 395, approved by the Privy Council in *Motor & General Insurance Co v Pavey* [1994] 1 W.L.R. 462 at 469; *Shinedean v Alldown Demolition* [2006] 2 All E.R. (Comm) 982 at [16]; *Kidsons v Lloyd's Underwriters* [2008] 1 All E.R. (Comm) 769 at [55]. However, see the discussion in *Astor Management AG v Atalaya Mining Plc* [2017] EWHC 425 (Comm); [2017] Bus. L.R. 1634 (not an insurance case) in which Leggatt J (as he then was) at [45]–[46] considered that Lord Denning MR's comments in *Barrett Bros* were obiter dicta that did not support the existence of a general "principle of futility" in English contract law (upheld on appeal [2018] EWCA Civ 2407; [2019] Bus. L.R. 106). In the Court of Appeal in *Astor Management AG*, Simon LJ and Dame Elizabeth Gloster (with whom Macur LJ agreed) at [24]–[28], drew a distinction between a requirement for the insurer to suffer prejudice before a condition precedent can be relied on, and the argument that, as a matter of construction, compliance is not required because it would be futile. By contrast, in Australia pursuant to s.54 Insurance Contracts Act 1984 an insurer must show prejudice before it can rely on a late notification defence to defeat a claim—see *Weir Services Australia Pty Ltd v AXA Corporate Solutions Assurance SA* [2017] NSWSC 259 at [181].

5. PARTICULARS AND PROOF OF LOSS

Whether notice a prerequisite to accrual of cause of action.

Replace footnote 238 with:

[238] *Ventouris v Mountain* [1992] 2 Lloyd's Rep. 281; *Bank of America National Trust & Savings Association v Chrismas* [1993] 1 Lloyd's Rep. 137, and authorities there cited. In liability insurance the relevant loss arises only when the insured's liability is ascertained by admission, agreement or judgment, and a cause of action arises in equity before the insured discharges it—*Firma C-Trade SA v Newcastle Protection & Indemnity Association* [1991] 2 A.C. 1. See also *Versloot Dredging BV & Anor v HDI Gerling Industrie Versicherung AG & Ors* [2016] UKSC 45; [2017] A.C. 1 at [24]. In Australia, the position is less clear. In *Globe Church Incorporated v Allianz Australia Ltd* [2019] NSWCA 27, the New South Wales Court of Appeal considered the position in various common law jurisdictions and held (by majority) that the cause of action accrued when the loss occurred, not when the insurer failed to pay within a reasonable time (at [209]–[210]).

21-055

6. FRAUDULENT CLAIMS

Introductory.

Replace footnote 246 with:

[246] The business of insurance is also affected by another category of fraudulent claims, namely those brought by third parties against insureds. Although outside the scope of this work, there is overlap between the court's powers under s.57 Criminal Justice and Courts Act 2015 to dismiss "fundamentally dishonest" personal injury claims, and the fraudulent claims rule considered in this chapter. See, for example, *Versloot Dredging BV v HDI Gerling Industrie Versicherung AG* [2016] UKSC 45; [2013] 3 W.L.R. 543 at [95] per Lord Sumption JSC (with whom Lord Clarke of Stone-cum-Ebony, Lord Hughes and Lord Toulson JJSC agreed); see also *London Organising Committee of the Olypmics and Paralymic Games (In Liquidation) v Sinfield* [2018] EWHC 51 (QB) at [54]. For the circumstances in which an insurer can recover exemplary damages in respect of its defence of such a fraudulent claim, see *AXA Insurance UK Plc v Financial Claims Solutions Ltd* [2018] EWCA Civ 1330.

21-057

Replace footnote 251 with:

[251] *Re B (Children)* [2009] 1 A.C. 11 at [64] per Baroness Hale of Richmond. For a detailed discussion of the approach to the standard of proof and the inherent probabilities in cases involving allegations of scuttling in marine insurance, see *Suez Fortune Investments Ltd v Talbot Underwriting Ltd (The "Brilliante Virtuoso")* [2019] EWHC 2599 (Comm); [2019] 2 Lloyd's Rep. 485 at [59]–[70] per Teare J.

(a)   The Common Law Rule

Collateral lies/fraudulent devices.

Replace footnote 257 with:

21-059   [257] *Versloot Dredging BV v HDI Gerling Industrie Versicherung AG* [2016] UKSC 45; [2013] 3 W.L.R. 543. The collateral lies rule articulated in *Versloot Dredging* was considered in the recent Scottish case *T & G Grampian Limited v Allianz Insurance Plc* [2018] SAC (Civ) 23. In that case, the Sheriff held at first instance (without reference to *Versloot Dredging*) that cover under a fire policy could be avoided due to "fraudulent devices". However, on appeal the Sheriff Appeal Court held that on the Sheriff's findings of fact no question of fraudulent devices arose, but the insurer was nonetheless entitled to avoid cover because the insured had failed to establish that the fire had an accidental cause, as required by the policy. The court did not need to consider the argument made by the insurer (at [11]) that the principle articulated in *Versloot Dredging* has no application where the question of fraudulent devices arises in the context of an express policy provision, rather than under the common law rule.

(d)   The Position Under the Insurance Act 2015

The new statutory regime.

After "... for which had crystallised before the fraudulent act.", add new footnote 314a:

21-069   [314a] In relation to the return of premiums, note also the Draft Insurable Interest Bill published by the Law Commission and Scottish Law Commission in June 2018, which contains specific provision in the case of fraudulent statements as to the insured's insurable interest in a contract of "life-related insurance". In such cases (save where the contract is a consumer insurance contract), if the Draft Bill is enacted, the contract will be treated as void but the insurer will not be required to return any premiums paid.

CHAPTER 22

THE CLAIMANT

1. ASSIGNMENT

(a) Voluntary Assignment

Assignment of the right of recovery.

Replace paragraph with:

If the insured validly assigns his right to recover under the policy, the assignee **22-009** becomes the payee of the proceeds, and the insurer will pay the assignor at his peril.[40] The assignee will, however, be bound to perform any conditions precedent to recovery, such as giving notice of loss, and, since he takes subject to equities, the insurers can rely on any breach of condition by the insured.[41] Moreover, since the assignor remains the insured, any cancellation of the policy by the assignee will be ineffective.[42] Whilst in accordance with ordinary contractual principles, an equitable assignee of the right to recover under the policy is not assigned the obligations under the policy, nonetheless the assignee cannot assert its rights inconsistently with its terms, and it therefore must do so subject to any conditions or qualifications to the exercise of those rights.[42a]

[40] *Watt v Gore District Mutual Insurance Co* (1861) 8 Gr. 523; *Greet v Citizens' Insurance Co* (1879) 27 Gr. 121, reversed on different grounds (1880) 5 O.A.R. 596.

[41] *Re Carr and Sun Fire Insurance Co* (1897) 13 T.L.R. 186; *Samuel & Co v Dumas* [1924] A.C. 431; *Williams v Atlantic Assurance Co Ltd* [1933] 1 K.B. 81; *McEntire v Sun Fire Office* (1895) 29 I.L.T. 103. When the right of recovery is assigned, the insurer owes a duty to act in good faith to the assignor before and after the assignment. When the insurance policy is assigned, the duty is then owed to the assignee—

The Good Luck [1988] 1 Lloyd's Rep. 514 at 546; [1989] 2 Lloyd's Rep. 238 at 264. Where payment is conditional on an obligation that is personal to the assignor, it has been held in New Zealand that the assignee is unable to recover, even if able to perform the obligation itself—*Bryant v Primary Industries Insurance Co* [1990] 2 N.Z.L.R. 142; *Xu v IAG New Zealand Ltd* [2017] NZHC 1964 (upheld on appeal by the Supreme Court of New Zealand [2019] NZSC 68), considered further in the first footnote to para.22-017 below.

[42] *Morrow v Lancashire Insurance Co* (1898) 26 O.A.R. 173; *Raiffeisen Zentralbank v Five Star Trading* [2001] 1 All E.R. (Comm) 961 at 982–983.

[42a] *Aspen Underwriting Ltd v Credit Europe Bank NV* [2020] UKSC 11; [2020] 2 W.L.R. 919 at [27]–[28] (assignee asserting right to receive policy proceeds not subject to exclusive jurisdiction clause in the policy where no present dispute about entitlement).

2.   LIMITED INTERESTS IN PROPERTY

(a)   Vendors and Purchasers

Insurance by vendor of land.

Replace footnote 69 with:

22-017   [69] *Paine v Meller* (1801) 6 Ves. Jr. 349; *Poole v Adams* (1864) 33 L.J.Ch. 639; *Rayner v Preston* (1881) 18 Ch. D. 1; *Bestquest Ltd v Regency Care Group* [2003] Lloyd's Rep. I.R. 392, where the vendor failed to note the purchaser's interest on its policy and thereby perfect the assignment of the policy as between them as required by the sale contract. In New Zealand, it has been held that even if there has been a valid assignment, the purchaser is not entitled to claim a reinstatement benefit under the policy as a clause providing for payment conditional on rebuilding the property imposes a personal obligation on the insured—*Bryant v Primary Industries Insurance Co* [1990] 2 N.Z.L.R. 142. Whilst this rule is grounded in policy, it can nonetheless be avoided by a suitably drafted clause—see *Xu v IAG New Zealand Ltd* [2017] NZHC 1964 (upheld on appeal [2018] NZCA 149; [2018] Lloyd's Rep. I.R. 710), in which such an argument did not succeed.

In *Xu v IAG New Zealand Ltd* [2019] NZSC 68, the Supreme Court of New Zealand by majority (William Young, O'Regan and Ellen France JJ) declined to overrule *Bryant* in a claim for reinstatement costs brought by a purchaser who had been assigned the seller's claims under a policy that entitled the insured to reinstatement costs conditional on actual reinstatement. The sale of the property occurred after the loss, but before any reinstatement had occurred. The majority held that the entitlement to reinstate and be paid the costs was a contingent right that was personal to the insured and therefore could not be assigned to the purchaser (at [45]–[46]). The majority decision was influenced by considerations of moral hazard, on the basis that if an assignee was permitted to reinstate and recover the cost the insurer would be assuming a risk it had not had an opportunity to bargain for (at [12] and [21]). By contrast, the minority (Glazebrrok and Arnold JJ) would have allowed the appeal and overruled *Bryant*, on the basis that the right to reinstate the property and claim the reinstatement costs was an "already accrued right" that was not personal and was capable of assignment ([96]).

(c)   Mortgagor and Mortgagee

Loss payable clause.

After ", or release of the insurers' rights of subrogation.[155]", add:

22-041   The mere assertion of a right to payment as loss payee/assignee of a policy does not, however, make the assignee bound by an exclusive jurisdiction clause in the policy, in circumstances where there is no present dispute as to the loss payee's entitlement.[155a]

[155a] *Aspen Underwriting Ltd v Credit Europe Bank NV* [2020] 2 W.L.R. 919 at [29] per Lord Hodge DPSC (with whom Lord Reed PSC, Lord Kerr of Tonaghmore, Lord Lloyd-Jones, Lord Kitchin, Lord Sales JJSC and Baroness Hale of Richmond agreed).

(d) Landlord and Tenant

Insurance by landlord.

Replace footnote 168 with:

¹⁶⁸ *Mark Rowlands Ltd v Berni Inns Ltd* [1986] Q.B. 211 at 225–228; and see comment in [1986] C.L.J. **22-044**
23. The position would seem to be a fortiori where the lease requires the landlord to use reasonable
endeavours to ensure that the tenant is named as an assured, as was the case in *Quirkco Investments Ltd*
v Aspray Transport Ltd [2013] Lloyds Rep. I.R. 55 at [43]–[44]. Where the insurance is for the joint
benefit of the landlord and tenant, in most cases it will be impossible for the landlord (or his insurers
by way of a subrogated action) to recover damages from the tenant in respect of an insured loss caused
by his negligence—*Mark Rowlands Ltd v Berni Inns Ltd* at 232–233. This was described as the
"Rowlands Principle" by Holgate J in *Frasca-Judd v Golovina* [2016] EWHC 497 (QB); [2016] 4
W.L.R. 107 at [33], in which the principles relevant to construing a tenancy agreement for this purpose
are summarised at [48]. For a case in which such a claim succeeded in respect of damages to the part
of a building to which the obligation to insure did not apply see *Prezzo Ltd v High Point Estates Ltd*
[2018] EWHC 1851 (TCC); [2019] Lloyd's Rep. I.R. 202. See also *Cape Distribution Ltd v Cape*
Intermediate Holdings Plc [2016] EWHC 1119 (QB). It appears unlikely that the Rowlands Principle
can operate to confer immunity from liability on a landlord sued by the tenant for negligence, at any
rate, where the property is underinsured—that was the conclusion reached (obiter) by Andrew Burrows QC (as he then was) in *Palliser Ltd v Fate Ltd & Ors* [2019] EWHC 43 (QB); [2019] Lloyd's Rep.
I.R. 341 at [20]–[24]. See also para.24-093 below.

3.   CLAIMS BROUGHT BY THIRD PARTIES PURSUANT TO THE CONTRACTS (RIGHTS OF THIRD PARTIES) ACT 1999

Failure of third-party claims.

Replace footnote 251 with:

²⁵¹ See M.C. Hemsworth, "Life Assurance and the Cohabitant: The Law Commission's Reforms on Priv- **22-066**
ity" (1998) 57(1) Camb.L.J. 55. But if C was B's registered civil partner she would have an unlimited
interest in B's life under s.253 of the Civil Partnership Act 2004. In June 2018, the Law Commission
published a Draft Insurable Interest Bill. The Draft Bill applies to contracts of "life-related insurance"
and provides that an insured has an insurable interest in such a contract "if there is a reasonable prospect
that the insured will suffer economic loss if the insured event occurs". Section 2(3)(a)(ii) specifically
provides that the spouse or civil partner of the insured, or an individual who lives with the insured as a
spouse or civil partner, will have an insurable interest. At the time of writing, the consultation process
for the Draft Bill is ongoing. See also para.1-117.

CHAPTER 23

REINSTATEMENT

1. GENERALLY

Introduction.

Replace footnote 1 with:

23-001 ¹ Especially where the insurance provides a monetary indemnity based on replacement value such that a monetary payment would enrich the claimant beyond an indemnity for the value of the property as it was at the time of the loss, and hence create an incentive for fraudulent claims: see *Tower Insurance Ltd v Skyward Aviation 2008 Ltd* [2015] Lloyd's Rep. I.R. 283 (NZSC); *Prattley Enterprises Ltd v Vero Insurance New Zealand Ltd* [2016] NZSC 158 at [38]; *Xu v IAG* [2018] NZCA 149; [2018] Lloyd's Rep. I.R. 710 at [20], referring to the "heightened moral risk" faced by insurers in relation to reinstatement.

Reinstatement clause.

Replace footnote 4 with:

23-002 ⁴ By contrast, for a case involving a reinstatement clause that did not provide the insurer with an option but entitled the insured to be indemnified for the cost of reinstating the lost or damaged property see *Western Trading Ltd v Great Lakes Reinsurance (UK) Plc* [2015] EWHC 103 (QB); [2015] Lloyd's Rep. I.R. 561 at [131]. The Court of Appeal agreed that the measure of indemnity under the policy was the cost of reinstatement: see *Western Trading Ltd v Great Lakes Reinsurance (UK) Plc* [2016] EWCA Civ 1003; [2016] Lloyd's Rep. I.R. 643 at [63]. On the question of whether a right to reinstate and claim an indemnity for the reinstatement costs is assignable, see *Xu v IAG* [2019] NZSC 68, considered in the first footnote to para.22-017 above.

Measure of insurer's obligation.

After ", the insurer must reinstate them on the the same site.", add new footnote 51a:

23-012 ⁵¹ᵃ Cf. *Sartex Quilts and Textiles Ltd v Endurance Corporate Capital Ltd* [2019] EWHC 1103 (Comm) at [89], in which evidence of an intention to reinstate a manufacturing facility abroad was not fatal to a claim for an indemnity on the reinstatement basis.

CHAPTER 24

SUBROGATION

1. INTRODUCTION

Difference between subrogation and abandonment.

Replace footnote 17 with:

[17] *Rankin v Potter* (1873) L.R. 6 H.L. 83 at 118 per Blackburn J approved by Brett LJ in *Kaltenbach v Mackenzie* (1878) 3 C.P.D. 467 at 471; *Chitty on Contracts*, 33rd edn and First Supplement (London: Sweet and Maxwell, 2019), para.42-114 (salvage). Sed quaere. The example given by Blackburn J of the cession of rights is *Mason v Sainsbury* (1782) 3 Doug. K.B. 61, a case of ordinary subrogation, and it may be that he was referring only to the exercise by the insurer of the insured's rights of action in order to try to salve something of value from the aftermath of the loss. His language is strikingly similar to s.79 of the Marine Insurance Act 1906. The same comment applies to his citation from *Randal v Cockran* (1748) 1 Ves. Sen. 98, unless that case is interpreted as one of abandonment of the insured vessel to underwriters after her loss by capture to the Spaniards. In *Dane v Mortgage Insurance Corp* [1894] 1 Q.B. 54 at 61, Lord Esher MR appears to use the expression "salvage" to describe the exercise by insurers of subrogation rights. *Holmes v Payne* [1930] 2 K.B. 301 turned upon a replacement agreement concluded after the claim was lodged. The insured voluntarily tendered the brooch when it was found, and the issue of ownership did not arise for decision.

24-008

Difference between subrogation and assignment.

Replace footnote 26 with:

[26] *Chitty on Contracts*, 33rd edn and First Supplement (London: Sweet and Maxwell, 2019), para.19-039; *Central Insurance Co Ltd v Seacalf Shipping Corp* [1983] 2 Lloyd's Rep. 25 at 33–34.

24-012

Subrogation an equitable doctrine?

Replace footnote 58 with:

24-017 ⁵⁸ *Chitty on Contracts*, 33rd edn and First Supplement (London: Sweet and Maxwell, 2019), para.19-039; *Central Insurance Co Ltd v Seacalf Shipping Corp* [1983] 2 Lloyd's Rep. 25 at 33–34.

Subrogation a principle of law?

Replace footnote 61 with:

24-018 ⁶¹ *Yorkshire Insurance Co v Nisbet Shipping Co Ltd* [1962] 2 Q.B. 330 at 339–340. See also *AXA SA v Genworth Financial International Holdings Inc* [2019] EWHC 3376 (Comm) at [132].

The conflicting theories—a suggested reconciliation.

Replace paragraph with:

24-020   It is submitted on the basis of House of Lords authority⁶⁵ and as a matter of legal history that subrogation in insurance law is a legal doctrine by origin. Equity later came to play a useful supporting role in the development of the doctrine. Equity's effective performance in that role may have created the impression that subrogation was an entirely equitable doctrine, but equity should not be permitted to upstage the common law in that way. The court's "task nowadays is to see the two strands of authority, at law and in equity, moulded into a coherent whole".⁶⁶

⁶⁵ *Hobbs v Marlowe* [1978] A.C. 16; *Napier and Ettrick v Hunter* [1993] A.C. 713. See also *AXA SA v Genworth Financial International Holdings Inc* [2019] EWHC 3376 (Comm) at [135].

⁶⁶ *Napier and Ettrick v Hunter* [1993] A.C. 713 at 743. As noted by Bryan J in *AXA SA v Genworth Financial International Holdings Inc* [2019] EWHC 3376 (Comm) at [130]: "There are two types of subrogation recognised by the law: contractual subrogation and equitable subrogation. In *Banque Financiere de la Cite SA v Parc (Battersea) Ltd* [1999] 1 AC 221, Lord Hoffman at 231-2 described the two types of subrogation as '*radically different institutions. One is part of the law of contract and the other part of the law of restitution.*' Equitable subrogation, whose foundation is to reverse unjust enrichment caused by defective transactions, has no application to the present dispute; this case is concerned only with contractual subrogation." See the helpful discussion and analysis of the juridical basis of contractual subrogation from [131]–[142]. At [141], Bryan J concluded that: "I am satisfied that Lord Hoffmann's summary in *Banque Financiere de la Cite SA v Parc (Battersea) Ltd* accurately states the true position, that the type of subrogation under consideration is based on the common intention of the parties to a contract and as such where subrogation rights are not conferred expressly (by an express term of a contract) any subrogation rights are to be implied (by an implied term) so as to reflect the (objective) common intention of the parties. The House of Lords in *Lord Napier* and *Ettrick* rejected the exclusivity of the contractual analysis, (because equity also has a role to play), but maintained that the doctrine derives from the common intention of the parties embodied by the contract. A right of subrogation is conferred by the contract pursuant to which the relevant indemnity is paid, either as an express or implied term reflecting the common intention of the parties. The role of equity is supplemental. Equity gives effect to rights by providing remedies for their enforcement, but the rights themselves stem from the common intention of the parties reflected in the contract."

The role of equity.

Replace footnote 79 with:

24-023 ⁷⁹ *Banque Financière de la Cité v Parc (Battersea) Ltd* [1998] 1 All E.R. 737 at 744–745. As noted by Bryan J in *AXA SA v Genworth Financial International Holdings Inc* [2019] EWHC 3376 (Comm) at [130]: "There are two types of subrogation recognised by the law: contractual subrogation and equitable subrogation. In *Banque Financiere de la Cite SA v Parc (Battersea) Ltd* [1999] 1 AC 221, Lord Hoffman at 231-2 described the two types of subrogation as '*radically different institutions. One is part of the law of contract and the other part of the law of restitution.*' Equitable subrogation, whose foundation is to reverse unjust enrichment caused by defective transactions, has no application to the present dispute; this case is concerned only with contractual subrogation." See the helpful discussion and analysis of the juridical basis of contractual subrogation from [131]–[142] and the further detail at fn.66 to para.24-020 above. As to equitable subrogation as a remedy for unjust enrichment, see *Swynson Ltd v Lowick Rose LLP (In Liquidation) (formerly Hurst Morrison Thomson LLP)* [2017] UKSC 32; [2018] A.C. 313.

2. CONDITIONS PRECEDENT TO THE EXERCISE OF RIGHTS OF SUBROGATION

(a) Contract of Indemnity

Replace footnote 81 with:

24-025

[81] *Burnand v Rodocanachi* (1882) 7 App. Cas. 333 at 339; *Simpson v Thomson* (1877) 3 App. Cas. 279 at 284. The doctrine of subrogation is not, of course, confined to contracts of insurance. If a broker compensates an insured he may acquire subrogation rights, see *Nahhas v Pierhouse* (1984) 270 E.G. 328. As noted by Bryan J in *AXA SA v Genworth Financial International Holdings Inc* [2019] EWHC 3376 (Comm) at [145]: "The availability of contractual subrogation rights depends on the paying party having indemnified the receiving party in respect of a loss suffered by the receiving party. The foundation of the doctrine is that the party in receipt of the relevant payment obtains an indemnity for a loss which it itself has incurred."

(b) Payment to Assured

Replace footnote 95 with:

24-027

[95] *Simpson v Thomson* (1877) 3 App. Cas. 279 at 284; *Castellain v Preston* (1883) 11 Q.B.D. 380 at 389; *Driscoll v Driscoll* [1918] 1 I.R. 152 at 159; *Burnand v Rodocanachi* (1882) 7 App. Cas. 333 at 339; *Dickenson v Jardine* (1868) L.R. 3 C.P. 639 at 644. Motor insurers do not acquire rights of subrogation by paying for repairs to the insured vehicle which have not in fact been properly performed to the reasonable satisfaction of the insured, since he has not been indemnified against his loss—*Scottish Union and National Insurance Co v Davis* [1970] 1 Lloyd's Rep. 1. See also *AXA SA v Genworth Financial International Holdings Inc* [2019] EWHC 3376 (Comm) at [145]–[148].

3. EXERCISE OF RIGHTS OF SUBROGATION

(a) Claims Against Third Parties

Claims to which the insurer is subrogated.

Replace footnote 126 with:

24-036

[126] *Castellain v Preston* (1883) 11 Q.B.D. 380 at 388; *Morley v Moore* [1936] 2 K.B. 359. As noted by Bryan J in *AXA SA v Genworth Financial International Holdings Inc* [2019] EWHC 3376 (Comm) at [145] and [153]: "145. The availability of contractual subrogation rights depends on the paying party having indemnified the receiving party in respect of a loss suffered by the receiving party. The foundation of the doctrine is that the party in receipt of the relevant payment obtains an indemnity for a loss which it itself has incurred. ... 153. Contractual subrogation, by its very nature as a creature of contract, requires that the indemnified and the person who has the relevant rights against the third party are the same legal entity."

6. CLAIMS AGAINST ASSURED

No recovery pending full indemnity.

Replace footnote 218 with:

24-072

[218] See Marine Insurance Act 1906 s.81; *Arnould: Law of Marine Insurance and Average*, 18th edn and First Supplement (London: Sweet & Maxwell, 2016), para.31–56; and now see Arnould, *Law of Marine Insurance and Average*, 19th edn and Second Supplement (London: Sweet & Maxwell, 2020).

Replace footnote 224 with:

24-075

[224] An example is *Goole and Hull Steam Towing Co Ltd v Ocean Marine Insurance Co Ltd* [1928] 1 K.B. 589. Valued policies are almost entirely confined to the field of marine insurance. For discussion of the much criticised cases in which this principle was laid down, see *Arnould: Law of Marine Insurance and Average*, 18th edn and First Supplement (London: Sweet & Maxwell, 2016), Vol.2, Ch.31, para.31–55; and now see Arnould, *Law of Marine Insurance and Average*, 19th edn and Second Supplement (London: Sweet & Maxwell, 2020).

7. APPLICATION TO PARTICULAR CASES

Landlord and tenant.

After para.24-093, add new paragraph:

24-093A   For a recent case briefly considering both the decisions in *Berni Inns* and in *Frasca-Judd*, see *Prezzo Ltd v High Point Estates Ltd*.[281a] For an article considering the *Prezzo* case, see "Subrogation: Interested third parties" (2019) 31 I.L.M. 2.

[281a] *Prezzo Ltd v High Point Estates Ltd* [2018] EWHC 1851 (TCC); [2019] Lloyd's Rep. I.R. 202.

For a more recent case considering the decisions in *Berni Inns* and *Frasca-Judd* in more detail, see *Palliser Ltd v Fate Ltd (In Liquidation)*.[281b] The oddity in the *Palliser*case was that it was the landlord (Fate) who had been negligent in causing the fire to the premises and had taken out the insurance. As summarised by Andrew Burrows QC (as he was then, sitting as a Judge of the High Court) (at [20]):

"[T]here is a very significant difference between our facts and the facts in *Berni Inns* ... The significant difference is that in our case it is the landlord, who has been negligent, not the tenant. So it is the landlord who has taken out the buildings insurance who seeks to rely on that insurance as impliedly excluding its negligence liability to the tenant. It follows from this that the initial question being asked in those other cases of whether the insurance enures for the benefit of the person who has been negligent seems an odd question to ask in this case. Clearly the landlord (Fate) who has taken out and paid for the buildings insurance is taking out the insurance for its own benefit (albeit perhaps for the benefit of the tenant as well) and can obviously rely on it if it needs to cover refurbishment of the building because of a fire caused by its own negligence. This also explains why, this way round, it is surely irrelevant whether the tenant (here Palliser) has paid anything towards the insurance: as it is the landlord, not the tenant, who is seeking exclusion of liability, it makes no difference whether the tenant has paid towards that insurance or not."

[281b] *Palliser Ltd v Fate Ltd (In Liquidation)* [2019] EWHC 43 (QB); [2019] Lloyd's Rep. I.R. 341.

Mr Burrows QC went on (at [22]) to make two observations about the application of the *Berni Inns* defence this way around (i.e. where it is the insuring landlord who has been negligent, not the tenant):

"First, it must be rare in practice for this issue to arise and certainly I was not referred to any case where it has been in issue. This is because, where the landlord has taken out the buildings insurance, it will be in the landlord's interest to use the proceeds of the insurance to repair the building so as to remove any loss to the tenant that could otherwise be claimed against the landlord in the tort of negligence. The issue is therefore only likely to be raised where there is some problem with the buildings insurance (as, for example, where, as here, the landlord has underinsured). Secondly, the underlying practical issue in the *Berni Inns* [case] ... is whether the insurer, under the buildings insurance, has subrogation rights against the negligent tenant. But there is no question of subrogation operating in the situation with which we are dealing; ie there is no possibility of the insurer having subrogation rights against the negligent landlord who is the insured under the buildings insurance policy (as the insurer 'stands in the shoes' of the landlord, it would be suing itself which would be a nonsense)."

Mr Burrows QC did also consider, albeit briefly, the decisions in *Co-operative Retail Services Ltd v Taylor Young Partnership Ltd* and in *Gard Marine & Energy Ltd v China National Chartering Co Ltd (The Ocean Victory)*, drawing (at [18]) the following three helpful points from those authorities:

"The first is that one is looking to see whether the contractual arrangements between the parties are such that the parties have agreed that compensation should be dealt with by insurance payments rather than the normal rules of tort and breach of contract. In the words of Lord Hope in the *Co-operative* case at [48], '[the contractual arrangements in relation to insurance meant that] the ordinary rules for the payment of compensation for negligence and breach of contract have been eliminated.' Secondly, it may be illuminating to think in terms of whether there is a single 'fund' provided from insurance out of which the repairing of damage to the property is to be covered and which carries with it the consequence that subrogated claims are excluded. So, for example, Lord Bingham in the *Co-operative* case, at [7], spoke of the parties being 'indemnified by the insurers' provision of a fund enabling [payment] for repairing the fire damage. The insurers could not then make a subrogated claim against the [payee] …'. Thirdly, one can look at the issue in terms of whether the scheme of insurance comprises a comprehensive allocation of risk between the parties in place of litigation: see, for example, Lord Mance in the *Gard Marine* case who said, at [114], 'The scheme… is clearly intended to be comprehensive. Whatever the causes, both repairs and total losses fall to be dealt with in accordance with its terms, rather than by litigation to establish who might otherwise be responsible for undertaking them, for bearing the risk of their occurrence or for making them good.'"

Subrogation barred by the underlying contract.

Replace footnote 300 with:

[300] *Co-operative Retail Services Ltd v Taylor Young Partnership Ltd* [2002] UKHL 17; [2002] 1 W.L.R.   **24-102**
1419. See also *Rathbone Brothers Plc v Novae Corporate Underwriting Ltd* [2014] EWCA Civ 1464; [2015] Lloyd's Rep. I.R. 95; *Gard Marine & Energy Ltd v China National Chartering Co Ltd (The Ocean Victory)* [2017] UKSC 35; [2017] 1 W.L.R. 1793; and *Haberdashers' Aske's Federation Trust Ltd v Lakehouse Contracts Ltd* [2018] EWHC 558 (TCC); [2018] Lloyd's Rep. I.R. 382 at [63] and [66]–[69].

Replace footnote 305 with:

[305] *Gard Marine & Energy Ltd v China National Chartering Co Ltd (The Ocean Victory)* [2017] UKSC   **24-104**
35; [2017] 1 W.L.R. 1793. For a commentary on this case, see "Marine insurance: Subrogation" (2018) 30 I.L.M. 3. For a recent case following the decision in *Gard Marine*, see *Haberdashers' Aske's Federation Trust Ltd v Lakehouse Contracts Ltd* [2018] EWHC 558 (TCC); [2018] Lloyd's Rep. I.R. 382, addressed more fully at para.24-104A below. See also *SSE Generation Ltd v Hochtief Solutions AG* [2018] CSIH 26.

After para.24-104, add new paragraph:

In *Haberdashers' Aske's Federation Trust Ltd v Lakehouse Contracts Ltd*,[305a] the   **24-104A**
preliminary issue was whether the second defendant sub-contractor (CPR) was insured under a project-wide insurance policy provided by the third-party insurers (Project Insurers) in respect of construction works at a school (operated by Haberdashers). In summary of the facts, Lewisham Council contracted with a Local Education Partnership (LEP) to refurbish a school. LEP sub-contracted to Lakehouse for demolition and reconstruction work. LEP was required by cl.25 of the Design and Build Contract to take out and maintain insurance, with LEP and Haberdashers named as co-insureds and also a subrogation waiver clause in favour of LEP, Haberdashers "and their respective employees and agents, acting properly in the course of their employment or agency". Lakehouse sub-contracted to CPR to carry out roofing works. The sub-contract provided that CPR was required to obtain its own insurance cover in the sum of £5 million. There was a fire at the school after CPR had carried out "hot work" and the Claimants (Haberdashers and Lewisham) sought damages against Lakehouse and CPR. Lakehouse settled the proceedings by paying the Claimants £8.75 million (paid by the Project Insurers) and Lakehouse sought to recover £5 million from CPR under CPR's insurance.

Lakehouse sought contribution or indemnity from CPR and CPR sought a declaration that it could rely on the project insurance.

[305a] *Haberdashers' Aske's Federation Trust Ltd v Lakehouse Contracts Ltd* [2018] EWHC 558 (TCC); [2018] Lloyd's Rep. I.R. 382. Permission to appeal was granted and an appeal was listed before the Court of Appeal, but the case settled.

The question was, therefore, whether Lakehouse was entitled to contribution or indemnity from CPR, so that the Project Insurers had a subrogation claim in Lakehouse's name. CPR sought a declaration that the Project Insurers could not pursue an indemnity or contribution claim against it, arguing that it was co-insured under the Project Insurance and was entitled to the benefit of the subrogation waiver clause in that insurance. The Project Insurers argued that CPR could not rely upon the Project Insurance by reason of the fact that it was required to arrange its own insurance.

At [65], Mr Justice Fraser quoted from Lord Toulson's speech in *Gard Marine* (at [139]), including that "[t]he question in each case is whether the parties are to be taken to have intended to create an insurance fund which would be the sole avenue for making good the relevant loss or damage …". Fraser J concluded (at [70]) that:

> "How, it could be posed rhetorically, could the parties be taken to have intended to create an insurance fund which would be the sole avenue for making good the relevant loss or damage, when those parties had expressly agreed that CPR would obtain its own separate insurance? When looked at this way, Mr Bartlett's argument that CPR was deemed to have knowledge of the main contract conditions between LEP and Lakehouse (which included reference to Project Insurance) by virtue of clause 1.7 of the roofing sub-contract is, if anything, a point against CPR. This is because, with deemed (or actual) knowledge of the Project Insurance, CPR expressly agreed a term that governed its relationship with Lakehouse (and hence its involvement in the project) that it would have its own insurance. That is directly contrary to there being an intention that there would be an insurance fund which would be the sole avenue for making good the relevant loss and damage. It was an express agreement to create a second insurance fund."

See also the consideration of *Co-operative Retail Services Ltd v Taylor Young Partnership Ltd*,[305b] with Fraser J concluding (at [69]) that:

> "It is therefore obvious that the answer in the *Cooperative* case depended upon the actual contractual arrangements between the parties. Again and again throughout the authorities, emphasis is placed upon the fact that the answer in any particular case is one of construction, and it therefore critically depends upon the provisions of the particular contract in each case."[305c]

[305b] *Co-operative Retail Services Ltd v Taylor Young Partnership Ltd* [2002] UKHL 17; [2002] 1 W.L.R. 1419 at [66]–[69].

[305c] For a commentary on the *Haberdashers'* case, see "Insurance law in 2018: a year in review" by Alison Padfield QC and Miles Harris, p.17.

In *Palliser Ltd v Fate Ltd (In Liquidation)*, Andrew Burrows QC (sitting as a Judge of the High Court) considered, albeit briefly, (at [18]) the decisions in *Co-operative Retail Services Ltd v Taylor Young Partnership Ltd* and *Gard Marine & Energy Ltd v China National Chartering Co Ltd (The Ocean Victory)*, and drew three helpful points from those authorities, as addressed at para.24-093A above.

CHAPTER 25

RIGHTS OF TWO OR MORE INSURERS

1. INTRODUCTION

Several liability of insurers.

Replace paragraph with:

Double insurance and contribution are closely linked. Double insurance occurs **25-001** when the insured insures against the same risk on the same interest in the same subject-matter with two or more independent insurers.[1] Over-insurance by double insurance occurs when the aggregate of all the insurances is more than the total value of the insured's interest. Apart from express condition, both double insurance and over-insurance are perfectly lawful; one may insure with as many insurers as one pleases and up to the full amount of one's interest with each one.[2] If a loss occurs, the insured may, in the absence of a pro rata contribution clause, select any one or more insurers and recover from him or them the total amount of the loss.[3] If he fails to recover his whole loss from those against whom he has proceeded in the first instance, he may recover the balance from any one or more of the others. But in no event is he entitled to recover more than his loss because each contract is a contract of indemnity only, and, therefore, when he has recovered his total loss from one or more of his insurers his claims against the others abate.[4] The right to sue his insurers in any order is a valuable right for the insured, for it protects him against loss in the event of one or more of his insurers becoming insolvent; but as it would have been a considerable hardship on the insurers that one alone of several co-insurers should bear the whole loss, the doctrine of contribution was evolved, apparently by Lord Mansfield, who held that in marine insurance an insurer who paid more than his rateable proportion of the loss should have a right to recover the excess from his co-insurers, who had paid less than their rateable proportion.[5] The same general principles of liability and contribution have been held to apply to fire insurance[6] and liability insurance.[7] As a rule, however, insurers are not content to leave their liability on this basis, and have accordingly inserted conditions in their policies to protect themselves as far as possible against fraudulent over-insurances,

[87]

and at the same time to obtain the maximum benefit from the contributory liability of co-insurers.[8]

[1] See *International Energy Group Ltd v Zurich Insurance Plc UK Branch* [2015] UKSC 33; [2016] A.C. 509 at [57], citing with approval *National Farmers Union Mutual Insurance Society Ltd v HSBC Insurance (UK) Ltd* [2010] EWHC 773 (Comm).

[2] *Albion Insurance Co v Government Insurance Office of New South Wales* (1969) 121 C.L.R. 342 at 345.

[3] *Godin v London Assurance Co* (1758) 1 Burr. 489; 1 Wm. Bl. 105; *Bank of British North America v Western Assurance Co* (1884) 7 Ont.R. 166; *International Energy Group Ltd v Zurich Insurance Plc UK* [2015] UKSC 33; [2016] A.C. 509 at [26] and [60].

[4] *Bovis Construction Ltd v Commercial Union Assurance Co Plc* [2001] 1 Lloyd's Rep. 416 at 418; *Sickness and Accident Assurance v General Accident Assurance* (1892) 19 R. 972 at 977; *Austin v Zurich General Accident & Liability Insurance Co* [1945] 1 K.B. 250 at 258.

[5] *Godin v London Assurance Co* (1758) 1 Burr. 489 at 492; *Newby v Reed* (1763) 1 Wm. Bl. 416; *Rogers v Davis* (1777) 2 Park 601; *Davis v Gildard* (1777) 2 Park 601; *International Energy Group Ltd v Zurich Insurance Plc UK* [2015] UKSC 33; [2016] A.C. 509 at [26]. In marine insurance the principles of double insurance and contribution have been codified in ss.32 and 80 of the Marine Insurance Act 1906. The "considerable hardship" point was recently cited with approval by the High Court of New Zealand in *Body Corporate 74246 v QBE Insurance (International) Ltd and Another* [2017] NZHC 1473 at [29]; affirmed by the Court of Appeal in *QBE Insurance (International) Ltd v Allianz Australia Ltd* [2018] NZCA 239.

[6] *North British and Mercantile Insurance Co v London, Liverpool and Globe Insurance Co* (1877) 5 Ch. D. 569 at 583 per Mellish LJ; 587 per Baggallay JA.

[7] *Commercial Union Assurance Co v Hayden* [1977] 1 Lloyd's Rep. 1; *Sickness and Accident Assurance v General Accident Assurance* (1892) 19 R. 972 at 977 per Lord Low, Lord Ordinary. In *Albion Insurance Co v Government Insurance Office of New South Wales* (1969) 121 C.L.R. 342 it was said that contribution applied to all types of indemnity insurance (1969) 121 C.L.R. 342 at 345. The cautionary remarks of Hamilton J in *American Surety Co of New York v Wrightson* (1910) 16 Com. Cas. 37 at 51 and 56 were prompted by radical differences in coverage afforded by the two policies before the court and not to any doubt that contribution was in principle applicable to fidelity risks.

[8] This sentence was recently cited with approval by the High Court of New Zealand in *Body Corporate 74246 v QBE Insurance (International) Ltd and Another* [2017] NZHC 1473 at [30]; affirmed by the Court of Appeal in *QBE Insurance (International) Ltd v Allianz Australia Ltd* [2018] NZCA 239. For a commentary on the *Body Corporate* case, see "Double insurance and contribution: Date of inception of cover" (2018) 30 I.L.M. 2.

Policy conditions.

Replace footnote 9 with:

25-002   [9] This paragraph up to the end of (2) was recently cited with approval by the High Court of New Zealand in *Body Corporate 74246 v QBE Insurance (International) Ltd and Another* [2017] NZHC 1473 at [30]; affirmed by the Court of Appeal in *QBE Insurance (International) Ltd v Allianz Australia Ltd* [2018] NZCA 239. For a commentary on the *Body Corporate* case, see "Double insurance and contribution: Date of inception of cover" (2018) 30 I.L.M. 2.

2.   DOUBLE INSURANCE

The same risk.

Replace footnote 25 with:

25-006   [25] See the decision of the High Court of New Zealand in *Body Corporate 74246 v QBE Insurance (International) Ltd* [2017] NZHC 1473 for a case where it was held that the intention had been to provide seamless rather than overlapping cover; affirmed by the Court of Appeal in *QBE Insurance (International) Ltd v Allianz Australia Ltd* [2018] NZCA 239. For a commentary on the *Body Corporate* case, see "Double insurance and contribution: Date of inception of cover" (2018) 30 I.L.M. 2.

After para.25-023, add new paragraph:

25-023A **Competing clauses.**   In the recent New South Wales Court of Appeal case of *Al-*

lianz Insurance Australia Ltd v Certain Underwriters at Lloyd's of London,[73a] there were "competing" clauses: one policy (the Allianz policy) was stated to be in excess of any other insurance and the other policy (the Lloyd's policy) excluded cover in the event of other insurance. The issue of such "competing clauses" has not been directly considered in the English authorities. In summary of the facts, Mr Dempsey was working on the construction of a road and was seriously injured when hit by a car. He received approximately AUS\$1 million in damages from the builders of the road (Baulderstone). Baulderstone had two relevant insurance policies: the Allianz policy and the Lloyd's policy. Payment was made by Allianz, which sought contribution from Lloyd's. The Allianz policy provided in relevant parts as follows:

"8.17 Difference in Conditions Cover

In circumstances where an Underlying Insurance has been arranged, this Policy shall be deemed to be the 'Master Policy'.

(a) In the event of the Insured being indemnified by an Underlying Insurance in respect of a claim for which indemnity is available under this Master Policy, the insurance afforded by this Policy shall be excess insurance over the applicable limit of indemnity of the Underlying Insurance.

(b) Coverage under this Master Policy shall not apply unless and until a claim for payment is made under the Underlying Insurance up to the amount of the Underlying Limit which, save for the limit of indemnity of the Underlying Insurance, would be covered by this Master Policy.

(c) Should any such Underlying Insurance, by virtue of its scope of cover, definitions, deductibles or excesses, conditions or limits of indemnity, not indemnify the Insured in whole or in part in respect of a loss, damage, liability, costs or expenses indemnifiable under this Master Policy, this Master Policy will provide indemnity to the extent that such indemnity is not provided by the terms and conditions of such Underlying Insurance. For the purpose of clarity, it is intended that indemnity by this Policy extends to cover losses not covered under the Underlying Insurance by virtue of the fact that such Underlying Insurance has a higher deductible or excess than the Excess under this Master Policy.

...

8.20 Where allowable by law, this Policy is excess over and above any other valid and collectible insurance and shall not respond to any loss until such times as the limit of liability under such other primary and valid insurance has been totally exhausted ...".

"Underlying Insurance" was defined in cl.10.5 as a "policy of insurance arranged by or on behalf of an Insured either voluntarily or pursuant to a Contract ... that provides cover to the Insured for a risk, which save for the Underlying Insurance, would be covered by this Policy". The Lloyd's policy provided in relevant part: "10. General exclusions: This Policy does not cover liability: 10.5 which forms the subject of insurance by any other policy and this Policy shall not be drawn into contribution with such other insurance."

At first instance, Rees J relied on the *New Zealand authority of Commercial Union Assurance Co of New Zealand Ltd v Murphy*[73b] and held that cl.8.17(c) meant that if the other policy contained an exclusion clause preventing coverage of liability that fell within the Allianz policy, then the Allianz policy responded to the claim. Rees J, therefore, held that there was no double insurance at all. The majority of the Court of Appeal reversed Rees J's decision (Macfarlan JA dissenting). The majority held that the effect of cl.10.5 of the Lloyd's policy and cl.8.20 of the Allianz policy was to deny liability under each policy because of the existence of the other. Applying the rule of construction in *Weddell v Road Transport and General Insurance Company Ltd*, the clauses cancelled each other out with the result that both policies responded and Allianz, having met the claim, was entitled to contribution from the Lloyd's Underwriters. Further, the Lloyd's policy was not "Underlying Insurance" as defined in the Allianz policy because, by virtue of cl.10.5 of the Lloyd's policy, the insurance did not provide cover for the risk in question. Clause 8.17 of the Allianz policy therefore had no application in relation to it.

The decision of the Court of Appeal is helpfully summarised and analysed in "Double insurance: the effect of 'other insurance' clauses" (2020) 32 I.L.M. 5, as follows:

> "First, a policy term under which there is an exclusion of liability 'which forms the subject of insurance by any other policy and this Policy shall not be drawn into contribution with such other insurance' refers to another policy that actually responds to the loss. So, if there is any other policy that covers the actual claim – and not merely a policy in existence that might cover the claim – the clause operates to exclude liability so that there can be no question of contribution. That was the effect of the judgments of Meagher JA and Macfarlan JA. Bathurst CJ took a different view, but nothing turned on the point. Secondly, an excess clause and an exclusion clause are, taken together, self-cancelling. That was the unanimous view of the court. The majority construed clause 8.17 of the Allianz policy as a pure excess clause, namely, one that operated as an excess provision only where there was another valid insurance in place. The minority view of clause 8.17 was that it operated to reinstate cover where there was no underlying policy."

[73a] *Allianz Insurance Australia Ltd v Certain Underwriters at Lloyd's of London* [2019] NSWCA 271; reversing the first instance decision of Rees J: [2019] NSWSC 453.

[73b] *New Zealand authority of Commercial Union Assurance Co of New Zealand Ltd v Murphy* [1989] 1 NZLR 687.

3. CONTRIBUTION

(a) Introduction

After para.25-032, add new paragraph:

25-032A Limitation and contribution   In *RSA Insurance Plc v Assicurazioni Generali SpA*,[98a] the issue arose as to the operation of the Limitation Act 1980 in respect of a contribution claim by one employer's liability insurer against another. Mr Merritt was employed by AWL for the period 1975 to 1986 and was exposed to asbestos and contracted mesothelioma. During that period, AWL had employer's liability insurance as follows: October 1975 to June 1979, Aviva; June 1979 to March 1981, no insurer traced; April 1981 to March 1983, Generali; April 1983 to March 1985, no insurer traced; and April 1985 to September 1985, RSA. As he was entitled to do pursuant to the decisions in *Fairchild* and in *IEGL* (see para.25-054 below), Mr Merritt pursued his entire claim against RSA alone and RSA paid that claim in 2011. In 2017, RSA then commenced contribution proceedings against both Generali and Aviva, seeking contribution from them on a "time on risk" basis. It appears that Aviva paid, but Generali did not pay and instead asserted that the claim was time-barred. Generali argued that the right of contribution fell within s.1(1) of the Civil Liability (Contribution) Act 1978, superseding the equitable right of contribution by reason of s.7(3), and was subject to a two-year limitation period under s.10(1) of the Limitation Act 1980, running from the date of the settlement. It was held, in relevant part, that RSA's claim did fall within s.1(1) of the 1978 Act. The claim by AWL against RSA was one for damages and not debt. There was a long line of cases confirming that the liability arising under an insurance contract of indemnity sounds in damages. It was common ground that if the liability of RSA to AWL was one sounding in damages rather than debt, then RSA's right of contribution fell within s.1 of the 1978 Act and was statute-barred, RSA's liability having accrued on the date of settlement in 2011. This decision would appear to give rise to complications in the case of first party insurance, if it is right in such cases that the claim for contribution would have to be made within two years from the date of the loss. This and other related issues will no doubt be matters for further consideration when such cases arise.

[98a] *RSA Insurance Plc v Assicurazioni Generali SpA* [2018] EWHC 1237 (QB); [2019] Lloyd's Rep. I.R. 264.

(c) Contribution Without Average

Mesothelioma and the Fairchild enclave.

Replace fourth paragraph with:

   Whilst an interesting and important case, Lord Mance stated in terms (at [1]) that **25-054** "[t]his appeal and the conclusions I reach on it are concerned exclusively with situations falling within the special rule" and Lord Hodge stated (at [109]) that "[t]he court is crafting a solution for the problems that stem from the alteration of the rules of causation and the solution applies only to cases to which the altered rules of causation apply". There were further issues relating to defence costs and the Third Parties (Rights against Insurers) Act 1930, but these are beyond the scope of this chapter. The 1930 Act point did not need to be resolved because IEG was solvent, but the difficult issues involving the 1930 Act were considered by Lord Mance at [83]–[93]. As Lord Mance noted at [85], "[w]hether an insurer's right to contribution against the insured constitutes a full or partial answer to a victim's policy claim based on such a transfer [under the 1930 Act] is a question of great potential importance". See now also *RSA Insurance Plc v Assicurazioni Generali SpA*,[125a] addressed in more detail at para.25-032A above, with HHJ Rawlings (obiter) setting out (at [122]) the reasons for rejecting the argument (on the facts of that case) that if Generali did have an obligation to contribute towards the monies that RSA paid to Mr Merritt, outside of the 1978 Act, it would be appropriate to reduce the level of that contribution to reflect the fact that RSA have not pursued previous employers of Mr Merritt or Electrolux/Philips as occupiers of factories in which Mr Merritt was exposed to asbestos dust whilst employed by the Company (AWL).

[125a] *RSA Insurance Plc v Assicurazioni Generali* [2019] Lloyd's Rep. I.R. 264 at [116]–[122].

Replace first paragraph with:

   This area of the law continues to develop. On 17 April 2019, the Court of Ap- **25-056** peal handed down judgment in *Equitas Insurance Ltd v Municipal Mutual Insurance Ltd*.[125b] This is addressed in further detail at para.35-080A below. The Court of Appeal had previously (on 4 May 2018), given permission to appeal in *Equitas Insurance Ltd v Municipal Mutual Insurance Ltd*,[125c] appealing against an arbitration award dated 7 April 2017 made by Flaux LJ sitting as a judge-arbitrator. The dispute raised questions concerning the treatment of mesothelioma claims for the purposes of certain contracts of employers' liability (EL) reinsurance; and more specifically: (i) whether MMI was entitled to present each outwards reinsurance claim to any single triggered reinsurance contract of its choice (i.e. whether it may "spike" the claims); and (ii) if so, how the resultant rights of recoupment and contribution, arising from the Supreme Court decision in *IEGL v Zurich* are to be calculated.

[125b] *Equitas Insurance Ltd v Municipal Mutual Insurance Ltd* [2019] EWCA Civ 718; [2020] Q.B. 418.

[125c] *Equitas Insurance Ltd v Municipal Mutual Insurance Ltd* [2018] EWCA Civ 991; [2018] Lloyd's Rep. I.R. Plus 26.

In the second paragraph, replace "Flaux J held in his award that:" with:
Flaux LJ held in his award that:

Replace third paragraph with:
When granting permission to appeal, the Court of Appeal held that permission would be given because, of relevance for present purposes: (1) there was force to the submission that, if it was determined that the reinsured had choice as to how to allocate its losses to its reinsurers, there could be some basis for a duty of good faith in order to restrain the manner of exercise of the freedom of choice; and (2) there were three potential problems with the tribunal's determination of the recoupment and contribution issue: (a) there was nothing in the existing authorities (and specifically *IEGL v Zurich*) which assisted on the issue of retentions; (b) there was a strong argument that the position, when it comes to recoupment and contribution in insurance and reinsurance, was different within the *Fairchild* enclave; and (c) it was arguable that Flaux LJ was wrong in his conclusion that there was no principled basis for the "top down" approach, in that there was considerable force in the submission that the higher layers of reinsurance in subsequent years should be made good first in any contribution and recoupment process, on the basis that they should always be furthest from the risk.

After the third paragraph, add new paragraph:
In its decision on the substance of the appeal,[125d] the Court of Appeal allowed the appeal and held, in summary, that the practice of "spiking" mesothelioma claims, whereby employers were entitled to present claims to any policy year of their choice, did not extend to the reinsurance context. In this regard, the court observed that the practice of spiking, and the anomalies that it caused, served a purpose at the insurance level, but that it was unnecessary to perpetuate those anomalies at the reinsurance level. It was therefore desirable, if possible, to revert to the principles of the common law, such that liability would be apportioned by reference to contribution to the risk. The court held that the insurer's right to present its reinsurance claims was subject to an implied term that the right must be exercised in a manner which is not arbitrary, irrational or capricious. In mesothelioma claims, rationality required that claims be presented by reference to each year's contribution to the risk, which would normally be measured by reference to time on risk unless in the particular circumstances there was a good reason for some other basis of presentation. The court stressed that the implication of such a term was specific to the *Fairchild* enclave and would not have wider ramifications for the law of reinsurance.

[125d] *Equitas Insurance Ltd v Municipal Mutual Insurance Ltd* [2019] EWCA Civ 718; [2020] Q.B. 418.

Males LJ addressed contribution and recoupment (at [119]–[128]), holding (at [122]) that

> "... the guiding principle is clear, which is that the objective must be to achieve a just solution. That solution will eliminate so far as possible the anomalies resulting from the *Fairchild* jurisprudence and will take account of the reality of the underlying claims, that

is to say that nobody can know in which year the critical exposure occurred in the case of any given victim and that considering the position of victims as a group, such exposures will have occurred in a variety of years. The best available measure of such exposures is by reference to each policy year's contribution to the risk. That is not to revert to the now discredited theory of liability for making a material contribution to risk but recognises the artificiality of saying that an exposure which in fact occurred only once, even if we do not know when, is regarded in law as having occurred in each and every year."

Males LJ suggested that there were two errors in Flaux LJ's reasoning on this issue, the second of which was that he had applied too closely the concept of double insurance in which only one retention would be applied.

After the final paragraph, add new paragraph:

Permission to appeal to the Supreme Court was granted and the appeal was due to be heard in July 2020. However, it is understood that the matter settled and the Supreme Court hearing did not proceed.

CHAPTER 26

LIFE INSURANCE

1. PROOF OF DEATH AND AGE

Presumption of death.

Replace footnote 19 with:

26-005

[19] The Presumption of Death Act 2013 introduced a statutory procedure enabling a declaration to be obtained that a missing person is to be deemed to have died. The procedure may be invoked when a missing person has not been known to be alive for seven years or more. A more detailed account may be found in H.M. Malek, J. Auburn, R. Bagshaw, *Phipson on Evidence*, 19th edn (London: Sweet & Maxwell, 2018), para.6-10. For an example of this procedure, see *Re Irish* [2019] EWHC 2508 (Ch); [2019] 4 W.L.R. 122; and *Re Irish* [2020] EWHC 456 (Ch). As to Scotland, see paras 26-014 and following, below.

4. CLAIMANT'S TITLE TO POLICY

(d) Equitable Discharge

(2) Purchaser of the policy.

Replace footnote 135 with:

26-055

[135] See Ch.1. In June 2018, the Law Commission published a Draft Insurable Interest Bill, which proposes that in contracts of "life-related insurance", the insured has an insurable interest "if there is a reasonable prospect that the insured will suffer economic loss if the insured event occurs". The Draft Bill provides specific circumstances in which the insured will have an insurable interest, including in the cases of the spouse, civil partner, child or grandchild of the insured. The Draft Bill also provides that in cases where the insured did not have an insurable interest at the relevant time, the contract will be void, but not illegal. This latter point reflects the present position in Scotland, but not in England and Wales. At the time of writing, the consultation process in relation to the Draft Bill remains ongoing.

7. TRUSTS AND SETTLED POLICIES

(b) Particular Types of Trust Policy

(1) Child Endowment Policies.

Replace footnote 410 with:

26-161

[410] *Halford v Kymer* (1830) 10 B. & C. 724; and see paras 1-090 to 1-100 above. In June 2018, the Law Commission published a Draft Insurable Interest Bill, which provides a statutory definition and specific examples of insurable interest in relation to contracts of "life-related insurance". The Draft Bill provides that the insured will have an insurable interest where (inter alia) the individual who is the subject of the contract is the child or grandchild of the insured, or is a member of a pension or other group scheme administered by the insured (whether as trustee or otherwise). At the time of writing, the consultation process for the Draft Bill remains ongoing.

CHAPTER 28

PROPERTY INSURANCE: FIRE POLICIES

2. CAUSATION OF LOSS

Burden of proof.

Replace footnote 47 with:

28-019 [47] The authorities are considered in the third footnote to para.21-010 above. See also *McGregor v Prudential Insurance Co Ltd* [1998] 1 Lloyd's Rep. 112 where the equivalent paragraph in the 8th edition of this work (para.1881) was cited by the learned judge. It is the same in marine insurance where fire is a specified peril—see *National Justice Cia v Prudential Assurance Co* [1995] 1 Lloyd's Rep. 455. The same approach was followed in *Shakur v Pilot Insurance Co* (1991) 73 D.L.R. (4th) 337 at 344, Ont.C.A. In many cases, it will not be necessary for the insurer to establish that the fire was caused by the insured's wilful act to avoid cover; depending on the terms of the policy, it may be sufficient for the insured to fail to establish that the cause of the fire was accidental, even if the true cause cannot be determined. For a recent Scottish case in which that was the result, see *T & G Grampian Ltd v Allianz Insurance Plc* [2018] SAC (Civ) 23 at [13].

3. PERILS COMMONLY EXCEPTED

Other risks and exceptions.

Replace footnote 120 with:

28-045 [120] *David Allen & Sons (Billposting) v Drysdale* [1939] 4 All E.R. 113. On the meanings of "subsidence" and "settlement", see *Contact (Print and Packaging) Ltd v Travelers Insurance Co Ltd* [2018] EWHC 83 (TCC); [2018] Lloyd's Rep. I.R. 295 at [50]–[56]; *Guastalegname v Australian Associated Motor Insurers Ltd* [2017] V.S.C. 420 (whether "soil movement" exclusion limited to movement of a mass of soil to a different location).

CHAPTER 29

PROPERTY INSURANCE: OTHER INSURANCES ON PROPERTY

1. BURGLARY AND THEFT

Loss of chattels from any cause.

Replace footnote 32 with:

[32] *Holmes v Payne* [1930] 2 K.B. 301; *Webster v General Accident Fire and Life Assurance Corp Ltd* [1953] 1 Q.B. 520 at 532. See also *Mobis Parts Australia Pty Ltd v XL Insurance Co SE* [2019] Lloyd's Rep. I.R. 162 at [105], in which the New South Wales Court of Appeal held that to describe the recovery of insured property as "uncertain" is to attribute an equal probability to recovery and non-recovery.   **29-010**

Replace footnote 37 with:

[37] See, in that respect, *Mobis Parts Australia Pty Ltd v XL Insurance Co SE* [2019] Lloyd's Rep. I.R. 88 at [98]–[105]. In *Parkin v Vero Insurance New Zealand Ltd* [2015] NZHC 1675 at [37]–[38], Mander J referred to Lord Atkinson's comments in *Moore v Evans* (at 191) and held that in order to determine whether property has been damaged, the court must ask itself whether it has suffered damage in the ordinary sense of the word, namely "whether the physical state has been altered in a negative way, in which case the item is prima facie damaged".   **29-011**

CHAPTER 30

THIRD PARTY RISKS

1.   LIABILITY INSURANCE GENERALLY

(a)   Accrual of Cause of Action

Legal liability.

Replace footnote 30 with:

30-007   [30] *Tesco Stores Ltd v Constable* [2008] Lloyd's Rep. I.R. 302; *AXA Insurance UK Plc v Thermonex* [2013] Lloyd's Rep. I.R. 323 at [60]–[65]; *MJ Gleeson Group Plc v Axa Corporate Solutions Assurance SA* [2013] Lloyd's Rep. I.R. 677; *Aspen Insurance v Sangster & Annand Ltd* [2019] Lloyd's Rep. I.R. 217.

Liability and global settlements.

Replace footnote 35 with:

30-008   [35] It has been supported, on an obiter basis, in *AIG Europe (Ireland) Ltd v Faraday Capital Ltd* [2007] Lloyd's Rep. I.R. 267; reversed on other grounds [2008] Lloyd's Rep. I.R. 454. See also *AstraZeneca Insurance Co Ltd v XL Insurance* [2013] Lloyd's Rep. I.R. 290 at [90]–[96]; *Cultural Foundation v Beazley Furlonge* [2018] Bus. L.R. 2174 at [217].

(b)   Rights of Third Party Against Insurer

Liability to be established first.

Replace footnote 56 with:

30-014   [56] Companies Act 1989 s.141, amending s.651 of the Companies Act 1985. The application procedure is now governed by s.1030 of the Companies Act 2006. No order can be made by the court if the action would, in any event, be time-barred—s.1030(2) of the Companies Act 2006. But if it is arguable that such action would not be time-barred, or that any primary time-limit might be disapplied, an order should be made: *Re Workvale Ltd* [1992] 1 W.L.R. 416. The power to restore to the register under s.1030 of the Companies Act 2006 now permits an insurer who is liable under the Third Parties (Rights against Insurers) Act 2010 in respect of the liability of a dissolved company for personal injury to restore that company to the register for the purposes of seeking a contribution from third parties: see s.1030(1)(b) (as amended by the Third Parties (Rights Against Insurers) Act 2010 (Consequential Amendment of Companies Act 2006) Regulations 2018 (SI 2018/1162)).

Third party in no better position than the insured.

Replace seventh paragraph with:

There is conflicting first instance authority as to the circumstances in which an **30-020** insurer is entitled to set off of claims for unpaid premiums or defence costs against its liability to a third party under the 1930 Act.[84] By contrast, the 2010 Act regime establishes a specific right to set off.[84a]

[84] In *Murray v Legal & General Assurance Society Ltd* [1970] 2 Q.B. 495, it was held that a third party is not affected by a counterclaim which the insurer has against the insured for premiums, at any rate where the right to set off such sums as are due is not a condition of the policy. The reasoning was that the Act transfers only the particular rights and liabilities "in respect of the liability" incurred to third parties. Rights in connection with premiums are not referable to such liability unless there is an express clause making payment of outstanding premium a condition precedent to payment. Sed quaere. The Act does not speak of a transfer of liabilities, as opposed to rights. The third party is assigned rights subject to any defences which the insurers possess against the insured, and these include, it is submitted, general equitable rights of set-off. *Murray* was not followed in *Cox v Bankside Members Agency Ltd* [1995] 2 Lloyd's Rep. 437 at 451 (at first instance), however in *Denso Manufacturing UK Ltd v Great Lakes Reinsurance (UK) Plc* [2017] EWHC 391 (Comm); [2018] 4 W.L.R. 93, Sara Cockerill QC (sitting as a Deputy High Court Judge) preferred (obiter) *Murray*, accepting the argument that *Cox* was distinguishable on this point as it did not concern set-off of a premium, but of the effect on a third -party of a costs-inclusive excess. These authorities were considered in *Cultural Foundation v Beazley Furlonge Ltd* [2018] Bus. L.R. 2174 at [394]–[408], in which Andrew Henshaw QC (sitting as a Deputy High Court Judge) declined to follow the construction of the 1930 Act adopted in *Murray*, holding that it is consistent with the policy of the 1930 Act for the third party to take the transferred rights subject to any defences, including set-off, which the insurer would have had available to it in respect of the claim. The question of whether equitable set-off was available therefore fell to be addressed by reference to the principles of set-off, rather than under the 1930 Act. Andrew Henshaw QC also distinguished *Murray* and *Denso* on the basis that in both those cases the liability which the insurer sought to set off was covered by the policy excess, whereas in both *Beazley* and *Cox* the right to set-off arose from costs incurred by the insurer outside the scope of the policy (at [407]).

It appears that legal set-off, as a procedural rather than substantive right, falls outside the scope of the statutory transfer via the 1930 Act: see *IEG v Zurich Insurance Plc* [2015] UKSC 33; [2016] A.C. 509 at [89] per Lord Mance JSC; and *Cultural Foundation v Beazley Furlonge* [2018] Bus. L.R. 2174 at [393]–[394].

[84a] Section 10 of the Third Parties (Rights against Insurers) Act 2010; see para.30-037 below.

Settlements.

Replace footnote 95 with:

[95] *Normid Housing Association v Ralphs* [1989] 1 Lloyd's Rep. 265; *Jackson v Greenfield* [1998] **30-023** B.P.I.R. 699 (rights against insurers were assets in an individual voluntary arrangement of the insured, and prior to ascertainment of liability to the claimant third party could be compromised). In *AB v Transform Medical Group (CS) Ltd* [2020] CSOH 3; [2020] P.N.L.R. 20, the Court of Session rejected the submission that a settlement agreement between and insured and its insurer should be set aside on the basis that it constituted an attempt to defraud the pursuer out of rights it would otherwise have been transferred under the 1930 Act. Lord Tyre (at [39]) declined to hold that a settlement could never be challenged on that basis, but held that that would be an "extreme situation".

Claim for declaratory relief.

After "Where the court", add new footnote 103a:

[103a] It has been held that an Employment Tribunal constitutes a court for the purposes of the Third Par- **30-027** ties (Rights Against Insurers) Act 2010, as the contrary conclusion would cut against a purpose of the 2010 Act in promoting a "single forum" for issues of liability as between third parties and the insurers of insolvent insureds to be addressed: see *Watson v Hemingway Design Ltd* [2020] I.C.R. 1063 at [32]– [43] per Kerr J.

Power of Secretary of State to enlarge or remove circumstances resulting in a transfer of rights.

After the fourth paragraph, add new paragraph:

30-033   Section 19(8) provides a general power to make other consequential regulations. One example of a circumstance in which this power has been invoked is to amend the Companies Act 2006 to permit insurers subject to personal injury liability via the statutory transfer of rights under the 2010 Act to restore the company (its insured) to the register in order to seek a contribution from third parties in respect of the liability.[107a]

[107a] Companies Act 2006 s.1030(1)(b), as amended by the Third Parties (Rights Against Insurers) Act 2010 (Consequential Amendment of Companies Act 2006) Regulations 2018 (SI 2018/1162).

(c)   Terms in Liability Policies

Notice to insurers.

Replace footnote 117 with:

30-040   [117] See *HLB Kidsons v Lloyd's Underwriters* [2009] Lloyd's Rep. I.R. 178 for a detailed consideration by the Court of Appeal as to the nature of the test where a clause required notice of circumstances which "may give rise to a loss or claim", which Rix LJ described as "a fairly loose and undemanding test". In *McManus v European Risk Insurance Company* [2013] Lloyd's Rep. I.R. 533, the policy provided cover for "circumstances" that had been first notified to the insurer during the period of the insurance, where "circumstances" meant "an incident, occurrence, fact, matter, act or omission which may give rise to a claim". The insured's solicitors firm sent a "blanket notification" letter to its liability insurers estimating that there were some 5,000 files which might be the subject of claims for negligence, malpractice and breach of contract by reason of suspected endemic failings in a firm whose business and goodwill had been acquired by the claimants and for which the claimants would consequently be liable. The letter did not identify any specific underlying facts or occurrences on any of those files. HHJ Rose QC held that the notification was a sufficient notification. That determination was not challenged on appeal [2014] Lloyd's Rep. I.R. 169 and the Court of Appeal expressed no doubts about its correctness (see [21] in the judgment of Davis LJ). In *Quantum Claims Compensation Specialists Ltd v Wren Insurance Services Ltd* [2012] Lloyd's Rep. I.R. 242, the Inner House of the Court of Session had to consider a clause which required the insured to seek the insurer's consent to any costs incurred "after the Insured and/or their Client becomes aware of any fact or matter which adversely affects the prospect of success in any Legal Action". It was held that "prospects of success" should be given its natural and familiar meaning, which was the likelihood of the claimant establishing liability on the part of the defendant. See also *AXA Insurance UK Plc v Thermonex* [2013] Lloyd's Rep. I.R. 323 at [78].

In *Euro Pools Plc (in administration) v Royal and Sun Alliance Insurance Plc* [2019] EWCA Civ 808, the Court of Appeal (Dame Elizabeth Gloster DBE, with whom Lord Justice Hamblen and Lord Justice Males agreed) summarised (at [39]) the principles relevant to clauses of this type, and endorsed the proposition articulated by HHJ Rose QC in *McManus* that a notification can be valid in relation to later claims arising from the circumstances notified "even though the notification had not even referred to the transaction from which the later claim arose, let alone identified a defect in relation to the handling of that particular client as likely to give rise to a claim by that client". The earlier notification was held to extend to the claims because there was a causal as opposed to "merely coincidental" link between the notified circumstances and the later claim (at [39(v)] and [55]), applying the reasoning in *Kajima UK Engineering Ltd v Underwriter Insurance Co Ltd* [2008] EWHC 83 (TCC); [2008] Lloyd's Rep. I.R. 391.

Lord Justice Males (with whom Hamblen LJ agreed) held (at [94]) that it is entirely appropriate for the insured to notify a problem to insurers when it was not aware of the cause of the problem or its consequences (so called "hornet's nest" notifications):

> "'Circumstances' is a broad term. Sometimes the insured will be able to specify with a high degree of precision what it is that gives rise to the possibility of a Claim. On other occasions, however, it may be able to do little more than to point to the fact that something is not working for a reason which has yet to be ascertained – sometimes referred to as a 'can of worms' or 'hornet's nest' notification. Provided that this is something which might reasonably be expected to produce a Claim by a customer for which the insurer may (not necessarily will, but may) be liable under the policy, there is no reason in principle why a notification should not be in these terms. The insured does not need to appreciate the cause of the problem or the consequences that may result."

For a recent summary of the relevant authorities, see *Cultural Foundation v Beazley Furlonge* [2018] Bus. L.R. 2174 at [154]–[163] (holding at [154] that the insured must have been aware of the matters in question at the time of the notification).

After the second paragraph, add new paragraph:

The question of whether, absent wording to the contrary, an insured can notify claims to two different policy periods and elect which is to provide cover, is unresolved in England and Wales.[123a]

[123a] The statement of Lord Mance JSC in *IEG v Zurich Insurance Plc* [2016] A.C. 509 at [43] that "[i]t is contrary to principle for insurance to operate on a basis which allows an insured to select the period and policy to which a loss attaches" might be said to support the argument that such a course is not permissible, even in the absence of an express prohibition in the policy. However, in *Cultural Foundation v Beazley Furlonge* [2018] Bus. L.R. 2174 at [168]–[170], Andrew Henshaw QC held (obiter), following the reasoning of the Supreme Court of South Africa in *Immerzeel v Santam Ltd* [2007] Lloyd's Rep. I.R. 106, that it is open to an insured in such circumstances to "renotify" circumstances to a subsequent policy period.

Whether prejudice to insurers required.

Replace first paragraph with:

In *Barrett Bros Taxis (Ltd) v Davies*,[124] an insured was required to forward to his **30-041** motor insurers any legal process received with regard to an accident, but failed to do so. The Court of Appeal held that the insurers waived that non-compliance in subsequent correspondence, and that the insurers had received the requisite information from the police. Lord Denning MR went on to say[125] that in any event the insurers could not rely on breach of the policy condition to defeat his claim unless they were prejudiced by it. Since they had been told of the intended prosecution by the police, there was no prejudice. These remarks have been interpreted subsequently as obiter dicta which ought not to be followed.[126] Where it is a condition precedent that insurers are to be provided with information within a reasonable time, there is no governing principle that the condition is only breached if insurers can show prejudice resulting from delay.[127]

[124] *Barrett Bros Taxis (Ltd) v Davies* [1966] 1 W.L.R. 1334.

[125] *Barrett Bros Taxis (Ltd) v Davies* [1966] 1 W.L.R. 1334 at 1340. Danckwerts LJ agreed generally with Lord Denning's judgment. Salmon LJ agreed only on the ground of waiver.

[126] *Farrell v Federated Employers' Insurance Association Ltd* [1970] 1 W.L.R. 498; [1970] 2 Lloyd's Rep. 170 (the report at [1970] 1 W.L.R. 1400 reports the constitution of the court inaccurately); *The Vainqueur Jose* [1979] 1 Lloyd's Rep. 557 (where Mocatta J did not reject the obiter dicta, but strained to find prejudice); *Pioneer Concrete (UK) Ltd v National Employers' Mutual General Insurance Association* [1985] 1 Lloyd's Rep. 274 at 281; *Motor and General Insurance Co v Pavey* [1994] 1 W.L.R. 462 at 469, in which the insurers were told by a third party what the insured should have told them; *Total Graphics Ltd v AGF Insurance Co Ltd* [1997] 1 Lloyd's Rep. 599. Cf. *CNA International Reinsurance Co Ltd v Companhia de Seguros Tranquilidade SA* [1999] Lloyd's Rep. I.R. 289, where it was not necessary for the court to decide the point, and *HLB Kidsons v Lloyd's Underwriters* [2009] Lloyd's Rep. I.R. 237, where the court rejected an argument that a contract term was intended to introduce a requirement of prejudice. See also para.21-045, above. In *Bass Brewers v Independent Insurance Co* 2002 S.L.T. 512, it was held that where one co-insured told the insurers of damage to insured property, but the other did not, the latter was in breach of a condition precedent, and lost his claim. This result is difficult to reconcile with the proposition to be derived from *Barrett Bros Taxis* (above), that the insurers cannot rely on a failure to notify where they have received the requisite information from a source other than the insured. See further *AXA Insurance UK Plc v Thermonex* [2013] Lloyd's Rep. I.R. 323 at [77]–[78], where HHJ Simon Brown QC distinguished *Barrett Bros Taxis (Ltd)* on the basis that the clause in question required *the insured* to give notice, rather than merely that notice be received from someone. See also the discussion in *Astor Management AG (formerly MRI Holdings AG) v Atalaya Mining Plc (formerly Emed Mining Public Ltd)* [2018] EWCA Civ 2407; [2019] Bus. L.R. 106 at [24]–[28].

[127] *Shinedean Ltd v Alldown Demolition Ltd* [2006] Lloyd's Rep. I.R. 846. It is possible that as a matter of construction the condition precedent may, in light of certain circumstances, cease to apply or no longer have effect—see *Astor Management AG (formerly MRI Holdings AG) v Atalaya Mining plc (formerly Emed Mining Public Ltd)* [2019] Bus. L.R. 106 at [33] per Simon LJ and Dame Elizabeth

Gloster (with whom Macur LJ agreed). It is submitted that a notification condition precedent is unlikely to be construed in this way, save in rare circumstances.

Conduct of proceedings.

Replace footnote 151 with:

30-050 [151] *Groom v Crocker* [1939] 1 K.B. 194 at 203 per Lord Greene MR. A bona fide settlement by the insurer, where he has a right to conduct the defence and settle claims, will bind the insured even if he has to pay part of the damages awarded himself (e.g. the first £5): *Beacon Insurance Co v Langdale* [1934] 4 All E.R. 204. It appears that, when the insurer takes over conduct of the insured's defence, each party comes under an obligation, as a matter of contractual implication, to act in good faith with due regard to the interests of the other: *K/S Merc-Scandia XXXXII v Lloyd's Underwriters* [2001] 2 Lloyd's Rep. 563 at 572 and 574. Generally the interest of insurer and insured will coincide. However, there is potential for conflict (e.g. if the limit of cover is likely to be exceeded). In this event, the insurer should pay regard to the separate interest of the insured, as well the insurer's own interest: *Cormack v Washbourne* [2000] Lloyd's Rep. P.N. 459 at 466 (CA). Cf. *Distillers Co Biochemical (Australia) v Ajax Insurance* (1974) 48 A.L.J.R. 136 (High Court of Australia). Similar considerations arise under claims co-operation clauses in reinsurance: *Gan v Tai Ping* [2001] Lloyd's Rep. I.R. 667 (CA). See also *Ramsook v Crossley* [2018] UKPC 9 at [27]: "A [claims control] clause ... is not carte blanche to insurers to conduct proceedings in their own interests, without regard to reality or to the insured's account of events ...".

Senior Courts Act 1981 s.51(1).

30-056 *After "In certain", delete "exceptional".*

Replace second paragraph with:

30-057 The features which should normally be present for costs to be awarded against a liability insurer have been held by the Court of Appeal[171] to be as follows:

(1) the insurers determined that the claim would be defended;
(2) the insurers funded the defence;
(3) the insurers had the conduct or control of the litigation;
(4) the insurers fought the claim exclusively to defend their own interests; and
(5) the defence failed in its entirety.

[171] *Murphy v Young & Co's Brewery Plc* [1997] 1 W.L.R. 1591; *TGA Chapman Ltd v Christopher* [1998] 1 W.L.R. 12. In *Cormack v Washbourne* [2000] Lloyd's Rep. P.N. 459 the Court of Appeal treated an insurer's overriding self-interest as being a key constituent of the relevant exceptional circumstances. In *Worsley v Tambrands Ltd* [2002] Lloyd's Rep. I.R. 382, an unusual decision by legal expenses insurers to increase the insured limit of indemnity to allow a claim to proceed was held not to be motivated overridingly by self-interest, and thus not to give rise to liability under s.51(1).

Replace fourth paragraph with:

The other features are primary material factors which will generally be determinative. The discretion should only be exercised where the circumstances are sufficiently exceptional.[175] However, these features should not be regarded as a series of conditions that must be fulfilled before an order for costs can be made. In a non-insurance context, it has been held that the discretion is a broad one, and the only immutable principle is that it must be exercised justly.[176] Each of these principles (including the requirement of exceptionality) must now be read subject to the Supreme Court's judgment in *Travelers v XYZ* (considered at para.30-057A below).

[175] *Cormack v Washbourne* [2000] Lloyd's Rep. P.N. 459, where the Court of Appeal rejected a test based merely upon considerations of broad fairness. The applicable principles were comprehensively reviewed in *Herridge v Parker* [2014] Lloyd's Rep. I.R. 177 (Cardiff County Court) by Recorder James Thom QC, which is the first reported decision on an application under s.51 against insurers in the context of "after the event" (ATE) insurance for litigation (see further at para.33-046 below). Thom QC reviewed the extensive case law beginning with *Aiden Shipping* (above) and distinguished between various classes of case as regards the circumstances in which a third party who has in some way funded or assisted a claim may be held liable for the successful defendant's costs. In the case of a liability insurer, he held

(at para.[87(2)]): "where cover is unlimited, or the claim and costs do not exceed the limit of cover, the successful party's costs will form part of the claim. Where cover is limited, an order can be made against the insurers, even if this causes them to pay out more than the policy limit, if they are the or at least a 'real party' to the proceedings, having regard to the motivation for and conduct of the proceedings", citing as authority the cases of *Chapman*, *Citibank* and *Cormack* (citations given in fnn.168–169). He further held that those under a contractual liability to indemnify the unsuccessful party against the successful party's entitlement to costs—which would include liability insurers generally and an ATE insurer—could be subjected to a s.51 non-party costs order as a convenient way of enforcing their contractual liability (para.[87(5)]), whilst (without more) s.51 could not be invoked if in fact there was no contractual liability, e.g. if the insurer validly exercised a right to avoid the policy. Thom QC went on to hold that an ATE insurer does not, merely by acting as such, expose itself to a s.51 order on any wider basis than as a convenient way of enforcing the indemnity in favour of the insured, if and to the extent that the insured is entitled to be indemnified. On the facts of Herridge itself, the insurers had validly avoided the policy for fraud and Thom QC was not persuaded that any sufficient grounds existed for making a s.51 order which would in practice have amounted to the same thing as ordering the insured to pay out under the policy when no liability to pay existed (para.[93]).

[176] *Deutsche Bank AG v Sebastian Holdings Inc* [2016] EWCA Civ 23; [2016] 4 W.L.R. 17 at [62].

Replace fifth paragraph with:

In light of the Supreme Court's judgment in *Travelers v XYZ*, the approach to the question of what type of conduct justifies the imposition of a non-party costs order is context-specific and, in the case of liability insurers, will take into account the nature of their role in litigation (see further, para.30-057A below). In *TGA Chapman Ltd v Christopher*,[178] Phillips LJ commented: "It must be rare for litigation to be funded, controlled and directed by a third party motivated entirely by its own interests." He explained that the basis for rejecting the argument that a limit in the policy should be respected was not that the policy was being re-written, but that a liability was being imposed on underwriters independent of the policy. The requirement that insurers have conduct of the proceedings is likely to involve an analysis of the nature of the instructions given to the solicitors retained to defend the claim. The insurers may have overall control and conduct of the matter notwithstanding the fact that the insured provides information and assistance to solicitors.[179]

[178] *TGA Chapman Ltd v Christopher* [1998] 1 W.L.R. 12 at 20.

[179] *Citibank NA v Excess Insurance Co Ltd* [1999] Lloyd's Rep. I.R. 122; *Monkton Court Ltd v Perry Prowse (Insurance Services) Ltd* [2001] 1 All E.R. (Comm) 566. In *Citibank*, at 136, Thomas J suggested that the terms of any joint retainer of solicitors should be clearly spelt out, and that insurers and insured should set out their involvement in decision-making in written form.

Replace footnote 180 with:

[180] See for example, apart from authorities mentioned above, *Tharros Shipping Co Ltd v Bias Shipping A.G.* [1997] 1 Lloyd's Rep. 246; *Pendennis Shipyard v Magrathea* [1998] 1 Lloyd's Rep. 315; *Citibank NA v Excess Insurance Co Ltd* [1999] Lloyd's Rep. I.R. 122 (application allowed in part—order made for period after judgment on liability, as the circumstances then became exceptional); *Gloucestershire Health Authority v MA Torpy and Partners Ltd* [1999] Lloyd's Rep. I.R. 203 (application refused—no exceptional features); *Monkton Court Ltd v Perry Prowse (Insurance Services) Ltd* [2000] 1 All E.R. (Comm) 566 (application granted—claim was fought almost exclusively to defend the insurer's interests); *Worsley v Tambrands* [2002] Lloyd's Rep. I.R. 382 (application refused); *Palmer v Palmer* [2008] Lloyd's Rep. I.R. 535 (application allowed); *XYZ v Travelers Insurance Company Ltd* [2017] EWHC 287 (QB) (application allowed where insurer had conduct of uninsured claims and insurance position not disclosed to claimants) (affirmed *XYZ v Travelers Insurance Company Ltd* [2018] Lloyd's Rep. I.R. 636). For a recent case in which an award of costs under s.51 against an insurer was upheld on appeal, see *Legg v Sterte Garage Ltd* [2016] EWCA Civ 97; [2016] 2 Costs L.O. 167. Following *Palmer v Palmer*, David Richards LJ held that there was ample material from which the judge could decide against insurers on the "critical issue" of whether they were acting exclusively or predominantly in their own interests in defending the claims ([51]–[52]).

After para.30-057, add new paragraph:

In *Travelers v XYZ*,[181a] the Supreme Court considered the principles applicable **30-057A** to non-party costs orders under s.51, in the specific context of liability insurers. That case arose in circumstances where the insurer bore the defence costs of 623 claims in group litigation arising out of defective breast implants, however the insured comprised only 197 of the claimants for whom the insurer bore costs. At first instance, Thirwall LJ (sitting as a High Court Judge) acceded to an application for non-party costs pursuant to s.51, holding that it was not necessary for the applicants to establish that the insurers controlled the litigation, and that an order was justified taking into account the insurers' influence on the litigation (including, in particular, the fact that if it had been disclosed earlier that some of the claims were uninsured, that would have led to those claims not being pursued).

[181a] *Travelers v XYZ* [2019] 1 W.L.R 6075.

On appeal to the Court of Appeal, Lewison LJ (with whom Patten LJ agreed), rejected the submission that in an insurance context the discretion is guided by established principles such that it can only be exercised against a liability insurer who funds an unsuccessful defence where that insurer: (a) controlled the litigation in its own interest; and (b) did not pay appropriate regard to any inconsistent or contrary interest of the insured, with the result that the insurer could properly be regarded as the real party [7]–[9]; [30]. In rejecting this submission, Lewison LJ considered the authorities and held that the only one which might arguably support the imposition of a series of conditions before a non-party costs order could be made on this context was *Citibank NA v Excess Insurance Co Ltd*[181b] but to the extent it did it was wrong and should not be followed (at [30]). In upholding the decision to order the insurer to pay the costs of the uninsured claims, Lewison LJ placed particular importance on the "principle of reciprocity", namely that if a person stands to benefit from and funds legal proceedings, justice requires that if they fail he should pay the successful party's costs ([32]). The fact that had the insurer succeeded it would have recovered, via its insured, its own costs of defending the uninsured claims made it just that it should also bear the burden of failure.

[181b] *Citibank NA v Excess Insurance Co Ltd* [1999] Lloyd's Rep. I.R. 122.

Lord Briggs (with whom Lady Black and Lord Kitchin JJSC agreed) gave the leading judgment in the Supreme Court, allowing the appeal. Rather than review the principles applicable to the exercise of the discretion under s.51 generally, Lord Briggs focused on the specific context of applications for non-party costs orders against liability insurers (at [30]). At [31], Lord Briggs described the distinct position of liability insurers as follows:

> "Liability insurance serves an obvious public interest. It protects those incurring liability from financial ruin. More importantly, it serves to minimise the risk that persons injured by the insured will go uncompensated as a result of the insured's lack of means. Unlike ATE insurance it is not primarily aimed at making a profit by assisting in the funding of litigation but, where liability becomes the subject of litigation, the insurance typically contains provision under which the insurer is obliged to fund the insured's defence and, as an inevitable concomitant, entitled to exercise substantial (although not always complete) control over the conduct of its insured's defence. The liability insurer is therefore typically an involuntary rather than voluntary funder of litigation, and the control which the insurer habitually exercises over the conduct of its insured's defence arises from a pre-existing contractual entitlement, rather than from a freely-made decision to intermeddle."

In his analysis, Lord Briggs (at [51]) deprecated the notion that a loose concept of exceptionality was sufficient to guide the circumstances in which liability insurers should be liable to pay non-party costs, and held (at [52]), that the two bases of liability identified in *Chapman v Christopher*,[181c] namely where the insurer: (1) "intermeddles"; or (2) becomes the "real defendant", represents a principled approach to the engagement of the jurisdiction as against liability insurers. Where the claim falls within the scope of cover, the real defendant test will normally be appropriate, whereas were one is dealing with an uninsured claim (as was the case in *Travelers v XYZ*), it is the intermeddling principle that applies. In this latter context, the question of whether the insurer's involvement was consistent with, rather than beyond, its contractual obligations, is likely to be decisive (at [55]).

[181c] *TGA Chapman Ltd v Christopher* [1998] 1 W.L.R. 12.

Lord Briggs concluded by summarising his analysis in seven propositions (at [76]–[82]):

1) The underlying question of whether the non-party has either become the real defendant in relation to an insured claim, or has intermeddled in an uninsured claim, is fundamental to the exercise of the discretion in insurance cases.

2) The *Chapman* principles are useful guidelines for establishing whether the liability insurer has become the real defendant, in a case where some part of the claim lies outside the scope of cover.

3) The *Chapman* principles are unlikely to be of assistance where the question is whether the insurers crossed the line in becoming involved in the funding or defence of wholly uninsured claims, as opposed to claims where there is limited cover. In those cases, the insurer may cross the line by conduct that falls short of total control of the litigation, where it intermeddles in the uninsured claim in a manner it cannot justify.

4) Where there is a connection between insured and uninsured claims, however, the legitimate interests of the insurer might justify some involvement in decision-making and even funding the costs of the uninsured claims, without exposing the insurer to liability for costs.

5) The existence of a causative link between the conduct of the non-party and the incurring of the costs sought to be recovered is an important element of the analysis under s.51. If the costs would have been incurred in any event, it is unlikely that an order under s.51 will be made.

6) The non-disclosure of the limits of cover by the defendant at the request of the insurer is unlikely to amount to relevant conduct, insofar as the non-disclosure is legitimate under the general law.

7) Asymmetry or lack of reciprocity in costs risk as between the uninsured claimant and the defendant's insurer is unlikely on its own to be a reason for the making of a non-party costs order against the insurer where the asymmetry arises because a claimant sues an uninsured and insolvent defendant and incurs several-only costs liability in group litigation.

Liability for costs.

Replace footnote 184 with:

30-058

[184] *Cox v Bankside Members Agency* [1995] 2 Lloyd's Rep. 437 at 460–463; *Cultural Foundation v Beazley Furlonge* [2018] Bus. L.R. 2174 at [338]–[390]. But see *TGA Chapman Ltd v Christopher* [1998] 1 W.L.R. 12.

Recklessness required to avoid liability.

Replace footnote 219 with:

30-072

[219] *Fraser v B.N. Furman (Productions) Ltd* [1967] 1 W.L.R. 898. This principle has been followed in Australia in a number of cases: see, for example, *Barrie Toepfer Earthmoving and Land Management*

Pty Ltd v CGU Insurance Ltd [2016] NSWCA 67, and the authorities cited at [108] of *Manitowoq Platinum Pty Ltd v WFI Insurance Ltd* [2017] WADC 32 (reversed on appeal: [2018] WASCA 89).

2. PROFESSIONAL INDEMNITY POLICIES

Duty to disclose negligence and circumstances likely to give rise to a claim.

Replace footnote 309 with:

30-104   309 *Kajima UK Engineering v Underwriter Insurance Co* [2008] Lloyd's Rep. I.R. 391, considering a similar though not identical clause to that in *HLB Kidsons v Lloyd's Underwriters* [2008] 1 All E.R. (Comm) 769. See also *Euro Pools Plc (In Administration) v Royal and Sun Alliance Insurance Plc* [2019] EWCA Civ 808, in which (allowing the appeal) the Court of Appeal held that the requisite causal link was satisfied on the judge's findings of fact (see the summary of the relevant principles from *HLB Kidsons* [2008] Lloyd's Rep. I.R. 237; and *Kajima* [2008] Lloyd's Rep. I.R. 391 at [39]); see also *Cultural Foundation v Beazley Furlonge* [2018] Bus. L.R. 2174 at [153]–[170].

Replace footnote 312 with:

30-106   312 For a recent case where a similar approach was adopted, see *McManus v European Risk Insurance Company* [2013] Lloyd's Rep. I.R. 533 upheld on appeal (where the first instance decision on the notification point was not challenged) at [2014] Lloyd's Rep. I.R. 169. For a recent brokers' negligence case concerning a failure to provide a "block notification" of potential claims within the policy period see *Ocean Finance & Mortgages Ltd v Oval Insurance Broking Ltd* [2016] EWHC 160 (Comm); [2016] Lloyd's Rep. I.R. 319. See also *Euro Pools Plc (In Administration) v Royal and Sun Alliance Insurance Plc* [2019] EWCA Civ 808 (the insured was entitled to rely on a "can of worms" or "hornet's nest" notification made in an earlier policy year in circumstances where it was aware of the problem but not of the cause of the problem or the consequences that may result).

3. EMPLOYERS' LIABILITY POLICIES

Compulsion to insure.

Replace footnote 322 with:

30-110   322 Employers' Liability (Compulsory Insurance) Act 1969 s.1(1). In *BAI (Run-Off) Ltd v Durham* [2012] Lloyd's Rep. I.R. 371 on appeal from *Employers Liability Policy Trigger Litigation* [2011] Lloyd's Rep. I.R. 1 CA, on appeal from Burton J in *Durham v BAI (Run-Off) Ltd* [2009] Lloyd's Rep. I.R. 295, the Supreme Court held (reversing both Burton J and a majority of the Court of Appeal, and upholding the dissenting judgment of Rix LJ on this point) that s.1(1) of the 1969 Act requires an employer to insure against liability for disease that is *caused* during the policy period, even if the disease only manifests itself at a later time. The *BAI* case concerned whether the insurance policies in question responded to claims in respect of the relevant employers' liability for mesothelioma. The principal issue turned on the construction of various policy wordings, some of which provided cover for injury or disease "sustained" during the policy period, and some for injury or disease "caused" during the policy period. Burton J had held that the commercial purpose of employers' liability insurance required that expressions such as "injury *sustained*" in the policy period be given the same meaning as "injury *caused*". A majority of the Court of Appeal (Rix and Stanley Burnton LJJ, Smith LJ dissenting) rejected that purposive construction, holding that under "injury *sustained*" wording liability is triggered only upon the actual onset of the disease, and not by the tortious exposure to asbestos fibres causative of the eventual disease. Rix LJ had considered that despite the commercial purpose being to insure the employer against liability which its activities as an employer engendered during the policy period ([219]), in the context of standard wordings renewed year after year and where other tariff wordings were available it was extremely difficult to conclude that anything had gone wrong with the language, and the more natural or literal interpretation of "sustained" as referring to the later manifestation of the disease was not absurd or meaningless ([234]–[235]). Lord Mance, with whom the other members of the Supreme Court agreed, held (at [26]) that in light of the Supreme Court's recent decision in *Rainy Sky SA v Kookmin Bank* [2011] UKSC 50; [2012] 1 Lloyd's Rep. 34, the approach of the majority in the Court of Appeal gave too little weight to the implications of the rival interpretations and to the principle that "where a term of a contract is open to more than one interpretation, it is generally appropriate to adopt the interpretation which is most consistent with business common sense". The Supreme Court's ruling on this point removes what would otherwise have been a lacuna in the protection to employees: since the actual onset of mesothelioma usually occurs many years after an employee has been exposed to asbestos fibres, it is likely that persons developing mesothelioma as a result of negligent exposure to asbestos fibres in the course of their employment will no longer be employed by the employer responsible at the time of the actual onset of the disease, such that on the approach taken by the majority in the Court of Appeal, the liability of the employer who caused the exposure to asbestos would not be covered by insurance if that employer had later ceased carrying on business in the UK or indeed had switched to a policy with "causation" wording. In those circumstances, the negligent former employer of such a person (if still existing) would be without cover for its liability to the former employee; and if the former employer were insolvent, the victim of the tort would have had no claim under the Third Parties (Rights Against Insurers) Act 1930 (or under the 2010 Act where it applies, as to which see paras 30-024 and following, above). For an illuminating discussion of *BAI (Run-Off) Ltd v Durham* in particular on the question of what will suffice to satisfy the "causal requirement" for a liability insurer of an employer to be liable to indemnify the insured, see *International Energy Group Ltd v Zurich Insurance Plc UK* [2013] EWCA Civ 39; [2013] Lloyd's Rep. I.R. 379.

The present position in relation to liability insurers in respect of mesothelioma claims was summarised in *Equitas Insurance Ltd v Municipal Insurance Ltd* [2019] EWCA Civ 718 (a case concerning the implications of the special rules for causation applicable in such claims to the allocation of losses under reinsurance contracts) by Mance LJ at [5]:

"The position which the law has reached so far is that any employer who has exposed a victim to asbestos in breach of duty, for however short a period, is liable in full to a victim of mesothelioma, while any EL [employers' liability] insurer of such an employer is liable in full to indemnity the employer, again regardless of the period for which it has provided insurance and received premium. Provided, therefore, that there is at least one solvent employer or solvent EL insurer who can be identified as having provided cover at some time during the period of wrongful exposure, the victim will have a remedy against a defendant who is good for the money."

In that case, considered further at Ch.35 below, the Court of Appeal (Mance LJ, Leggatt LJ and Patten LJ) held that the practice of "spiking", whereby a liability insurer, relying on the special rules of causation applicable to mesothelioma claims, sought to allocate its losses in claims under a reinsurance contract to particular policy years so as to maximise recovery from reinsurers, was a breach of an implied restriction on the exercise of a contractual discretion (at [114]–[116] per Mance LJ, with whom Legatt LJ and Patten LJ agreed, and at [162] per Leggatt LJ, with whom Patten LJ agreed).

CHAPTER 31

MOTOR VEHICLE INSURANCE

1. RISKS COVERED

Compulsory cover against third-party risks.

Replace footnote 13 with:

31-002 [13] "Motor vehicle" is defined by s.185(1) as "a mechanically propelled vehicle intended or adapted for use on roads". A vehicle without its propulsive unit may be within the section if there is reasonable prospect of it being made mobile again (*Newberry v Simmonds* [1961] 2 Q.B. 345; *Law v Thomas* (1964) 108 S.J. 158) but not otherwise: *Lawrence v Howlett* [1952] 2 All E.R. 74; *Smart v Allan* [1963] 1 Q.B. 291. A fortiori, a vehicle with its propulsive unit but otherwise propelled is inside the section: *Floyd v Bush* [1953] 1 W.L.R. 242. A vehicle is "intended" for use on the road if that was reasonably to be contemplated as one of its uses. It is "adapted" to that end if fit and apt for road use: *Burns v Currell* [1963] 2 Q.B. 433 at 441. A farm tractor has come within the section (*Woodward v James Young* 1958, S.C. (J) 28), while dumper trucks, a go-kart and a Ford Anglia prepared for racing were not (*Daley v Hargreaves* [1961] 1 W.L.R. 487; *Burns v Currell*, above; *Brown v Abbott* (1965) 109 S.J. 437), nor was a motor cycle adapted for "scrambling": *Chief Constable of Avon and Somerset v Fleming* [1987] 1 All E.R. 318; however, a dumper truck stolen from a quarry and driven on a road was: *Lewington v MIB* [2017] EWHC 2848 (Comm) at [72]–[73]. A pedestrian-controlled motor mower is not a motor vehicle: see s.189. The position in relation to automated and electronic vehicles is considered at para.31-006A below.

Essentials of valid policy.

Replace (i) of the list with:

31-005 (i) against liability[44] in respect of death or bodily injury to any person or damage to property caused by, or arising out of,[45] the use[46] of the vehicle[47] on a road or other public place[48] in Great Britain[49]; "person" includes any passenger,[50] but not the driver[51]; "arising out of the use of the vehicle" does not cover the situation where a vehicle stops to pick up a passenger who is injured when crossing the road to reach the vehicle[52];

[44] Including liability to a husband for the loss of the society and services of his wife: *Ladd v Jones* [1975] R.T.R. 67.

[45] The case law bearing on what meaning should be given to the words "arising out of" in s.145(3)(a) was reviewed in detail by Silber J in *AXN v Worboys* [2013] Lloyd's Rep. I.R. 207. Silber J held that in

light of both English and Australian authority, "arising out of" in this context should be interpreted as wider than a test of proximate causation, having regard to all material circumstances, and in particular bearing in mind that the purpose of the user of the motor vehicle is relevant and that where injury has occurred the focus is on whether the injury was a matter arising out of the way the vehicle was being used at the time when the injury was sustained (see [58]). In *R&S Pilling (t/a Phoenix Engineering) v UK Insurance Ltd* [2019] UKSC 16; [2019] 2 W.L.R. 1015, the Supreme Court (per Lord Hodge JSC, with whom Baroness Hale of Richmond PSC, Lord Wilson, Lady Arden and Lord Kitchin JJSC agreed) held that liability caused by a fire arising from repairs conducted on a vehicle in a warehouse for the purposes of enabling it to pass its MOT did not constitute liability "caused by or arising out of the use of the vehicle on a road or other public place" as the causal link was too remote. The Supreme Court (at [42]–[43]) approved the analysis (of the equivalent provision in the Road Traffic Act 1930) in *Romford Ice and Cold Storage Co Ltd v Lister* [1956] 2 Q.B. 180, in which the Court of Appeal had held that an accident in a yard of a slaughterhouse did not arise out of the use of the vehicle on the road. Lord Hodge summarised the requirements of s.145(3) as follows (at [45]):

> "In summary, section 145(3) must be interpreted as mandating third party motor insurance against liability in respect of death or bodily injury of a person or damage to property which is caused by or arises out of the use of the vehicle on a road or public place, including where he or she parks an immobilized vehicle in such a place (as the English case law required), and the relevant damage has to have arisen out of that use."

See also *Carroll v Taylor* [2020] EWHC 153 (QB) (injuries suffered by drunk passenger after disembarking from taxi did not arise out of use on a road or public place).

[46] See further para 31-006 below. The CJEU has held that the "use" of a vehicle is an autonomous Community law concept for the purposes of art.3(1) of the First Directive, now art.3(1) of the Consolidated Directive 2009/103/EC: see *Vnuk v Zavarovalnica Triglav DD* (C-162/13) EU:C:2014:2146; [2015] Lloyd's Rep. I.R. 142 at [41]–[42], and should be interpreted to include any use that is consistent with the normal function of the vehicle: see [56]. However, permitting the use of a vehicle is not "use" of the vehicle for the purposes of s.145(3)(a)—see *Sahin v Havard* [2016] EWCA Civ 1202 at [20].

[47] "Vehicle" is defined by s.185(1); see the fourth footnote to para.31-002 above.

[48] See the fifth footnote to para.31-002 above. Following the CJEU's judgment in *Vnuk v Zavarovalnica Triglav DD* (C-162/13) [2015] Lloyd's Rep. I.R. 142 (see para.31-006 below) it is now beyond doubt that the limitation on the scope of the compulsory insurance regime to the use of vehicles "on a road or in other public place" is incompatible with the Consolidated Directive: see *R&S Pilling (t/a Phoenix Engineering) v UK Insurance Ltd* [2019] 2 W.L.R. 1015 at [40] (considered at the third footnote to para.31-006 below); *Motor Insurers Bureau v Lewis* [2019] EWCA Civ 909 at [63]; see also *RoadPeace v Secretary of State for Transport* [2018] 1 W.L.R. 1293 at [6]. This reflects recent CJEU authority— see *Nunes Torreiro v AIG Europe Ltd* (C-334/16) EU:C:2017:1007; [2018] Lloyd's Rep. I.R. 418 (concept of "use" not limited to use on a road); *Fundo de Garantia Automovel v Juliana* (C-80/17) EU:C:2018:661; [2018] 1 W.L.R. 5798 at [56]–[57] (compulsory insurance required where car parked on private property for long period of time and owner did not intend to drive it).

[49] Section 145(3)(a).

[50] Unless they are covered by an effective employer's liability policy as described below. It does not matter that the vehicle is not designed to carry passengers: *Farrell v Motor Insurers Bureau of Ireland* (C-356/05) [2007] Lloyd's Rep. I.R. 525, where the European Court of Justice so held, construing art.1 of the Third Motor Insurance Directive (90/232/EEC).

[51] *R. v Secretary of State for Transport, Ex p. National Insurance Guarantee Corp Plc, The Times,* 3 June 1996. However, it does include the owner of the vehicle, who is treated as a third party for these purposes when struck by his own car being driven by a thief—*Delgado Mendes v Credit Agricola Seguros-Companhia de Seguros de Ramos Reais SA* (C-503/16) EU:C:2017:68; [2018] Lloyd's Rep. I.R. 16.

[52] *Slater v Buckinghamshire County Council* [2004] Lloyd's Rep. I.R. 432; compare *Dunthorne v Bentley* [1999] Lloyd's Rep. I.R. 560 (driver leaving vehicle parked when ran out of fuel and crossing the road to get help); see also *Wastell v Woodward (Deceased)* [2017] Lloyd's Rep. I.R. 474 (use of a van parked in a layby as a hamburger van was "use of the vehicle on the road").

After the final paragraph, add new paragraph:

Where a policy contains a certificate confirming compliance with the requirements of the RTA, but the policy wording itself appears to provide cover on a narrower basis, the court may construe the cover under the policy as extending to meet the compulsory insurance requirements of s.145(3).[68a]

[68a] This was the result in *R&S Pilling (t/a as Phoenix Engineering) v UK Insurance Ltd* [2019] 2 W.L.R. 1015. However, the Supreme Court declined to construe the clause on a broader basis (as the Court of

Appeal had done), such that it would be compliant with the requirements of EU law under the Consolidated Directive (at [49]; [52]).

Replace third paragraph with:

31-006   The case law on the meaning of "use" in light of the CJEU's judgment in *Vnuk* is still developing, however, the overall trend has been towards broadening the circumstances in which compulsory insurance is required.[71] It is in any case clear that the restriction of the UK compulsory insurance regime to use of a vehicle "on a road or other public place" in s.145 cannot stand.[72]

[71] The CJEU has considered the meaning of "use of a vehicle" for the purposes of the compulsory insurance requirement in a number of recent cases, applying the *Vnuk* test. That test was held to be satisfied in the following cases: *BTA Baltic Insurance Co AS v Baltijas Apdrosinasanas Nams AS* EU:C:2018:917; [2019] 4 W.L.R. 48 at [34]–[37]; [48] (the act of opening a door by a passenger while the car was stationary constituted "use"); *Fundo de Garantia Automovel v Juliana* (C-80/17) [2018] 1 W.L.R. 5798 at [42] (a vehicle capable of being driven but parked on private land without an intention by the owner to drive it required compulsory insurance); *Linea Directa Aseguradora, SA v Segurcaixa, Sociedad Anónima de Seguros y Reaseguros* (C-100/18) EU:C:2019:51 at [42]–[44] (compulsory insurance required to cover risks eventuating from vehicle parked in private garage between two journeys). However, in in *Rodrigues de Andrade v Salvador* (C-514/16) EU:C:2017:908; [2018] 4 W.L.R. 75, the CJEU held that the stationary use of a tractor with its engine running for the purposes of spraying herbicide was not "use" within the meaning of the *Vnuk* test. The reasoning of Bryan J in *Lewington v MIB* [2017] EWHC 2848 (Comm) goes some way to reconciling these different results. In *Lewington*, the issue was whether a stolen dumper truck being driven on the road was "use" for the purposes of a claim against the MIB. Bryan J held (at [53]) that the distinction in *Vnuk* was between matters which relate to the "normal use of a vehicle" and "the vehicle being used in a way where it is not being used as a vehicle as such". The example given, of climbing on a tractor so that it is being used as a ladder rather than as a vehicle, is consistent with the result in *Rodrigues de Andrade*.

[72] This has been accepted by the UK Government: see *RoadPeace v Secretary of State for Transport* [2018] 1 W.L.R. 1293 at [6]. See further the authorities at the seventh footnote to para.31-005 above.

After para.31-006, add new paragraph:

31-006A Automated and electric vehicles.   On 19 July 2018, the Automated and Electric Vehicles Act 2018 (AEVA 2018) received Royal Assent. At the time of writing, it has not yet entered into force. The purpose of the AEVA 2018 is to make provision for the liability of insurers in respect of accidents caused by automated vehicles, as well as the insurer's right to recover against third parties in respect of any such liability. Section 2(1) provides that where an accident is caused by an automated vehicle when driving itself on a "road or other public place"[73a] in Great Britain, the vehicle is insured at the time of the accident, and the insured or any other person suffers damage as a result, then the insurer is liable for that damage. In this context, "caused" includes accidents that are partly caused by the automated vehicle.[73b] Pursuant to s.2(2), if an automated vehicle is uninsured and none of the exceptions to the compulsory insurance requirements of s.143 apply, then the owner is liable for the damage. Any liability caused by or arising out of any one accident involving an automated vehicle is subject to the limit in s.145(4)(b), which at the time of writing is £1.2 million.[73c] Save in the circumstances set out in s.4 (which preserves the insurer's right to exclude or limit liability in respect of accidents arising from impermissible software alterations, or failures to install safety-critical software), it is not possible to exclude liability under s.2 by reference to a term of the policy or otherwise.[73d]

Section 3 preserves the right of the owner of the vehicle or the insurer to reduce their liability under s.2 as a result of the injured party's contributory negligence. Section 2(2) makes specific provision for circumstances in which the accident was caused wholly due to the person in charge of the vehicle's negligence in allowing the vehicle to begin driving itself when it was not appropriate to do so. In those circumstances, neither the insurer nor the owner is liable.

The AEVA 2018 also contains provisions regarding the insurer's or owner's rights to recover from third parties in respect of their liability to the injured party.[73e]

[73a] In that respect, the AEVA 2018 mirrors the limitation on the scope of compulsory insurance pursuant to s.145(3)(a) of the RTA 1988, which has been held to be incompatible with EU law. See para.31-006 above.

[73b] AEVA 2018 s.8(3)(b).

[73c] AEVA 2018 s.2(4). See the nineteenth footnote to para.31-005 above.

[73d] AEVA 2018 s.2(6).

[73e] AEVA 2018 s.5.

2. Policy "In Force"

Insurance certificate.

After the second paragraph, add new paragraph:

31-010 After a car has been seized pursuant to s.165A, its retention and disposal is governed by regulation.[93a]

[93a] Road Traffic Act 1988 (Retention and Disposal of Seized Motor Vehicles) Regulations 2005 (SI 2005/1606) reg.5 provides that the car may be recovered by a person who satisfies the authority that he is the registered keeper or owner, pays any charge pursuant to reg. 6, and produces a "valid" certificate of insurance. In *R. (on the application of Linse) v Chief Constable of North Wales* [2020] EWHC 1288 (Admin), HHJ Jarman QC (sitting as High Court Judge) held (at [22]–[32]) (referring to para.31-008 of the 14th edition of this work) that a policy voidable on grounds of misrepresentation was nonetheless "valid" for the purposes of these regulations, in circumstances where it had not yet been avoided by insurers.

3. Persons Entitled to Indemnity or Compensation from Motor Insurers

Liability of insurer to third party under the 1988 Act.

Replace footnote 162 with:

31-025 [162] The court will not grant a declaration in favour of the claimant pending judgment to the effect that, if a judgment be obtained subsequently, the insurer will be liable to meet it: *Carpenter v Ebblewhite* [1939] 1 K.B. 347. This is a specific feature of the UK statutory scheme, and reflects several aspects of UK motor insurance law and practice—see *Cameron v Liverpool Victoria Insurance Co Ltd* [2019] UKSC 6; [2019] 1 W.L.R. 1471 at [5]. This means that, as was held in *Cameron v Hussain* [2017] EWCA Civ 366; [2018] 1 W.L.R. 657, if it is not possible to establish liability against the insured (for example, because the insured cannot be identified for the purposes of effecting service of proceedings), then the only recourse will be against the MIB pursuant to the Untraced Drivers Agreement, considered further at para.31-052 below.

Replace first paragraph with:

31-026 For s.151 to operate, it appears that there must be an apparently valid policy which in terms covered the use to which the insured vehicle was being put at the time, but assuming, for the purposes of the section, that the policy covers driving by any person regardless of whether or not that person holds a valid driving licence.[169] On the other hand, under the Act, the insurers are not disentitled from reliance on a non-disclosure or misrepresentation or breach of warranty which would entitle them to avoid or cancel the policy as against their insured, provided the declaration of avoidance was obtained before the accident, in accordance with s.152(2).[170] The third party is further assisted by s.148(1) and (2) which avoid certain terms of policies otherwise providing a defence to insurers against claims made on the policy.[171]

[169] The section assumes that the insurer was on risk under a validly concluded contract: *Norman v Gresham Fire & Accident Insurance Society* [1936] 2 K.B. 253 at 277–278; *Spraggon v Dominion Insur-*

ance Co Ltd (1941) 69 Lloyd's Rep. 1. It seems that it will still not apply to a user outside the policy terms, e.g. other than for social domestic and pleasure purposes: *Jones v Welsh Insurance Corp Ltd* [1937] 4 All E.R. 149. If the act giving rise to liability was intentional the insurer has a defence to a claim by the insured for reasons of public policy but would remain liable to an injured third party under the principles stated in *Hardy v MIB* [1964] 2 Q.B. 745 and *Gardner v Moore* [1984] A.C. 548. See Ch.14, above.

[170] See para.31-029 below, and *Motor & General Insurance Co v Pavy* [1994] 1 W.L.R. 462 at 473–474. However, it is now clear that this contrary to EU law. In *Fidelidade-Companhia de Seguros SA v Caisse Suisse de Compensation* (C-287/16) EU:C:2017:575; [2017] R.T.R. 26 (20 July 2017), the CJEU held that it was not compatible with art.3(1) of the First Directive and art.2(1) of the Second Directive for an insurer to rely on Portuguese law providing for the nullity of the insurance contract on the basis of misrepresentations as to the identity of the owner of the vehicle and of its usual driver to avoid liability to a third-party victim. The CJEU did not consider this conclusion to be affected by the potential availability to the victim of compensation from the Fundo de Garantia Automóvel (the Portuguese equivalent of the MIB) (at [35]). Following acceptance by the UK Government that s.152(2) did not meet the requirements of the Directive and required amendment in *RoadPeace v Secretary of State for Transport* [2017] EWHC 2725 (Admin) at [70], s.152(2) was amended with effect from 1 November 2019. See also *Cameron v Liverpool Victoria Insurance Co Ltd* [2019] 1 W.L.R. 1471 at [3]. See also *Colley v Shuker* [2019] EWHC 781 (QB) at [28] and [33]–[34], in which the court rejected the proposition that a purposive interpretation of s.152(2) prior to amendment could be adopted to render it compatible with EU law by implying into it a residual discretion to set aside or disapply a declaration of non-liability made pursuant to s.152(2).

[171] See paras 31-031 to 31-036, below.

Replace second paragraph with:

In order to bring a claim against an insurer under s.151, it is necessary first for liability to be established against the driver; the insurer's obligation under s.151 is to satisfy judgments. For the purpose of establishing liability against the driver, it is not sufficient for the driver to be identified by a description of the type "the person unknown driving vehicle registration [X] who collided with vehicle registration [Y] on [N] date". In those circumstances, the only recourse is against the MIB pursuant to the Untraced Drivers Agreement.[172]

[172] This was held in *Cameron v Liverpool Victoria Insurance Co* [2019] 1 W.L.R. 1471. The Court of Appeal had held (by majority, Sir Ross Cranston dissenting), that a claimant injured in an accident should be permitted to amend her claim to identify the defendant driver by reference to description (namely, the licence registration of the vehicle and date of the accident) in circumstances where the driver's identity could not be found, and the purpose of the amendment was for the insurer to be required to satisfy the judgment under s.151. The majority (Gloster LJ and Lloyd Jones LJ) did not consider that the availability of a claim against the MIB under the Untraced Drivers Agreement altered the position. By contrast, Sir Ross Cranston considered that the "grain" of the s.151 regime required that the defendant must be named and that there would be no real injustice to the claimant by not permitting the amendment, as compensation could be claimed from the MIB pursuant to the Untraced Drivers Agreement (at [106]–[112]). The Supreme Court (per Lord Sumption JSC, with whom Lord Reed, Lord Carnwath, Lord Hodge and Lady Black agreed) allowed the appeal, holding that such an approach was contrary to the normal principle that for alternative service to be valid, the mode of service should be such as can reasonably be expected to bring the proceedings to the attention of the defendant, and there was nothing in the statutory scheme that altered the position (at [21]). This was supported by the availability of compensation from the MIB via the Untraced Drivers Agreement, which made it unnecessary to construe the statute so as to circumvent the ordinary service rules (at [22]).

Qualifications upon insurer's liability to satisfy a judgment.

Replace (d) of the list with:

31-029   (d)   if before the happening of the event which was the cause of death or bodily injury, the insurer has obtained a declaration[187] that he is entitled to avoid the policy for non-disclosure of a material fact or material misrepresentation.[188]

[187] s.152(2). Section 152(2) was amended by the Motor Vehicles (Compulsory Insurance) (Miscellaneous Amendments) Regulations 2019 (SI 2019/1047), which entered into force on 1 November 2019. Prior to that amendment, s.152(2) permitted avoidance where the action for declaratory relief was commenced not later than three months after the commencement of the proceedings in which judgment was

given. The amendment reflected the Government's concession in *RoadPeace v Secretary of State for Transport* [2017] EWHC 2725 (Admin) at [70] that previous s.152(2) was incompatible with EU law.

[188] Defined in s.152(2), as amended by the Road Traffic Act 1991 Sch.4. Prior to its amendment with effect from 1 November 2019, it had been held that s.152(2) could not be read as incorporating as residual discretion to set aside or disapply such a declaration, in order to ensure compatibility with EU law—see *Colley v Shuker* [2019] EWHC 781 (QB) at [33]–[34]. See further the third footnote to para.31-026 above. On 1 July 2019, the Motor Vehicles (Compulsory Insurance) (Miscellaneous Amendments) Regulations 2019 (SI 2019/1047) were laid before Parliament. Pursuant to those regulations, from 1 November 2019 s.152(2) was amended such that insurers are no longer able to obtain a declaration of avoidance after an accident in order to avoid meeting an insured's liability to the third party.

Delete paragraph 31-031: "Notice of proceedings to plaintiff.".

Action for declaration.

Replace footnote 205 with:

[205] *Merchants & Manufacturers' Insurance Co v Hunt* [1941] 1 K.B. 295; *Zurich General Accident & Liability Insurance Co v Morrison* [1942] 2 K.B. 53 at 58, 60, 65; *General Accident Fire and Life Assurance Corp v Shuttleworth* (1938) 60 Lloyd's Rep. 301 at 304. However, now the general law on non-disclosure and misrepresentation is to similar effect; see paras 17-028 and 20-050, above. After acceptance by the UK Government that the previous version of s.152(2) was incompatible with EU law in *RoadPeace v Secretary of State for Transport* [2017] EWHC 2725 (Admin) at [70], s.152(2) was amended pursuant to the Motor Vehicles (Compulsory Insurance) (Miscellaneous Amendments) Regulations 2019 (SI 2019/1047) such that since 1 November 2019 s.152(2) insurers have no longer been able to obtain a declaration of avoidance after an accident in order to avoid meeting an insured's liability to the third party. See also *Fidelidade-Companhia de Seguros SA v Caisse Suisse de Compensation* (C-287/16) EU:C:2017:575; [2017] R.T.R. 26. On 1 July 2019, the Motor Vehicles (Compulsory Insurance) (Miscellaneous Amendments) Regulations 2019 (SI 2019/1047) were laid before Parliament. Pursuant to those regulations, from 1 November 2019 s.152(2) will be amended such that insurers will no longer be able to obtain a declaration of avoidance after an accident in order to avoid meeting an insured's liability to the third party. **31-032**

5. TERMS AND CONDITIONS OF MOTOR POLICIES

User of the vehicle—private, social, domestic and pleasure purposes.

Replace footnote 405 with:

[405] *Seddon v Binions* [1978] 1 Lloyd's Rep. 381. See also *AXA Insurance UK Ltd v EUI Ltd (t/a Elephant Insurance)* [2020] EWHC 1207 (QB); [2020] 1 W.L.R. 3048 (driving home from work was "business" use notwithstanding a detour to give a lift to a friend). **31-075**

Dual purposes.

After the first paragraph, add new paragraph:

Where the essential character of the journey consists of use for a criminal purpose, the use is neither "social, domestic and pleasure" nor "business".[408a] **31-076**

[408a] *Caroll v Taylor* [2020] EWHC 153 (QB) at [86]–[87], referring to *Keeley v Pashen* [2005] 1 W.L.R. 1226 at [19].

CHAPTER 32

AVIATION INSURANCE

Aviation Insurance

Liability insurance.

After "... as supplemented by the Civil Aviation (Insurance) Regulations 2005 (SI 2005/1089).", add new footnote 11a:

32-005   ^{11a} Both reg.785/2004 on insurance requirements for air carriers and aircraft operators [2004] OJ L/138 and the Civil Aviation (Insurance) Regulations 2005 (SI 2005/1089) have been amended by the Civil Aviation (Insurance) (Amendment) (EU Exit) Regulations 2018 (SI 2018/1363), and the Civil Aviation (Insurance) (Amendment) (EU Exit) Regulations 2020 (SI 2020/692) (the latter of which is not yet in force, and was made in response to amendments to reg.785/2004 which entered into force after the 2018 Regulations). The amending regulation is made pursuant to s.8(1) of the European Union (Withdrawal) Act 2018, and the amendments will come into force on the day the UK exits the EU. The purpose of the amendments is to ensure that the existing scheme of regulation will be retained following withdrawal, and the amendments reflect the fact that after the UK exits the EU many of the functions previously performed by the Commission (including the power to amend the minimum insurance requirements) will be performed by the Civil Aviation Authority and/or the Secretary of State. The amending regulation makes no changes to the substantive minimum insurance requirements set out in reg.785/2004. An explanatory memorandum is available at *http://www.legislation.gov.uk/uksi/2018/1363/pdfs/uksiem_20181363_en.pdf* [Accessed 9 July 2019].

Standard policies.

Replace footnote 15 with:

32-007   ¹⁵ *Kuwait Airways Corp v Kuwait Insurance Co S.A.K.* [1999] 1 Lloyd's Rep. 803 at 809. For a recent example of a claim under a policy of this type arising from a confiscation, see *Toby v Allianz Global Risks US Insurance Company* FSD 152 of 2013 (IMJ) (29 August 2018) (Grand Court of Cayman Islands) at [73]–[74].

Add new footnote 32a after paragraph title:

Exceptions.^{32a}

32-014   ^{32a} For a recent case involving the application of a number of different exclusions in an aviation hull policy, see *Toby v Allianz Global Risks US Insurance Company* FSD 152 of 2013 (IMJ) (29 August 2018) (Grand Court of Cayman Islands). The claim failed on several grounds, including that the insured's failure to pay import duty was a proximate cause of the loss that fell within a "financial cause" exclusion, and that the insured had breached conditions requiring it to use all reasonable efforts to comply with the laws of any country within whose jurisdiction the aircraft may be, and requiring it to use due diligence to avoid the loss (see summary at [778]–[781]).

Leased aircraft extension.

After ", thus seeking to provide continuity of cover in these circumstances", replace "circumstances" with:

32-017   circumstances.

CHAPTER 33

INSURANCE AGAINST PECUNIARY LOSS

1. BUSINESS INTERRUPTION INSURANCE

Add new paragraph:

Policy coverage—Covid-19 pandemic. *Financial Conduct Authority v Arch*   **33-001A**
Insurance (UK) Ltd[9a] was a test case brought to determine a number of issues of
principle relating to the cover provided under business interruption policies
consequent on interruption to businesses caused by the Covid-19 pandemic. The
court considered 21 policies issued by eight defendant insurers. In addition to questions of construction, the case considered issues of causation,[9b] although in respect
of the large majority of policies the latter were held not to be relevant as cover was
determined solely by the construction of the cover provided. There were complex
questions of construction; the following brief summary seeks to highlight the most
important ones.

A key pervasive issue was to determine the "counterfactual". As described in the
following paragraphs, to ascertain the amount of loss it is necessary to work out
what the insured's revenue would have been had the insured event not occurred,
which is typically done by looking backwards to see how the business had
performed before the occurrence of the insured peril. There is also usually a
"trends" clause (see para.33-005) which allows account to be taken of exceptional
events that may have depressed or increased revenue in the earlier period, and also
to take account of anticipated exceptional events in the current indemnity period.
The effect is to require a "counterfactual", namely to consider what would have happened but for the occurrence of the insured peril. It was therefore necessary to define
what was the "insured peril".

The policy terms were grouped into three categories: "disease clauses", "hybrid
clauses" and "prevention of access (and similar) clauses". It is necessary to read the
detailed judgment to see the terms of the policies considered and the variation
amongst the different wordings.

Although the wording of each policy considered was by no means identical, a large number of them basically covered interruption to or interference with the business of the insured following the occurrence of a notifiable disease (it was accepted that Covid-19 was such). The courts held that the proper construction of this sort of wording was that the insured peril included the outbreak of the disease as well as the lockdown that followed it. Therefore, the counterfactual disregarded both lockdown and disease and what was relevant was what would have happened if there had been no disease and no lockdown.

However, all the policies required in addition that disease occurred either within a specified radius of the insured's premises (normally 25 miles) or in the vicinity of the premises.[9c] An important distinction was between those policies where cover was triggered by a generalised outbreak of an infectious disease, which necessarily affected the locality of the premises as opposed to those where cover was triggered because something specific had happened in the locality of the premises. Wordings having the former effect were those which referred generally to interruption following the occurrence of the disease within the locality. If there was a generalised outbreak of disease (as with Covid-19), as long as there was one instance of it in the relevant locality then there was cover. A causal connection between the local occurrence and the interruption of business was not necessary. Wordings which had the latter effect were those that clearly linked the interruption to local events. A reference to an "event" or "incident" in the locality sufficed, as those words contemplated a single specific happening. Similarly, the requirement that interruption was the result of an occurrence, manifestation or threat of disease at the premises or in their locality focused only on local events, and such events must have been the cause of the interruption.

In addition, the court held the following in respect of common words or expressions found across many of the policies under consideration. First, there was a distinction between the "occurrence" of disease and the "manifestation" of disease. An "occurrence" required actual infection, whether or not manifest or diagnosed, whereas a "manifestation" required either symptoms or diagnosis. Secondly, a distinction had to be drawn between "prevention" and "restriction" of access or use of the insured's business. The word "prevention" meant a complete ban on access, whereas a "restriction" was a hindrance to access. However, the prevention related to the insured business, and so it was necessary to examine that business to see whether it was prevented or restricted. If, for example, the insured's business was a restaurant, the closure of the restaurant amounted to prevention of the insured business, and the fact that the restaurant could operate on a takeaway basis only did not preclude a finding of "prevention" because the previous business could not continue. Thirdly, the word "interruption" did not require a complete closure of business. Fourthly, "restriction imposed" referred to something enforceable by law and not merely advisory, so guidance from the government but before regulations requiring restrictions were in force was not sufficient.

[9a] *Financial Conduct Authority v Arch Insurance (UK) Ltd* [2020] EWHC 2448 (Comm).

[9b] As to this, see para.21-001, above.

[9c] Where this was used, "vicinity" was not defined in terms of a specific distance, but in one instance as "an area surrounding or adjacent to an Insured Location in which events that occur within such area would be reasonably expected to have an impact on an Insured or the Insured's Business". It was held that where a disease was of a such a nature that any occurrence in England and Wales would reasonably be expected to have an impact on the business of an insured, all occurrences of Covid-19 were within the relevant "vicinity".

CHAPTER 34

CONTRACTORS' RISKS POLICIES

After ", albeit inaccurately, as a 'contractors' all risks policy'.", add new footnote 16a:

[16a] This can often give rise to double-insurance issues, for example, when the insured also has cover **34-005** under a separate liability policy that contains an "other insurances" exclusion. It has been held that an all risks policy covering damage and a third-party liability policy are not insurances on the same property and against the same risk and therefore do not give rise to double insurance so as to fall within such a clause—see *Petrofina (UK) Ltd & Ors v Magnaload Ltd & Anor* [1984] Q.B. 127. This issue is considered in greater detail above at para.25-007. For a recent application of this principle in a contractors' all risks context, see *Alliance Australia Ltd v Certain Underwriters at Lloyd's Subscribing to Policy Number B105809GC0M0430* [2019] NSWSC 453.

Faulty design.

Replace footnote 34 with:

[34] See, for example, *Seele Austria GmbH & Co v Tokio Marine Europe Insurance Ltd* [2008] Lloyd's **34-010** Rep. I.R. 372, reversed in part by the Court of Appeal [2008] Lloyd's Rep. I.R. 739. A majority of the Court of Appeal held that the insured was entitled to recover for part of the damage under a clause which provided additional cover in respect of intentional damage caused to the insured property in order to enable the replacement, repair or rectification of defective insured property. An analogous problem arose under the Liner Negligence Clause inserted into marine hull policies. The current Inchmaree clause is contained in cl.6.2, Institute Time Clauses (Hulls) 1995—see Arnould, *Law of Marine Insurance*, 18th edn (London: Sweet & Maxwell, 2013), para.22-06. Where there is an exclusion of loss or damage to insured property in a defective condition due to a defect in design or workmanship, the exclusion will not apply if the defect relates to part of the works separate from the part which has suffered damage: *C.A. Blackwell (Contractors) Ltd v Gerling General Insurance Co* [2007] Lloyd's Rep. I.R. 511; [2008] Lloyd's Rep. I.R. 529; *Corbett v Vero Insurance New Zealand Ltd* [2020] Lloyd's Rep. I.R. Plus 6 (NZHC).

Latent defects.

After "... from a latent defect in machinery or materials.", add new footnote 34a:

[34a] For a case in which the issue was whether the contract required a party to take out latent defects insur- **34-011** ance as part of its obligation to insure, see *Harrow LBC v Engie Regeneration (Apollo) Ltd* [2018] EWHC 2575 (TCC).

Damage to property.

Replace footnote 53 with:

34-019   [53] *James Longley & Co v Forest Giles Ltd* [2002] Lloyd's Rep. I.R. 421. Note the consideration of this case by the Victoria Supreme Court in *Metricon Homes Pty Ltd v Great Lakes Insurance SE* [2017] VSC 749 at [71]–[79] (distinguishing *James Longley* and rejecting the argument that the damage arose from a failure by the contractor to construct the house in accordance with its contractual obligations, rather than from "damage to property" within the meaning of the insuring clause).

CHAPTER 35

REINSURANCE

TABLE OF CONTENTS

1. REINSURANCE TERMINOLOGY

Definition.

Replace paragraph with:

In these early descriptions of reinsurance, certain accepted characteristics of **35-002** modern reinsurance contracts can be perceived. The object of the reinsurance is to indemnify the reinsured against liability which may arise on the primary insurance.[5] The reinsurance is a separate contract from the original insurance,[6] so that there is no privity of contract between the insured and the reinsurer.[7] This distinguishes it from double insurance and solvency insurance.[8] It is neither an assignment nor transfer of the original insurance business from one insurer to another,[9] nor is it a relationship of partnership or agency between insurers.[10] It is essentially an independent contract of insurance whereby the reinsurer engages to indemnify the reinsured wholly or partially against losses for which the latter is liable to the insured under the primary contract of insurance.[11] Accordingly, it is subject to the general principles and rules of law applying to insurance contracts, such as the principles of utmost good faith[12] and subrogation, and the rules relating to insurable interest and illegality.

[5] *South British Fire and Marine Insurance Co of New Zealand v Da Costa* [1906] 1 K.B. 456 at 460 per Bigham J; *Wasa International Insurance Co v Lexington Insurance Co* [2008] 1 All E.R. (Comm) 1085 at 1102, [48]–[49] per Sedley LJ. *Wasa International Insurance Co v Lexington Insurance Co* was overturned by [2010] 1 A.C. 180 but in the judgement it was stated that reinsurance contracts should be "construed so as to be consistent with the terms of the insurance contract on the basis that the normal commercial intention was that they should be back-to-back". However, it was also stated that it still remained a question of construction where the law applicable to the insurance and reinsurance contracts were different. See also fn.213 to para.35-061, below and the recent decision of the New South Wales Court of Appeal in *MetLife Insurance Ltd v RGA Reinsurance Company of Australia Ltd* [2017] NSWCA 56. For a commentary on the *MetLife* case, see "Reinsurance: Back-to-back coverage" (2017) 29 I.L.M. 8.

[6] *British Dominions General Insurance Co Ltd v Duder* [1915] 2 K.B. 394 at 400, 405. The two contracts may be subject to different systems of law—see, e.g. *Citadel Insurance Co v Atlantic Union*

Insurance Co [1982] 2 Lloyd's Rep. 543; *Forsikringsaktieselskapet Vesta v Butcher* [1989] A.C. 852 (see para.35-068, below).

[7] *Re Norwich Equitable Fire Assurance* (1887) 3 T.L.R. 781; *Re Law Guarantee Trust & Accident Society* [1914] 2 Ch. 617 at 647–648; *English Insurance Co v National Benefit Assurance Co* [1929] A.C. 114 at 124; *Versicherungs und Transport AG Daugava v Henderson* (1934) 39 Com. Cas. 312 at 316. Since enforcement of contractual rights by third parties has become possible under the Contracts (Rights of Third Parties) Act 1999 it may now be possible for the original insured to claim directly against his insurer's reinsurer under a "cut through" clause in a reinsurance subject to English law, but even so the clause may be invalid under the relevant insolvency regime. See para.22-067 above. For a recent case concerning a "cut-through" clause, see *Randgold Resources Ltd v Santam Ltd* [2018] EWHC 2493 (Comm); [2019] Lloyd's Rep. I.R. 467. The judgment considers the application of the 1999 Act and the availability (or otherwise) of various forms of declaratory relief sought. This case is helpfully summarised and analysed in "Reinsurance: cut-through clauses" (2019) 31 I.L.M. 11.

[8] J.A. Park, *Marine Insurance* (1842), Vol.2, pp.599–600.

[9] *Re Lancashire Plate Glass Fire and Burglary Insurance Ltd* [1912] 1 Ch. 35.

[10] *Re Norwich Equitable Fire Assurance Society* (1887) 3 T.L.R. 781; *English Insurance Co v National Benefit Assurance Co* [1929] A.C. 114; *Motor Union Insurance Co v Mannheimer Versicherungs Gesellschaft* [1933] 1 K.B. 812; *Phoenix General Insurance Co v Halvanon Insurance Co* [1985] 2 Lloyd's Rep. 599 at 614.

[11] *Versicherungs und Transport AG Daugava v Henderson* (1934) 39 Com. Cas. 312 at 316; *Home Insurance Co of New York v Victoria Montreal Fire Insurance Co* [1907] A.C. 59 at 63. See also, *Equitas Insurance Ltd v Municipal Mutual Insurance Ltd* [2019] EWCA Civ 718; [2020] Q.B. 418 at [99]. However, a contract to indemnify in respect of liabilities assumed under contracts of insurance will not necessarily be a contract of reinsurance: *GMA v Storebrand & Kansa* [1995] L.R.L.R. 333.

[12] This is to be distinguished from a fiduciary relationship which is not created under a reinsurance treaty—*Law Guarantee Trust and Accident Society Ltd v Munich Reinsurance Co* [1914] 31 T.L.R. 572.

Reinsurance terminology and categories.

Replace footnote 41 with:

35-010　[41] R. Kiln and S. Kiln, *Reinsurance in Practice*, 4th edn (Witherby & Co, 2001); R. L. Carter, N. Ralph, L. Lucas, *Carter on Reinsurance*, 5th revised edn (Witherby Seamanship International Ltd, 2013); J. Butler and R. Merkin, *Butler and Merkin's Reinsurance Law* (London: Sweet & Maxwell, 2018); Barlow Lyle and Gilbert, *Reinsurance Practice and the Law* (Informa Law, 2018); C. Edelman, QC and A. Burns, *The Law of Reinsurance*, 2nd edn (Oxford: Oxford University Press, 2013); A. T. O'Neill and J. Woloniecki, *Law of Reinsurance in England and Bermuda*, 5th edn (London: Sweet & Maxwell, 2019).

4. TERMS OF THE CONTRACT

Incorporation of terms of underlying insurance.

Replace footnote 194 with:

35-055　[194] *Pine Top Insurance Co Ltd v Unione Italiana Anglo-Saxon Reinsurance Co Ltd* [1987] 1 Lloyd's Rep. 476. There are variants—e.g. terms "as original"—*Citadel Insurance v Atlantic Union Insurance* [1982] 2 Lloyd's Rep. 543, or "subject to the same clauses and conditions as original policy"—*Charlesworth v Faber* (1900) 5 Com. Cas. 408, or "conditions as underlying"—*Municipal Mutual Insurance Ltd v Sea Insurance Co* [1996] L.R.L.R. 265 (appealed on other grounds: [1998] Lloyd's Rep. I.R. 421). For a recent example, see *Munich Re Capital Ltd v Ascot Corporate Name Ltd* [2019] EWHC 2768 (Comm).

Intention as to incorporation.

Replace footnote 202 with:

35-058　[202] *AIG Europe (UK) Ltd v Ethniki* [2000] Lloyd's Rep. I.R. 343 at 351; *CNA International Reinsurance Co Ltd v Companhia de Seguros Tranquilidade SA* [1999] Lloyd's Rep. I.R. 289 at 299; *Groupama Navigation et Transports v Catatumbo CA Seguros* [2001] Lloyd's Rep. I.R. 141 at 146. For a recent example of a relatively unusual case, see *Munich Re Capital Ltd v Ascot Corporate Name Ltd* [2019] EWHC 2768 (Comm) and the commentary in "Reinsurance: back-to-back cover" (2019) 31 I.L.M. 12. The issue in the *Munich* case was that circumstances had changed, leading to an extension of the insurance, but no extension of the reinsurance. Mrs Justice Carr noted, at [54]–[56], in relevant parts, that:

"54. As the authorities [including *Bromarin AB v IMD Investments* [1999] STC 301 and *Debenhams Retail plc v Sun Alliance and London Assurance Company Ltd* [2005] EWCA Civ 868, [2006] 1 P & CR 8] suggest, the exercise of construction is therefore to consider how the Reinsurance Policy is to be construed in circumstances where, contrary to the original (objective) expectation of the parties, there has been an extension of the Insurance Policy period but not (for whatever reason) an extension of the Reinsurance Policy period. 55. It is a question of contractual interpretation in changed factual circumstances. The task of the court is to decide, in the light of the agreement that the parties made, what they must have been taken to have intended in relation to the events which have arisen which they did not contemplate, namely an extension to the Project Period in the Insurance Policy but no corresponding extension to the Project Period in the Reinsurance Policy. 56. As to assessing the parties' objective intentions at the time of Reinsurance Policy, the commercial context is important …".

5. LIABILITY OF REINSURER

Claims—timing and extent of reinsurers' liability: when right to indemnity arises.

After para.35-080, add new paragraphs:

In *Equitas Insurance Ltd v Municipal Mutual Insurance Ltd*,[291a] the Court of Appeal considered whether the rules on presentation developed within the "*Fairchild* enclave"[291b] in respect of presentation by employers also applied to reinsurance claims.

35-080A

[291a] *Equitas Insurance Ltd v Municipal Mutual Insurance Ltd* [2019] EWCA Civ 718; [2020] Q.B. 418.

[291b] The *Fairchild* enclave refers to the special rule of causation developed by the House of Lords in *Fairchild v Glenhaven Funeral Services Ltd* [2002] UKHL 22; [2003] 1 A.C. 32, which enabled claimants tortiously exposed to asbestos during their employment to recover damages for mesothelioma without needing to prove which employer caused the critical exposure. See paras 25-054 to 25-055 above.

The court held that the practice of "spiking" mesothelioma claims, whereby employers were entitled to present claims to any policy year of their choice,[291c] did not extend to the reinsurance context. In this regard, the court observed that the practice of spiking, and the anomalies that it caused, served a purpose at the insurance level, but that it was unnecessary to perpetuate those anomalies at the reinsurance level. It was therefore desirable, if possible, to revert to the principles of the common law, such that liability would be apportioned by reference to contribution to the risk.[291d]

[291c] The process of "spiking" had been approved in respect of insurance claims in *International Energy Group Ltd v Zurich Insurance Plc UK* [2015] UKSC 33; [2016] A.C. 509. See paras 25-054 to 25-055 above.

[291d] *Equitas Insurance Ltd v Municipal Mutual Insurance Ltd* [2019] EWCA Civ 718; [2020] Q.B. 418 at [92]–[94] per Males LJ, and at [168] per Leggatt LJ.

The court rejected the submission that an insurer's right to present its reinsurance claims to the policy year of its choice was subject to a principle of deemed allocation, whereby the value represented by the settlement consideration should be regarded as implicitly allocated in pro rata shares across all triggered years. The court considered that the permissibility of spiking at the insurance level precluded a principle of deemed allocation to avoid spiking at the reinsurance level. That conclusion followed from the nature of reinsurance as a form of insurance on the original subject matter insured.[291e]

[291e] *Equitas Insurance Ltd v Municipal Mutual Insurance Ltd* [2019] EWCA Civ 718; [2020] Q.B. 418 at [99]–[101] per Males LJ.

Instead, the court held that the insurer's right to present its reinsurance claims was subject to an implied term that that right must be exercised in a manner which is not arbitrary, irrational or capricious. In mesothelioma claims, rationality required that claims be presented by reference to each year's contribution to the risk, which would normally be measured by reference to time on risk unless in the particular circumstances there was a good reason for some other basis of presentation. The court stressed that the implication of such a term was specific to the *Fairchild* enclave and would not have wider ramifications for the law of reinsurance.[291f]

[291f] *Equitas Insurance Ltd v Municipal Mutual Insurance Ltd* [2019] EWCA Civ 718; [2020] Q.B. 418 at [114]–[116] per Males LJ, and at [159]–[162] per Leggatt LJ.

Permission to appeal to the Supreme Court was granted and the appeal was due to be heard in July 2020. However, it is understood that the matter settled and the Supreme Court hearing did not proceed.

6. MISCELLANEOUS

Contracts (Applicable Law) Act 1990.

Replace footnote 401 with:

35-105   [401]   In *Gan Insurance Co Ltd v Tai Ping Insurance Co Ltd* [1999] Lloyd's Rep. I.R. 472.

CHAPTER 36

INSURANCE COMPANIES

1. BACKGROUND

Introduction.

Replace paragraph with:

This chapter is concerned with giving a general introduction to the principal **36-001**
aspects of the legislation controlling insurance companies and protecting the
policyholders of such companies. The relevant legislation is now the Financial
Services and Markets Act 2000, as supplemented by a large volume of secondary
legislation and as amended by the Financial Services Act 2012. The 2000 Act
established a single regulatory structure across the whole of the financial services
industry; originally there was one regulator, the Financial Services Authority (FSA),
but the amendments made by the 2012 Act introduced a dual regulatory system
under the Prudential Regulation Authority (PRA), a division of the Bank of
England, and the Financial Conduct Authority (FCA). The regulation of insurance
companies in terms of authorisation and supervision falls under the jurisdiction of
the PRA.[1] Therefore, as much of the legislation is no longer particular to insurance companies, the chapter does not seek to cover it exhaustively nor to cover the
detail so far as it concerns the internal workings of an insurance company.[2] Earlier
editions of this work should be consulted for the history before the introduction of
modern companies legislation[3] or concerning the introduction of the legislation
particular to insurance companies.[4] A brief account of the European legislation that
underpins the system of regulation follows at paras 36-003 to 36-009. It is quite
uncertain at present as to what will be the effect on the regulation of insurance
companies of the UK's withdrawal from the EU on 31 January 2020. The
transitional period following that withdrawal ends at the end of 2020, unless an

extension is agreed. At the time of writing it is wholly uncertain what sort of deal for the future, if any, will be agreed with the EU. The law described in this chapter will therefore clearly be operational until at least 31 December 2020 and inevitably insurance companies will remain subject to detailed regulation thereafter. If the UK does leave the single European market completely, obviously the "passport rights" briefly described at paras 36-007 to 36-009 will no longer be applicable.[5]

[1] The scheme under the 2000 Act took effect from 1 December 2000. The amended scheme took effect from 1 April 2013. For the legislation, annotations and commentary, see the *Encyclopedia of Insurance Law* (Sweet & Maxwell).

[2] The chapter is also not concerned with the specialised law regarding friendly societies conducting industrial assurance business, although much of that has been brought within the framework established by the 2000 Act.

[3] As to this, see paras 2234–2238 of the 7th edition of this work.

[4] As to this, see paras 2239–2242 of the 7th edition of this work.

[5] A Temporary Permissions Regime was introduced, under the EEA Passport Rights (Amendment, etc., and Transitional Provisions) (EU Exit) Regulations 2018 (SI 2018/1149), to enable EEA firms already exercising passport rights into the UK to continue carrying on business in the UK after exit day while they become fully authorised in the UK. Firms that choose not to seek authorisation will be able to run off their UK business under the Financial Services Contracts (Transitional and Saving Provision) (EU Exit) Regulations 2019 (SI 2019/405). Both statutory instruments are amended by the Financial Services (Miscellaneous) (Amendment) (EU Exit) (No. 2) Regulations 2019 (SI 2019/1010).

Solvency II.

Replace footnote 29 with:

36-009 [29] Solvency 2 Regulations 2015 (SI 2015/575). See also Solvency 2 and Insurance (Amendment, etc.) (EU Exit) Regulations 2019 (SI 2019/407).

2.   REGULATION UNDER THE FINANCIAL SERVICES AND MARKETS ACT 2000

(e)   Transfers of Business and Winding Up

Insurance business transfer scheme.

Replace paragraph with:

36-030   Before making an order sanctioning an insurance business transfer scheme, the court must be satisfied that the appropriate certificates have been obtained and that, if appropriate, the transferee has or will have the necessary authorisation to carry on the transferred business.[91] It must also consider that, in all the circumstances of the case, it is appropriate to sanction the scheme.[92] The appropriate certificates are specified in Sch.12 and are essentially a certificate from the appropriate regulator that the transferee possesses the necessary margin of solvency and a certificate, in cases involving risks or firms located in another EEA state, that the host state regulator has consented to the transfer or failed to object to it within three months of being notified. The principles to be applied by the court in deciding whether or not to sanction a transfer are that it should take account of the fact that the board of the transferor company has exercised a commercial judgment that the transfer is beneficial and must consider whether any policyholders, employees or others may be adversely affected, although, even if they are, it does not follow that the scheme must be rejected. The most important criterion is the fairness of the scheme as between the different classes of affected persons and in deciding that, the most important material is the report of the actuary.[93] As long as a scheme results in a transfer of business, there is no requirement that it does anything else.[94] It has been held competent in an application under Pt VII of the 2000 Act to transfer only some of the rights and liabilities arising under a policy.[95] In the vast majority of reported cases, provided that the actuary's report supports the transfer and the regulators are satisfied, the court has approved the scheme. However, in *Re Prudential Assurance Company Ltd*,[95a] despite these requirements being satisfied, the court refused to approve a transfer of annuities where the objecting policyholders had chosen the insurer based on its age and reputation and the financial support it would be likely to receive from the group of which it formed part, should the need ever arise. The requirements described above have been considered and applied in a number of cases involving transfers of business to other EEA states in anticipation of the UK's departure from the EU, where a UK authorised insurer had clients in another EEA state.[95b]

[91] Financial Services and Markets Act 2000 s.111(2).

[92] Financial Services and Markets Act 2000 s.111(3).

[93] *Re Hill Samuel Life Assurance Ltd* [1998] 3 All E.R. 176; *Re AXA Equity and Law Life Assurance Society Plc* [2001] 2 B.C.L.C. 447 (following the unreported decision of Hoffmann J in *Re London Life Association Ltd* unreported 21 February 1989). For an extended consideration by the court of the actuary's report, see *The Standard Life Insurance Co, Petitioner* [2007] S.C.L.R. 581. Where not all policies issued by the transferor are the subject of the proposed transfer, for example because they have been issued to non-UK residents and it is not clear that the regulatory authorities in the appropriate jurisdiction will consent, the court must take account of this as it is an inherent and essential part of the scheme. Under similar provisions of former legislation it has been held that the court must consider whether there are objections to the proposal even if none has been raised by persons appearing before it (*Re Hearts of Oak and General Assurance Co Ltd* (1914) 30 T.L.R 436) and that a transfer to a company outside the jurisdiction cannot be sanctioned (*Re Prudential Assurance Co Ltd* [1939] Ch. 878), although the latter cannot now be an objection where the company is a properly authorised EEA insurer. See also *Re Norwich Union Linked Life Assurance Ltd* [2004] EWHC 2802 (Ch); *Re Allied Dunbar Assurance Plc* [2005] 2 B.C.L.C. 220; *Re Prudential Annuities Ltd* [2014] EWHC 4770 (Ch). See also *Re Royal Sun Alliance Insurance Plc* [2008] EWHC 3436 (Ch); *Re Aviva Annuity UK* [2016] EWHC 3574 (Ch); *Re the West of England Ship Owners Mutual Insurance Association (London) Ltd* [2017] EWHC 512 (Ch); *Re Scottish Equitable Plc* [2017] EWHC 1439 (Ch); *Re Prudential Assurance Company Ltd* [2019] EWHC 2245 (Ch) considered briefly below; and *Re Equitable Life Assurance Society* [2019] EWHC 3336 (Ch).

[94] *Re Norwich Union Linked Life Assurance Ltd* [2004] EWHC 2802 (Ch).

[95] *Save & Prosper Pensions Ltd & Prudential Retirement Income Ltd, Petitioners* [2007] CSOH 205 (Lord Glennie, Outer House, Ct of Session).

[95a] *Re Prudential Assurance Company Ltd* [2019] EWHC 2245 (Ch).

[95b] See, for example, *Re AIG Europe Ltd* [2018] EWHC 2818 (Ch); [2019] Bus. L.R. 307; *Re Royal London Mutual Insurance Society Ltd* [2019] EWHC 185 (Ch); [2019] 1 All E.R. (Comm) 909; and *Re Scottish Widows Ltd* [2019] EWHC 642 (Ch). The fact that the insureds affected would lose the protection of the Financial Services Compensation Scheme (see para.39-041) without having the equivalent in the transferee state was not a bar to approval, provided the scheme was fair overall and the independent report provided appropriate assurances.

(g)   Dispute Resolution and Complaints

Eligible complainants.

Replace paragraph with:

There are detailed rules determining who can complain to FOS.[197] As far as insur-   **36-057** ance business is concerned, the essential requirements are that the respondent has already sent the complainant its final response or eight weeks have elapsed since the respondent received the complaint[198] and that the complainant is a consumer, namely an individual acting for purposes outside his trade business or profession,[199] a micro-enterprise[200] which employs fewer than 10 persons and has a turnover or annual balance sheet of less than €2 million, a charity with an annual income of less than £1 million or a trustee of a trust with a net asset value of less than £1 million. This is a significant change from the jurisdiction of the former IOB, which, as indicated earlier, covered only complaints from private insureds. Potential, as well as actual, customers may be eligible to complain. In the insurance context this could be relevant, for example, to a complaint against an insurance intermediary for failure properly to effect insurance on behalf of the complainant. Further, complaints may be brought by a person with no actual or potential relationship themselves with the respondent, but who is a person for whose benefit a contract of insurance was taken out or was intended to be taken out or is a person on whom the legal right to benefit from a claim under a contract of insurance has been devolved by contract, assignment, statute or subrogation. The first category clearly includes, for example, a beneficiary under a group life insurance policy and a person named or described as entitled to benefit under a household insurance policy effected by their spouse or parent. The second would appear to include someone who has obtained rights under the Third Parties (Rights Against Insurers) Act 1930 or the Third Parties (Rights Against Insurers) Act 2010[201] or Pt IV of the Road Traffic Act 1988.[202]

[197] Dispute Resolution Rules, Ch.2.7.

[198] Dispute Resolution Rules, r.2.8.1. There are limitation periods in the same Ch.2.8.

[199] The beneficiary of a D & O policy was not acting as a consumer when the claim against him related to his conduct as a company director: *R. (on the application of Bluefin Insurance Ltd) v Financial Ombudsman Service Ltd* [2014] EWHC 3413 (Admin).

[200] Including a sole trader, a company, an unincorporated body and a partnership carrying on any trade or business.

[201] See paras 30-009 and following, above.

[202] See para.31-024, above.

Determination of complaints.

Replace footnote 203 with:

36-058   [203] *R. v Financial Ombudsman Services Ltd Ex p. IFG Financial Services Ltd* [2006] 1 B.C.L.C. 534, approved and followed in *R. v Financial Ombudsman Service, Ex p. Heather Moor & Edgecomb Ltd* [2008] EWCA Civ 642. See also *R. v The Financial Services Authority, Ex p. British Bankers Association* [2011] EWHC 999 (Admin); and *R. (on the application of Critchley) v Financial Ombudsman Service Ltd* [2019] EWHC 3036 (Admin), which involved unsuccessful challenges to the FOS's approach to the mis-selling of payment protection insurance.

CHAPTER 38

THE ROLE OF AGENTS IN INSURANCE BUSINESS

TABLE OF CONTENTS

2.   THE INSURED'S AGENT

Completion of proposal form and the duty of disclosure.

Replace footnote 98 with:

[98] *Jones v Environcom Ltd* [2010] Lloyd's Rep. I.R. 676. See also *Synergy Health (UK) Ltd v CGU* **38-028**
Insurance Plc [2011] Lloyd's Rep. I.R. 500; *Avondale Exhibitions Ltd v Arthur J Gallagher Insurance Brokers Ltd* [2018] EWHC 1311 (QB); [2019] Lloyd's Rep. I.R. 104; and *Dalamd Ltd v Butterworth Spengler Commercial Ltd* [2018] EWHC 2558 (Comm); [2019] P.N.L.R. 6.

Measure of damages payable by negligent agent.

Replace paragraph with:

The position is more complicated where, under the policy that the agent has **38-038** negligently failed to effect, the insurers could have repudiated liability for a breach of condition or warranty prior to the date of the loss. The court must then consider what were the chances of the particular insurers repudiating their liability in the ordinary course of business or, if no particular insurer was in contemplation, what were the chances of a typical reputable insurer of the risks in question doing so.[134] This approach was followed in a case where the loss for which the insured wished to claim fell inside an exclusion from cover[135] and in a case where the broker is in breach of the duty to advise fully as to the need for the insured to disclose material facts and the insurer has avoided the policy as a result.[135a] It is for the insured to adduce evidence that the insurers would not have exercised their legal right if the policy had been validly concluded, but would have paid the claim. The court may draw inferences in the absence of evidence from the insurers.[136] Having assessed the chances that the insurers would not have exercised their rights of defence to payment, the court then awards to the insured a corresponding proportion of their claim for damages.

[134] *Fraser v Furman, Miller Smith & Partners Third Party* [1967] 1 W.L.R. 898.

[135] *Dunbar v A&B Painters* [1986] 2 Lloyd's Rep. 38.

[135a] *Dalamd Ltd v Butterworth Spengler Commercial Ltd* [2019] P.N.L.R. 6.

[136] In a case where the claim for damages against the brokers is brought in the same proceedings in which insurers are seeking to avoid the policy the insurers' witnesses are available to give the evidence— see *March Cabaret Club v The London Assurance* [1975] 1 Lloyd's Rep. 169 concerning the same principles in respect of assessors.

After "... the court is in reality denying the", replace "plaintiff" with:

38-044   claimant

4.   STATUTORY REGULATION

Replace paragraph with:

38-073   Insurance intermediaries became subject to a plethora of regulations over the last 40 years. Now there is one statutory scheme. This was introduced pursuant to the Insurance Mediation Directive (IMD)[234] and implemented by the Insurance Mediation Directive (Miscellaneous Amendments) Regulations 2003[235] and the Financial Services and Markets Act 2000 (Regulated Activities) (Amendment) (No.2) Order 2003.[236] The IMD was replaced by the Insurance Distribution Directive (IDD),[236a] which was implemented in the UK on 1 October 2018 by the Insurance Distribution (Regulated Activities and Miscellaneous Amendments) Order 2018.[236b] The changes required to the regime in the UK did not need to be significant.[236c] Under the Financial Services and Markets Act 2000, as amended by the Financial Services Act 2012, intermediaries are regulated, both as to authorisation and conduct, by the Financial Conduct Authority.

[234] Insurance Mediation Directive 2002/92/EC.

[235] Insurance Mediation Directive (Miscellaneous Amendments) Regulations 2003 (SI 2003/1473).

[236] Financial Services and Markets Act 2000 (Regulated Activities) (Amendment) (No.2) Order 2003 (SI 2003/1476), defining "insurance mediation" and "reinsurance mediation". See para.38-075, below. For a brief account of the short-lived General Insurance Standards Council, see para.36-075 in the 10th edition of this work.

[236a] Directive 2016/97 on insurance distribution (recast) [2016] OJ L26/19.

[236b] Insurance Distribution (Regulated Activities and Miscellaneous Amendments) Order 2018 (SI 2018/546). See also the Insurance Distribution (Amendment) (EU Exit) Regulations 2019 (SI 2019/663).

[236c] Note that the European Court of Justice has given a wide construction to the meaning of "insurance mediation" in the IMD and, given the relevant wording is identical in the definition of "insurance distribution" in the IDD, this must also apply to the latter. In *Länsförsäkringar Sak Försäkringsaktiebolag v Dödsboet efter Mattsson* (C-542/16) EU:C:2018:369; [2018] Bus. L.R. 1653, it was held that the definition covers work preparatory to the conclusion of an insurance contract, even in the absence of any intention on the part of the insurance intermediary concerned to conclude a genuine insurance contract.

INDEX

This index has been prepared using Sweet & Maxwell's Legal Taxonomy. Main index entries conform to keywords provided by the Legal Taxonomy except where references to specific documents or non-standard terms (denoted by quotation marks) have been included. These keywords provide a means of identifying similar concepts in other Sweet & Maxwell publications and online services to which keywords from the Legal Taxonomy have been applied. Readers may find some minor differences between terms used in the text and those which appear in the index. Suggestions to *sweetandmaxwell.taxonomy@tr.com*.

Cyber Risks Insurance: Law and Practice, 1ˢᵗ edition
Celso de Azevedo
978-0-414-07034-9
July 2019
Hardback / Westlaw UK / ProView eBook

This new title is a comprehensive text clarifying the law and practice of cyber insurance. Written in an accessible and practical style designed to help you find answers quickly, it adopts a UK perspective with additional comparative analysis of the most significant cases in the US. Complete with sample clauses from leading industry organisations including the Lloyd's Market Association and International Underwriting Association, this is your definitive guide to understanding the law of cyber risks insurance.

The Law of Reinsurance, 5ᵗʰ edition
Terry O'Neill; Jan Woloniecki
978-0-414-06817-9
April 2019
Hardback / Westlaw UK / ProView eBook

The Law of Reinsurance has established itself as the definitive guide on reinsurance law and practice in England and Bermuda. This title not only addresses the core principles of reinsurance contracts and regulation but also relevant areas of agency law and dispute resolution procedure. It is relied upon as comprehensive and trusted text that continues to clarify a complex area of law.

Also available as a Standing order

Colinvaux's Law of Insurance, 1ˢᵗ supplement to the 12th edition
Robert Merkin
978-0-414-07909-0
September 2020
Paperback / Westlaw UK / ProView eBook

Colinvaux's Law of Insurance is a thorough examination of insurance contract law. This supplement keeps your copy up to date with the most recent and significant case law including: *AB v Transform Medical Group (CS) Ltd; Aspen Underwriting Ltd v Credit Europe Bank; Endurance Corporate Capital Ltd v Sartex Quilts & Textiles Ltd; Niramax Group Ltd v Zurich Insurance Plc;* and more.

Also available as a Standing order

Contact us: Tel: +44 (0)345 600 9355
Order online: *sweetandmaxwell.co.uk*